# AMERICA
and ZION

**MOSHE DAVIS.**
(Courtesy of the Hebrew University photo archive)

# AMERICA and ZION

Essays and Papers in Memory of
## MOSHE DAVIS

Edited by ELI LEDERHENDLER and JONATHAN D. SARNA

WAYNE STATE UNIVERSITY PRESS    DETROIT

Copyright © 2002 by Wayne State University Press, Detroit, Michigan 48201.
All rights are reserved.
No part of this book may be reproduced without formal permission.
Manufactured in the United States of America.

Library of Congress Cataloging-in-Publication Data

America and Zion : essays and papers in memory of Moshe
Davis / edited by Eli Lederhendler and Jonathan D. Sarna.
p. cm.—(America-Holy Land series)
Includes bibliographical references and index.
ISBN 0-8143-3034-7
1. Americans—Palestine. 2. Americans—Israel. 3. United
States—Relations—Palestine. 4. Palestine—Relations—United States.
5. United States—Relations—Israel. 6. Israel—Relations—United States.
7. Christian Zionism. 8. Pilgrims and pilgrimages—Palestine. 9. Pilgrims
and pilgrimages—Israel. 10. Jews, American—Palestine. I. Davis, Moshe.
II. Lederhendler, Eli. III. Sarna, Jonathan D. IV. America-Holy Land monographs
DS113.8.A4 A49 2002
303.48'27305694—dc21          2002004801

# Table of Contents

Acknowledgments   7

Foreword: America and Zion   9
*Eli Lederhendler*

## Part I: Moshe Davis: The Man and the Scholar

*Achavah* and History: Reflections on the
Historical Emphases of Moshe Davis   23
*Jonathan D. Sarna*

Vision and Persistence: Origins of the
America–Holy Land Studies Project   33
*Robert T. Handy*

Moshe Davis and the New Field of America–Holy Land Studies   39
*Michael Brown*

## Part II: Historical Studies

"Each mouldering ruin recalls a history": Nineteenth-Century Images of
Jerusalem and the American Public   49
*John Davis*

Historical Perspective Through the Study of Ordinary People:
William H. Rudy (1845–1915), a Member of the
American-Swedish Colony in Jerusalem   75
*Ruth Kark*

CONTENTS

Dedicating and Consecrating the Land:
Mormon Ritual Performance in Palestine   91
*Steven Epperson*

The Esco Fund Committee: The Story of an
American Jewish Foundation   117
*Marianne Sanua*

A Cultural Model for America–Holy Land Studies:
One Early Example   161
*Matthew Silver*

The Ambiguous Missionary: Robert Lindsey
in Israel, 1948–1970   185
*Yaakov Ariel*

American Olim and the Transfer of
Innovation to Palestine, 1917–1939   201
*Joseph B. Glass*

Armchair Travelers to the Holy Land: The Travel Accounts of
Rev. J. Lynch, OSF   233
*Margaret M. McGuinness*

The Franciscan Monastery in Washington, D.C.:
"The Holy Land of America"   243
*David Klatzker*

Jerusalem, Vilna, Chicago: Gedaliah Bublick's
Wartime Dilemma   255
*Gershon Greenberg*

Appendix: Primary Occupations of North American Applicants for
Immigration to Palestine, January 1, 1919–May 30, 1920   277

Notes on Contributors   279

Index   283

# Acknowledgments

Professor Moshe Davis was the initiator as well as the inspiration for this book. His dream of introducing a new generation of scholars into the study of the America–Holy Land relationship resulted in the 1996 Young Scholars' Conference in Jerusalem (as noted in the Foreword), from which half of the articles in this volume are drawn. Unfortunately, Professor Davis himself did not live to see the conference he had done so much to plan. He passed away in April 1996. This volume is therefore a memorial to him.

The editors of ths volume, ably assisted by Dr. Joseph Glass, now a lecturer at the Hebrew University, oversaw the Young Scholars' conference. We also participated in a memorial meeting for Professor Davis shortly after his death and secured scholarly papers and reminiscences from some of his closest friends and associates. These too have been incorporated into this volume, which as a result includes contributions from four generations of scholars with whom Professor Davis interacted.

Had we been able to publish all of the worthwhile contributions from the Young Scholars' Conference and from those associated with Professor Davis over the course of his long and varied career, this volume would have been many times its present length. We take this opportunity to thank all those who offered us articles and reminiscences, and we apologize to those whose work could not, for one reason or another, be included here.

The road to press for this volume has been extraordinarily long. We thank Professor Davis's widow, Mrs. Lottie Davis, for her many helpful suggestions and for her constant support. We hope that this book justifies her patient forbearance in the face of many wearisome delays.

## ACKNOWLEDGMENTS

The Institute of Contemporary Jewry at the Hebrew University, founded by Professor Davis, has been of inestimable support in preparing this volume for publication. We particularly thank Laurie Fialkoff and especially Alifa Saadya for their editorial assistance; Mr. Avraham Bargil, executive director of the Institute, for his administrative help; and Professor Sergio DellaPergolla, chair of the department, for assistance at critical moments. Some of the earlier editorial work on this volume was completed at Brandeis University under the auspices of its Department of Near Eastern and Judaic Studies. Brandeis University's president, Professor Jehuda Reinharz, a longtime friend of Professor Davis, took a lively interest in every stage of this project and made funds available through the Joseph H. and Belle R. Braun Chair in American Jewish History.

Arthur Evans and his able staff at Wayne State University Press shepherded this volume to publication. We particularly thank Dr. Lester I. Vogel for his careful reading of the manuscript on behalf of the press and all those who copyedited and prepared the manuscript for publication. Funds from the estate of the late Mrs. Rosemary Krensky, a longtime friend of the America–Holy Land Project, helped to support the publication of this volume as well as the original conference upon which it is based. We were also fortunate to obtain funds both for the conference and the publication of this book from the Jacob and Hilda Blaustein Foundation, whose long and fruitful relationship with Professor Davis and the Institute of Contemporary Jewry we acknowledge here with deep and abiding gratitude.

# Foreword: America and Zion

Eli Lederhendler
*Hebrew University*

This volume of essays is presented as a tribute to the late Professor Moshe Davis in recognition of his influence and inspiration, and in a spirit of lasting affection.

A man of intellectual vision and seemingly boundless energy, Davis succeeded during his lifetime in sowing the seeds of a variety of innovative, interdisciplinary projects in the field of contemporary Jewish studies. So peripatetic an imagination seemed only natural in a man who was as undaunted by geographical distance as he was unfazed by new media and undeterred by the skepticism of conservative academic establishments. The first native-born American to receive a doctorate from the Hebrew University, a pioneer in the establishment of Hebrew-speaking summer camps in America, an educator who very early on recognized the potential of radio and television for popular educational purposes, founder of the interdisciplinary Institute of Contemporary Jewry at The Hebrew University, and an eager advocate of the methods of oral history for the documentation of our own era, Moshe Davis seemed to think cross culturally and integrally as a matter of course. He made connections and syntheses the basis of his lifework, perhaps most of all in the way he sought to build bridges between his two spiritual homes: America and Zion. "I do think that I was actually born here," he said in Jerusalem, "even though on my birth certificate, they say, it states that I was born in Brooklyn."[1] Yet, he was at the same time passionately committed to the life of the American Jewish community, where he felt that positive cultural and religious creativity was possible:

One never knows what a community [like that] is capable of, what can transpire in that community, how history can influence it, how the Land of Israel itself can exert an influence [upon it].[2]

The majority of the essays included in the present volume were first delivered as lectures at a colloquium held in Jerusalem in 1996. Professor Davis had taken a personal role in planning the colloquium (ably assisted by Joseph Glass, whose own paper appears here, and with the assistance of the two co-editors of this volume). Characteristically, Davis had conceived the event as a collaborative project of two academic institutions, an American one and an Israeli one: Brandeis University and the Hebrew University of Jerusalem. The present volume, therefore, reflects that collaborative spirit.

Sadly, Davis did not live to take part in the colloquium itself, which centered on the topic of America–Holy Land studies, a subdiscipline of cross-cultural research that he had himself conceptualized and encouraged over the course of some three decades. The essays in this volume by Michael Brown and Robert Handy—complementing those belonging to the original group—amply express how his partners in the development of America–Holy Land studies felt about Davis's crucial role as the project's godfather and guiding light.

"Just what are America–Holy Land studies?" asks Michael Brown, who replies with the concise definition that Davis himself had formulated: "The Zion theme is part of the spiritual history of America [and] an important factor in the interplay of ideas among [the] . . . religious faiths." Clearly reflected in the essay by Handy, as well as in the ecumenical contents of this volume, is the fact that the America–Holy Land hypothesis was born out of Davis's and his colleagues' commitment to interfaith discourse. Because of his abiding interest in the topic, and because a colloquium on America–Holy Land studies was the form that he himself chose, in the last year of his life, in which to pass along something of his legacy to a younger generation of scholars, we have undertaken to publish the present volume as a testament to his work, although it clearly reflects only one facet out of many in Davis's long and fruitful career.

This choice is based, moreover, on the fact that the America–Holy Land focus represents the working-out of an *idea*, and as such remains open to further development and research. Much might have been written about Moshe Davis as an architect of academic and educational institutions, but discussion of this accomplishment would not have been as immediately interesting, as widely accessible to a varied readership, or as open to review and evaluation by other scholars as the intellectual discourse stimulated by Davis's efforts to bridge the worlds of America and Zion.

It is therefore worth pausing, by way of introducing the essays themselves, to consider the intellectual bases of this conjunction between Zionist historiography, on the one hand, and American cultural studies, on the other.

―――

The yoking together of two such disparate historical matrices via cross-cultural study ultimately rests upon a notion of the inter-permeability of Jewish and American experience, a notion that is basic to Jewish-American self-understanding. The hypothesis of a dual civilization, where two cultures not only coexist but also do so compatibly, was crucial to the theories of Mordecai M. Kaplan (as Jonathan Sarna points out in the volume's first essay).

Davis happily acknowledged his intellectual debt to Kaplan in an interview conducted in 1990:

> Mordecai Kaplan was my great exemplar as a teacher. He headed the [Jewish Theological Seminary's] Teachers' Institute, and I followed him in that post after [Kaplan's tenure of] thirty-five years—a task that I chose [willingly], because he was a man of vision, and for him research went hand in hand with practical work. . . . I, too, have a fairly clear ideology with regard to the Jewish people, one that runs together [with my work as a historian]—there are no separating boundaries there.[3]

Kaplan's own view, namely that Jews could simultaneously and authentically partake of Jewish and American civilization while being true to both, made sense to Davis, the historian, who knew that the experience of the Jews has been, on the whole, one of contact with and adaptation to their environment. "Jews are not an insular people," he once wrote.[4]

In the America–Holy Land construct, Kaplan's theory of compatibility of civilizations was objectified by referring specifically to one value-object: namely, the land of the Bible. This opened the possibility of viewing a Jewish value, such as the abiding attachment to Zion, from an American point of view. By implication, it also suggested the need to examine the extent to which the reciprocal notion could be documented for non-Jewish Americans. Certainly, such an enterprise was likely to reveal the extent to which America's culture could be defined as a "religious" one, as well as the degree to which certain religious or collateral ideas were felt to be more closely related to American culture than others.

The evidence that has been marshaled for this field of research is not of an abstract, Olympian quality, but rather of a very human nature. In practice, America–Holy Land studies are narratives almost wholly dependent upon individuals, rather than on institutional, governmental, or other large-scale structural elements. This principle is borne out by the essays contributed by Yaakov Ariel on the career of an American missionary in Israel; by Gershon Greenberg on the religious views of Gedaliah Bublick, a prominent Orthodox Jewish figure in Chicago during the Second World War; by Ruth Kark on the William H. Rudy group in Jerusalem's American colony in the 1880s; by Margaret McGuinness on one particular Holy Land traveler, Rev. J. Lynch; by Marianne Sanua on Frank and Ethel Cohen and their friends who comprised the Esco Fund Committee, a model of activist philanthropy; and by Matthew Silver on the frustrations and dilemmas that faced Harry Friedenwald, both as an American and as a Jew, when he occupied the chairmanship of the Zionist Commission in Palestine for a brief period in 1919. Each one of these essays focuses upon the concrete experience of one individual or a small group of intimate friends in a discrete sociohistorical context.

That this microhistorical—human and *humanistic*—temper is what best suits America–Holy Land studies is not coincidental, if we consider that Moshe Davis's own imagination was drawn to the importance of the individual's role in history, as we readily understand from Jonathan Sarna's essay on one of Davis's early pieces of scholarship. The larger point behind such microhistory is that beyond these "trees" a forest might be discerned, and this macro framework was indeed the object of Davis's ruminations on America and Zion. That framework was suggestive, however, rather than definitive. Davis expected that individual studies would flesh out the dimensions of his basic hypothesis. Here, I will point to some of the broader implications that may be drawn from the particular studies we have included in the present volume.

Apart from those essays that focus on Jewish personalities (including, beyond those already mentioned, Joseph Glass's study of North American Jewish immigrants—*olim* in Hebrew—in mandatory Palestine), it will be noted that most of the papers deal with American Protestants. David Klatzker's and Margaret McGuinness's essays on Franciscans are the exceptions to what is otherwise a field dominated by a non-Roman Catholic orientation to American spiritual involvement in the Holy Land. This in itself deserves further scrutiny, but suffice it to note for the present that it is not mainstream or establishment Protestantism in America that furnishes the most fertile field for those interested in America–Holy Land research. One finds, rather, a stress on those from outside the mainstream consensus or elite churches and institutions. This emphasis certainly applies to the present collection, which includes Stephen Epperson's examination of Mormon dedication rituals in nineteenth- and early twentieth-century Palestine; Ruth Kark's exploration of the unruly, sectarian, expatriate world of William H. Rudy (no "ordinary" person, despite the title of Kark's essay); and Yaakov Ariel's illuminating profile of the "ambiguous missionary," Robert Lindsey, a Southern Baptist Evangelical.

The marginal perspective constitutes an important clue as to the nature of the Holy Land linkage in the minds of these people and others described in the book. The land of the Bible is, for these Americans, a sort of alternative, better, domain (as they themselves were a type of alternative to mainstream American culture). Such people construed the Holy Land as an echo, or perhaps much more than merely an echo, of America's pre-industrial, pre-urban, pre-secularized identity: otherworldly where America itself had become worldly, more Christlike at a time when America had become less Christlike. In Steven Epperson's exacting investigation of Mormon rites of dedication of the Holy Land to Jewish restoration, the theme of self-distancing from established churches and from commercializing impulses in the political economy of American Protestantism is quite explicit. We find, as another example, William Rudy's coterie in the Jerusalem of the late nineteenth century, hankering after messianic redemption and living the communitarian life of Christian fellowship that eluded them in Chicago. To a very real extent, this construction was predicated on preserving an image of the Holy Land as embedded in ahistorical (scriptural) time, a place where time had stood still since Golgotha.

These needs were also catered to by those artists who created images of the Holy Land to be brought back to America, mainly for Protestant consumption, as John Davis so ably describes in his essay "Each mouldering ruin recalls a history." The carefully preserved ahistorical image was, indeed, more powerful and ultimately more meaningful than the reality. Visiting Jerusalem in the course of a year-long U.S. naval expedition to explore the Holy Land (1847–48), William F. Lynch wrote that Jerusalem was already so familiar to Americans through their scriptural education that "there is no reason to add a thing about the current situation of Palestina and its outlook for the future."[5] One is reminded, here, of the analogous way in which a more secular (and more elitist) American social set turned in the nineteenth century to the ruins of classical Italy for aesthetic inspiration, as historian Ann Douglas has pointed out:

> There was no country Americans had traveled to so often, loved so much, and written about so verbosely as Italy. . . . [But] they unanimously resented the encroachments of the present on the classical past. . . . In American eyes, Italy was an artistic resource for capitalist culture, and by definition both effeminate and ahistorical.[6]

The spiritualization of the Holy Land among American Christian sojourners, occasional visitors, and audiences back home appears to have been even more thoroughgoing than what is implied by Douglas for the Italian case. David Klatzker's insightful reading of the various Holy Land reconstructions and replicas appears to bear this out. Nevertheless, the American world of material and pragmatic concerns—money, management, and marketing—that was ostensibly being kept at bay did seep through. Ruth Kark's eminent communitarian, William Rudy, was trusted and valued by the fellowship he led partly, perhaps mainly, because of his legal and financial expertise (which also proved his ultimate undoing). The artists profiled by Jonathan Davis took great pains to market their images and landscapes commercially to as large a public as possible. Entrepreneurship, tourism, and institutional fundraising played a conspicuous role in the Holy Land activities of American Catholics, as we note in David Klatzker's essay.

Such wayward intrusions of capitalist subtexts into a non-worldly text lend the American Protestants' Holy Land image a certain ambiguity; nonetheless, one can still discriminate text from subtext, and it seems clear that for Americans in general, and non-mainstream Protestants in particular, the Holy Land's significance lay precisely in its remaining "other" than the America they knew. That they sometimes failed to uphold that separation simply indicates how deep was the inner conflict that dogged their project of self-demarcation from their wider, native environment.

Herein, too, lies the asymmetry between their Holy Land nexus and that of America's Jews. Where Christian sojourners or would-be sojourners in the Land expected to be lifted *out* of their ordinary lives and social settings, American Jews saw in their affinity with the Land of the Bible a strong *link* to their American environment. American Jews seem to have been more singularly focused on the worldly, structural-political (democratic), and pragmatic-scientific premises of America's heritage, and it was these that they also sought (with varying degrees of frustration) to project onto the Land. The papers in this volume support the idea that Jews saw in America's biblical heritage primarily a source of such operative values as democracy and freedom, fair play and equality, social vision and political covenant. Such is the conclusion we may draw from Joseph Glass's work on the attempts to implant American-style enterprise and know-how in the interwar economy of Palestine; Matthew Silver's sensitive reading of Harry Friedenwald's dilemmas regarding liberalism, democracy, and the exercise of imperial power; Marianne Sanua's analysis of the Esco Fund's activities, which also notes those setbacks encountered when American Jews faced incompatible cultural, political, and social mentalities in Israel; and even Gershon Greenberg's profile of Gedaliah Bublick, the Orthodox Jewish commentator and religious Zionist who keenly appreciated America's scripture-based civilization as the underlying guarantor of America's democracy. These were manifestly worldly, modern, less romanticized, and less eschatological concerns, in contrast with what we have noted regarding prevailing Protestant Holy Land notions. This asymmetry of approach is perhaps most poignantly brought out by the essay by Yaakov Ariel on the dilemmas facing an American evangelical missionary to the Jews in Israel.

The Christian-Jewish asymmetry is not the only one that is limned in these pages. The American influence is at work in an asymmetry that can be noted between American Jews and their Israeli counterparts. In the discourse between the two communities, much remained that separated the "the land of promise" of *freedom and opportunity* from "the promised land" of *commanded destiny and patriarchal inheritance*. The implications of such clashing images are what Matthew Silver takes up in his essay, as to some extent do Marianne Sanua and Joseph Glass in their respective papers. In a different though related vein, Gershon Greenberg notes that Gedaliah Bublick could not but contrast critically the Jewish life he observed in America with the ideal vision he harbored of Jewish life in the Holy Land. The notion of religious, symbolic, or historical compatibility between the two, Bublick perceived, could not be taken for granted.

After considering the issue for many years, Moshe Davis reached the conclusion that it was not a common religious faith as such that explained (or could sustain in future years) the close bonds that existed between American and Israeli Jews. His scholarly work on American Judaism and the years he spent in the service of American Jewish education, along with his observations of Israeli life (having settled permanently in Israel in 1959), had taught him that the religious tempers of Israeli and American Jews were quite different, mediated as they were by quite different social environments and historical circumstances.

As has so often been observed—and affirmed most recently by a Jewish candidate for the American vice-presidency—the dominant strains of American religion are oriented toward the social expression of religious values by individuals, based broadly on biblical premises (good works and a consensually binding code of ethics), as these were filtered by Enlightenment ideals and by Christianity's specific attention to individual salvation. These shared elements and mutual influences allow both the individual and religious groups ample ground outside the public realm for the elaboration of more specific rules and beliefs. For reasons having to do with the post-Reformation founding of American society, religion in America (even among Catholics and Jews) is adapted to the coexistence of heterodoxies: particular theologies, in both the "faith" and the "doctrinal" sense of the term, are left to be formulated in the privacy of individual consciences (a person's "religious persuasion," in American parlance) or in church groups organized, for the most part, non-exclusively, pluralistically, and—most importantly—without privileged status vis-à-vis political authority.

In the Holy Land, in contrast, postbiblical, collectivist paradigms reign supreme over biblical, individual-salvationist, or post-Reformationist models. While personal piety remains the touchstone of an authentic religious life anywhere, religion in the Holy Land is less an individual than a tribal affair. Symptomatically, such personal virtues as altruism or fortitude that, in America, are popularly conceived to be particularly rooted in "religious" traits, qualities of mind, or values, are not thus construed in the Middle East. In part, at least, the collective and institutional emphasis remains intact because the dominant religions of the Holy Land were shaped by (and have by and large remained in) pre-disestablishmentarian, orthodox modes (i.e., Orthodox Judaism, Sunni Islam, and, among Christians, the Orthodox, Armenian, and Latin churches, though Protestant churches are present, too).[7]

As most Americans, including American Jews, do not share the premises of this "oriental" religious model, it is difficult to postulate that religion alone might offer a common basis for empathy. If despite this disparity, American Jews and some of their non-Jewish fellow Americans have felt themselves linked to the Holy Land and have given expression to this feeling in their own lives as Americans—and this claim, of course, is what lies at the heart of the proposition that Davis and his colleagues have supported—then this phenomenon demands examination in a context that subordinates religion as such to a stronger, overriding motif or context.

In Davis's conception, the Land itself presented just such a key. On the face of it, such a hypothesis may appear as dubious as one based on an ostensible religious congruence: little, *objectively* speaking, might be said to link a tiny, semi-arid strip on the eastern shore of the Mediterranean to a continental nation on the other side of the globe. That still left open, however, the *subjective* realm of myth, metaphor, self-projection, and self-image that might, indeed, be explored from the point of view of the Land as a topography of common inspiration.

Even (or especially) as the America of material well-being crowded out the last vestiges of "a new heaven and a new earth," the older utopian and spiritual strain in American self-consciousness remained an avenue of possible refuge from the closing of frontiers, both real and symbolic.[8] Despite the risk of overstatement that threatened, out of sheer repetition, to overwhelm the modest reality behind the America–"promised land" analogy, that projected image continued to retain a certain resonance in American cultural terms, if only, as we have seen, on the margins of the Protestant establishment.

Moreover, while this mythic realm was certainly informed by religious tradition per se, it was at one remove from actual religion in the institutional sense. It did not, for example, impose a particular doctrine.

Different religious groups in America, for example, might easily relate in characteristically disparate ways to a metaphorical engagement with the Holy Land without thereby doing violence to their own individual agendas.

The notion of the Land as a powerful coordinate in cultural and historical discourse for Americans may well have been suggested to Davis, by way of analogy, by the teachings of Ben-Zion Dinur, a chief exponent of the Zionist-oriented "Jerusalem school" of modern Jewish historiography. As Jonathan Sarna reminds us, Davis learned little from Dinur insofar as American Jewish history was concerned; but he appears to have learned much from him about the construction of overarching historical models, and thus Dinur's influence is evident in Davis's own development as a historian. Dinur, under whose guidance Davis wrote his doctoral thesis, propounded the view that the Jews' return to their ancestral land was the axial core around which the entire modern epoch of the Jewish people might be defined. All other developments were subordinate and related to this main Palestinocentric axis.

By formulating an Americanist version of it, Davis sought to apply the Palestinocentric model even more expansively than had Dinur himself. One might say that America—the land itself—was clearly the main, if not the only organizing principle of American history. Thus, if Americans chose to relate to the Holy Land at all, it would likely be through the prism of their own historical experience of the "land where my fathers died." In that sense, even in faraway America, Jews and others might well feel the thrill of history turning on its hinges, challenging them to take part in the drama in some fashion, if only through their moral support, or perhaps by construing the modern Zionist saga of Jewish political redemption as an echo of what, closer to home, had begun in 1776.

That, in so many words, is what Moshe Davis had once actually suggested in a public statement that he gave on May 14, 1948, when the State of Israel was declared. Asked by a reporter for the *New York Times* for a usable paragraph, Davis (who was attending a Jewish convention in Chicago), stepped up to the microphone at 9 a.m. on that Friday morning and said, "It is the 1776 of the Holy Land."[9]

It is possible to suggest, too, that Davis used "the Land" in a way that was functionally equivalent to the way Kaplan, his other mentor, had used the term "civilization": namely, as a concept that transcended the narrow focus of "religion" by pointing toward something more expansive and inclusive, accessible at different levels for different purposes while remaining, all the while, an all-encompassing framework of discourse.

That leaves open a more basic question with regard to America–Holy Land studies: To what extent can we support an encompassing notion of discursive unity, given the asymmetries, differences of purpose, and individualized experiences involved? Moshe Davis, who clearly believed that boundaries were less important than bridges, was a strong advocate for an America–Holy Land hypothesis and saw it as a window into the history of America as well as Zion. By virtue of their excellence, the individual studies presented here vindicate Professor Davis's confidence in the intellectual potential of humanistic, cross-cultural research. They also leave open intriguing questions for those who would continue to follow in his footsteps.

## Notes

1. Moshe Davis, interview by Shlomo Sneh (in Hebrew), Jerusalem, 7 January 1990. Institute of Contemporary Jewry of the Hebrew University, Oral Documentation Division, transcript 59 (56), Part I, 7.

2. Ibid., 9.

3. Ibid., 4.

4. Moshe Davis, "Reflections on an Agenda for the Future," in Moshe Davis ed., *The Yom Kippur War and the Jewish People* (Jerusalem and New York, 1974), 337.

5. William Francis Lynch, *Narrative of the United States' Expedition to the River Jordan and the Dead Sea* (Philadelphia, 1849), cited in Benny Landau, "The Great Plan," *Haaretz Magazine,* 27 April 2001, 26–29.

6. Ann Douglas, *The Feminization of American Culture* (New York, 1977; repr. 1998), 283–84.

7. Jews in Israel are mainly the descendants of immigrants from East European and Middle Eastern countries—areas where a post-reformation religious mode never really penetrated traditional Jewish life. While Jews in the United States similarly derive mainly from Russia, Poland, and Austria-Hungary, they readily adapted (or their children did so) to non-orthodox religious patterns prevalent in their new environment. In Israel, the environmental influence served, if anything, to foster the status of orthodoxy.

The pro-orthodox and collectivist quality of Israel's religious cultures tends to privilege public expressions of religious discipline and fealty (from public prayer rituals through the observance of religious traditions by government bodies and representatives) to a degree that is not normally the case in American religious culture. Partly for this reason, the government of Israel has continued the historical practice of previous regimes (both the Ottoman Turkish and British) of granting legal and quasi-official status to the various religious establishments (Jewish and non-Jewish), and of designating a government ministry to assign budgets to them as providers of basic public services (in spheres such as education, marriage, divorce, and burial).

8. On the conflict between the agrarian and market cultures in nineteenth-century American society, see the illuminating discussion by Charles Sellers, *The Market Revolution: Jacksonian America, 1815–1846* (New York and Oxford, 1991).

9. Moshe Davis, interview by Shlomo Sneh (in Hebrew), Jerusalem, 7 January 1990. Oral Documentation, Institute of Contemporary Jewry, Hebrew University of Jerusalem, transcript 59 (56), Part II, 4.

# Moshe Davis:
# The Man and the Scholar

# *Achavah* and History

## Reflections on the Historical Emphases of Moshe Davis

Jonathan D. Sarna
*Brandeis University*

Of Moshe Davis's 250 publications, the one that taught me the most about his approach to history and Jewish life was his scholarly study of New York's *Achavah* Club (1909–1912), published in 1953. *Achavah*, Davis discovered, was an exclusive fraternity consisting of twenty-five of New York's foremost Jewish scholars, intellectuals and activists, all of them adherents of "National Judaism," who agreed to meet in one another's homes every two or three weeks to discuss what was simply called "Jewish matters." The club's membership included a galaxy of Jewish luminaries, including Judah Magnes, Louis Ginzberg, Mordecai Kaplan, Louis Lipsky, Alexander Marx, Israel Davidson, Israel Friedlaender, Chaim Zhitlowsky, David Pinski, Samson Benderly, Solomon Bloomgarden (known as Yehoash), and Max Radin. Davis, who might himself have been included in this august company had he been alive at that time, described the history of this unique club and filled in important details concerning its membership and raison d'être. For some of his information, he relied upon oral history, a methodology that in 1953 had not yet even been named. He also transcribed and published Israel Friedlaender's fascinating minute book of the club's meetings and activities. The article as a whole, published in the *Mordecai Kaplan Jubilee Volume*, represents a model of textual scholarship—the application of *Wissenschaft* methodologies to American Jewish history—while also displaying impressive erudition and a lively writing style. Beyond its technical and scholarly mastery, however, the article is deeply revealing of Moshe Davis's own values. From it, one can learn much about his understanding of history and his approach to contemporary Jewish life.[1]

Davis believed, as he once explained to Geoffrey Wigoder, that "history indicates lines and trends for the present." Indeed, he felt that "you can understand the past better if you experience the present" and you need as well "to study the present, in order to better understand the past."[2] History, for him, was thus an intensely "relevant" subject in that it yoked past and present together in a single continuum. In this, Davis was Mordecai Kaplan's disciple—even as he was a disciple of Benzion Dinur and Alexander Marx in his respect for facts and primary source documentation. Still, it is appropriate that his study of the *Achavah* Club appeared in the Kaplan festschrift, for in his approach to Jewish scholarship he clearly sympathized with Kaplan as against the more Germanic, aloof textual scholarship that dominated the Jewish Theological Seminary in his day.[3]

It is likely that *Achavah* appealed to Davis for another reason: the club was true to its name, which in Hebrew means fraternity or brotherhood. It brought together people from different walks of life—scholars, Zionists, and Jewish communal activists, men (no women) who on many issues fundamentally disagreed with one another—asking them, in Levi [Louis] Ginzberg's words, to "help clarify the profounder questions of Jewish life and, if possible, apply their views to the solution of those problems."[4] Davis's own lifework as a historian and institution-builder reflected this same conception. He firmly believed in *achavah*, particularly in the larger sense of bringing variegated individuals and institutions into communication and partnership with one another. He was also convinced that Jewish scholarship—history in particular—could speak to contemporary concerns and present-day questions. Years later, Davis himself founded a study circle at the home of the President of Israel that echoed much of what he thought the *Achavah* Club had represented.[5] Many of his other projects similarly reflected his understanding of the club's values, particularly its stress on excellence, its inner diversity, its commitment to the Jewish people *(klal yisrael)*, its confidence in the centrality of Zion, and its engagement with issues of present-day significance.

To borrow a phrase once applied to Louis Brandeis, Moshe Davis had a mind of one piece: his scholarship, his administrative under-

## *Achavah* and History

takings, his public activities, his religious faith—all reflected and reinforced one another. Coherence and intellectual consistency were among his most remarkable and endearing characteristics. The same values, the same lessons, the same stories and asides and words of wisdom characterized everything that he did. Nor is this an accident, for all of Davis's myriad activities flowed from a common set of assumptions and goals, very much the same ones, in fact, that underlay the club about which he so luminously wrote.

Davis's training as a historian took place both in America and in Israel, and from the beginning he took it as his personal mission to help each of these vital Jewish centers to understand the other. He was extremely proud of being "the first American to receive a doctoral degree from the Hebrew University of Jerusalem (1946)," and even today his dissertation ranks among the most important ones ever written in Hebrew in the field of American Jewish history.[6] When he entered that field in the 1930s, American Jewish history was just beginning to emerge as a scholarly discipline. Davis's teachers and later colleagues at the Jewish Theological Seminary shied away, for the most part, from anything after the French Revolution, while most of those who wrote in American Jewish history were amateurs or filiopietists more interested in apologetics than in scholarship.[7] At the Hebrew University, not surprisingly, the study of American Jewish history was completely unknown. None of the three great scholars who read his dissertation (Dinur, Yitzhak Baer, and Joseph Klausner) had ever made any original contributions on the subject. Consequently, as he would so often do later in life, Davis blazed his own trail. He utilized a wide range of sources, many of them never previously examined, and he drew upon the expertise of anyone who could help him. Salo Baron guided his American research. Davis also called upon Hyman Grinstein, Baron's first significant doctoral student in American Jewish history, as well as upon Jacob Rader Marcus, who, like Baron, had begun to devote himself to this field. Years later, Marcus still remembered reading every word of Davis's dissertation in Hebrew with the aid of a dictionary. Davis, for his part, remained deeply indebted to Marcus for many invaluable comments and corrections.[8]

What set Davis apart from others working in the field of American Jewish history in his day was his focus on the religious history of American Jews. This was a neglected aspect of American Jewish history, then and later, and Davis approached it with admirable breadth—focusing on individuals, ideas, movements, and institutions. In 1951, an expanded version of his dissertation appeared in Hebrew, entitled *Yahadut amerika behitpathutah* (The shaping of American Judaism) with a significant Hebrew subtitle: *Toldot haaskolah hahistorit beme'ah hatesha' 'esreh* ("A History of the Historical School of the Nineteenth Century"). The subtitle, in fact, captures Davis's central thesis: he felt that he could identify a "historical school" in nineteenth-century American Judaism that took issue with Reform, offered its own solutions to the problems affecting America's Jews, and ultimately became institutionalized in the Jewish Theological Seminary (1886) and in the Conservative movement. Davis thus offered the Conservative movement a usable past, a history that indicated "lines and trends for the present." Written for a select audience of Hebrew speakers, the volume concluded with a strong plea for the Hebrew language, Jewish peoplehood, and what we would today call Jewish continuity *(kiyum haumah)*. The more widely read English version, entitled *The Emergence of Conservative Judaism,* published in 1963 and rewritten for an American audience, closed with a somewhat different message, perhaps more appropriate to the 1960s era in American Jewish life. In this version, Davis called for unity among the diverse elements of the Conservative movement and quoted Sabato Morais's call to "work to preserve historical Judaism, though for its sake concessions for which we are unprepared may be demanded."[9]

Both the Hebrew and the English volumes proved somewhat controversial both in their use of the term "historical school," which some found anachronistic, and for their embrace of men such as Isaac Leeser, whom other historians considered more Orthodox than proto-Conservative.[10] Davis, however, held his ground. He maintained that his critics failed to sufficiently appreciate his method, which entailed the use of a historical construct to shed light on larger themes, and he stood by his interpretation of Leeser. The controversy itself, as Lloyd Gartner has suggested, "points paradoxically to the significance of Davis's book."[11] Rarely before had a theme in American Jewish history been presented in a manner that was meaningful and timely enough to engender controversy. Davis demonstrated the ongoing relevance of many issues that confronted nineteenth-century American Jews. And his did so based on a thorough mastery of primary sources—newspapers, sermons, obscure pamphlets, and correspondence—that had never before seen the light of day.

Davis continued to publish studies in American Jewish history throughout his tenure at the Jewish Theological Seminary. His best-known and most frequently reprinted work was a synthetic history of "Jewish Religious Life and Institutions in America" that appeared in Louis Finkelstein's *The Jews* (1949, 1955, 1960, 1971). Rewritten and separately issued in Hebrew, it served as a basic introduction to American Judaism for a full generation of Israelis.[12] He also authored other significant studies—including "*Ha-Zofeh Ba-Arez Ha-Hadashah:* A Source for East European Jewish Settlement in America," "Jewry East and West: The Correspondence of Israel Friedlaender and Simon Dubnow," "The Synagogue in American Judaism (A Study of Congregation B'nai Jeshurun, New York City)," and "The Human Record: Cyrus Adler at the Peace Conference, 1919"—all of which he later brought together in his Hebrew collection, *Beit yisrael beamerikah* (1970).[13]

Beyond this, Davis brought new excitement to the field of American Jewish history, particularly at the Jewish Theological Seminary. In 1953, together with chancellor Louis Finkelstein, he created the American Jewish History Center, funded by Louis M. Rabinowitz. The establishment of this center is of great interest, for its advisers from Columbia University included both the leading American historian of the day, Allan Nevins, and the leading Jewish historian, Salo Baron. Davis properly sought to locate American Jewish history within *both* disciplines, a point he made forcefully the following year at the Peekskill conference on "The Writing of American Jewish History," one of a series of events connected with the tercentenary of Jewish life in the United States.[14] At this conference, which he helped to organize and whose proceedings he co-edited, Davis argued:

> The first step to improve the quality of American Jewish historical writing is to regain the awareness that the Jewish experience in America should be studied as part of the larger scheme of American history as well as of world Jewish history. . . . The interaction between historians of American and Jewish life in their studies and writings will naturally wean away American Jewish historiography from its tendency to parochialism. In turn it will deepen and broaden the character of general American histories.[15]

In the reference to "interaction" we see again the theme of *achavah*. Indeed, Davis went further, calling at the conference for the establishment of a scholarly "collegium" designed to foster collaborative research, collaborative thinking, and collaborative historical study. It was an audacious vision, and it guided the approach that he would take in his own work for the next forty years.

From the late 1950s, when he settled in Israel, Davis's historical emphases shifted, and he pioneered two new areas of inquiry: contemporary Jewry and America–Holy Land studies. Since both of these subjects are addressed elsewhere in this volume, I will confine myself to a few points relevant to historical scholarship.

First, both of these new areas had been adumbrated in Davis's earlier writings and activities. His bibliography includes articles on contemporary social issues that date from the 1940s, and in 1952 he helped to establish the Seminary's Israel Institute, "to strengthen the spiritual and cultural bonds between the State of Israel and America . . . and to help develop a recognition of Israel as a spiritual center for Jewry everywhere."[16] What we see in his career, as in that of so many fruitful scholars, is the elaboration later in life of themes set down earlier on. A full reading of his oeuvre, especially his early writings in Hebrew, indicate that contemporary issues and Zion were never far from his mind even in the years when his primary scholarship focused elsewhere.

Second, both contemporary Jewry and America–Holy Land studies involved the same kind of interrelationship between past and present that is central to so much of Davis's work. His approach to contemporary Jewry was informed by history—his article on intermarriage is significantly subtitled "Historical Background to the Jewish Response,"[17]— and he encouraged the use of traditional historical methodologies on the part of his colleagues at the Institute of Contemporary Jewry (many of whom were, in fact, trained as historians). This approach distinguished the study of contemporary Jewry in Jerusalem from the more sociological approach characterizing the field in the United States, as even a cursory comparison between *Studies in Contemporary Jewry,* published by the Institute, and *Contemporary Jewry,* published by the Association for the Social Scientific Study of Jewry in the United States, amply reveals. Similarly, Davis understood that the relationship between America and Israel needed to be understood historically. Here again, through the America–Holy Land Project, he sought to place a subject of contemporary concern in a much broader historical and religious studies context.

Third, Davis insisted that both the Institute of Contemporary Jewry and the America–Holy Land Project focus on research based upon primary sources. Davis believed that in these new areas, as in American Jewish history, scholarship depended upon a firm foundation of data. When he was a student, Davis once recalled, he asked his teacher Allan Nevins, "Why is it that you never mention the Jews of the United

States in your writing?" "Mr. Davis," Nevins replied, "if you will mine the material, I will use it."[18] That answer made a great impression upon Davis—one that was doubtless reinforced by the worshipful emphasis on textual scholarship that characterized the Jewish Theological Seminary and the Hebrew University of his day. Having received essentially the same message from both his Jewish and his American history teachers, Davis internalized that message and made it his own. No matter what subject he subsequently researched, he invariably sought to "mine the material" by assembling primary data. The Institute of Contemporary Jewry's oral history collection, the America–Holy Land Project's archival guide, the Arno reprint series, the statistical data collected by the Institute of Contemporary Jewry over many years—these and many other data collection projects that he initiated and oversaw reflected Davis's lifelong belief that scholarship in any field was only as strong as the primary research in which it was grounded. Pragmatically, he also understood that in order to legitimate new fields of research at the Seminary and at the Hebrew University, he needed to root them in primary texts, for this was the sine qua non for acceptance. "Even Gershom Scholem," he once pointed out, had followed that route.[19]

Fourth, Davis believed in comparative study. Long before these became fashionable in American academic circles, he understood the value of interfaith and intercultural comparison. Davis resisted the narrow parochialism that Jewish historians, especially American Jewish historians, often fall prey to. Already in the 1950s, he co-taught a course with Robert Handy of the Union Theological Seminary that dealt with Jewish and Protestant perspectives on the Holy Land. Later, he insisted that the Institute of Contemporary Jewry work comparatively. He built comparative dimensions into the America–Holy Land Project. And from its inception, he made sure that the International Center for University Teaching of Jewish Civilization provided a global comparative perspective on Jewish studies. Two of Davis's most memorable and influential articles were also comparative in nature: "Centres of Jewry in the Western Hemisphere: A Comparative Approach," and the aforementioned "Mixed Marriage in Western Jewry."[20] Today, Israeli scholarship, especially in the area of contemporary Jewish studies, is almost reflexively comparative, in contrast to American Jewish scholarship. Davis alone may not be responsible for this difference—the multicultural nature of Israeli society, after all, fosters comparative research—but his role cannot be underestimated. In this, as in so many other areas, he was a pioneer.

Finally, in all of his later work—the Institute, the America–Holy Land Project, the International Center, and other projects—Davis emphasized collaborative and interdisciplinary research, the kind of "collegium" he had advocated back in 1954. The very last conference he planned, the junior scholars' colloquium on America and the Holy Land, typified his approach. It began with an institutional partnership (the Hebrew University and Brandeis University), drew scholars from different countries, utilized diverse methodologies, and brought together a rich mix of Jewish as well as Christian participants. While he did not live to see that colloquium, it totally reflected both in form and in content his vision and historical emphases.

Back in 1953, at the conclusion of his study of the *Achavah* Club, Moshe Davis observed that "breadth of understanding and freedom of intellectual exchange is a spirit to be appreciated wherever and whenever it existed." Seventeen years later, when the same article came out in Hebrew, Davis altered the final phrase, transforming the past tense ("existed") into the present: "breadth of understanding and freedom of intellectual exchange are worthy of appreciation wherever and whenever they *appear*."[21] The shift is both significant and revealing. Early in his career, through his historical scholarship, Davis illuminated a glorious moment in the past when the *Achavah* Club spirit "existed." Later, through his extraordinary vision and administrative accomplishments, he made many more such moments "appear," both in his own lifetime and beyond.

## Notes

1. Moshe Davis, "Israel Friedlaender's Minute Book of the *Achavah* Club (1909–1912)," in *Mordecai Kaplan Jubilee Volume* (New York, 1953), 156–213. A Hebrew translation appeared in idem, *Beit yisrael beamerika* (Jerusalem, 1970), 72–142.

2. Geoffrey Wigoder, "Moshe Davis and the Study of Contemporary Jewry: An Oral History," *Contemporary Jewry: Studies in Honor of Moshe Davis* (Jerusalem, 1984), 11–12.

3. Jonathan D. Sarna, "Two Traditions of Seminary Scholarship," in *Tradition Renewed: A History of the Jewish Theological Seminary,* edited by Jack Wertheimer (New York, 1998).

4. Davis, "Israel Friedlaender's Minute Book," 161.

5. Revealingly, the English title that he gave to the Hebrew version of his article was "Study Circle on World Jewish Issues: Minute Book of the *Achavah* Club."

6. See, for example, the biographical note appended to *Contemporary Jewry: Studies in Honor of Moshe Davis,* 10, and the emphasis on this point in the biographical sketch that opens his *Darkhei hayahadut beamerika* (Tel Aviv, 1953).

7. Sarna, "Two Traditions of Seminary Scholarship"; idem, *JPS: The Americanization of Jewish Culture* (Philadelphia, 1989), 61–62, 165; Jeffrey S. Gurock, "From *Publications* to *American Jewish History:* The Journal of the American Jewish Historical Society and the Writing of American Jewish History," *American Jewish History* 81 (Winter 1993–1994): 185–204.

8. Moshe Davis, *Yahadut amerika behitpathutah* (New York, 1951), xi–xiii; personal conversations with Jacob R. Marcus and Moshe Davis.

9. Davis, *Yahadut amerikah,* 318–19; idem, *The Emergence of Conservative Judaism* (Philadelphia, 1963), 326.

10. See especially Charles Liebman's review essay in *Tradition* 6 (Spring–Summer 1964): 132–40 and the comments of Lance J. Sussman in his *Isaac Leeser and the Making of American Judaism* (Detroit, 1995), 246–47.

11. Lloyd Gartner, "Professor Moshe Davis hahistoriyon" (Professor Moshe Davis the historian), *Hadoar,* 24 January 1992, 16.

12. Davis, *Darkhei hayahadut beamerika.*

13. All of Davis's publications to 1992 are listed in *Pirsume Moshe Davis* (Jerusalem, 1992).

14. Arthur Goren described the gathering at Peekskill as "the most impressive conference of historians ever held on the writing of American Jewish history." See Arthur A. Goren, "A Golden Decade for American Jews: 1945–1955," in *Studies in Contemporary Jewry,* vol. 8: *A New Jewry? America since the Second World War,* edited by Peter Y. Medding (New York, 1992), 13.

15. Moshe Davis and Isidore D. Meyer, *The Writing of American Jewish History* (New York, 1957), 9–10; the proceedings were also printed in *Publications of the American Jewish Historical Society* 46, no. 3 (March 1957).

16. Moshe Davis, ed., *Israel: Its Role in Civilization* (New York, 1956), x.

17. Moshe Davis, "Mixed Marriage in Western Jewry: Historical Background to the Jewish Response," *Jewish Journal of Sociology* 10 (December 1968): 177–80; reprinted in Hebrew in *Beit yisrael beamerika,* 276–342.

18. Geoffrey Wigoder, "Moshe Davis and the Study of Contemporary Jewry," 17.

19. Ibid.

20. Moshe Davis, "Centres of Jewry in the Western Hemisphere: A Comparative Approach," *Jewish Journal of Sociology* 5 (June 1963): 4–26; the Hebrew version is in *Beit yisrael beamerika,* 241–75.

21. Davis, "Israel Friedlaender's Minute Book," 171; idem, *Beit yisrael beamerika,* 91 [translation and italics J. Sarna]. A concluding paragraph found in the English article was dropped in the Hebrew, making the quoted passage the last words of the chapter.

# Vision and Persistence

## Origins of the
## America–Holy Land Studies Project

Robert T. Handy
*Union Theological Seminary*

---

The vision of scholarly, interfaith study of the many interrelationships between America and the Holy Land emanated from the mind and heart of Moshe Davis. I first learned about his plans to develop such a project when he was a young professor at the Jewish Theological Seminary (JTS) in New York, where he taught the history of American Jewish life and institutions, and served in several important administrative capacities. His aim was to work with scholars from many fields and backgrounds toward a fuller understanding of both lands—their cultures, religions, and diplomatic policies. As he and most of the partners and helpers he enlisted to move from vision to reality were committed to the use of historical method, that perspective was central (but not exclusive) as the project slowly unfolded. Very early, we soon realized that there was a wealth of background material worthy of study, and certain parameters were set: a geographical focus on the United States of America on the one hand, and on the other, the area long known as Palestine and sacred to three major historical faiths: Judaism, Christianity, and Islam. Chronological attention was given to the period 1620–1948, but with emphasis on the nineteenth and first half of the twentieth centuries.

Professor Davis and I had met in the early 1950s at gatherings of the faculties of his seminary and of the nearby Union Theological Seminary (UTS), where I was teaching courses in modern and American church history. Somewhat to my surprise, he invited me to give a lecture at JTS in 1955, suggesting that I speak on "Zion in American Christian Movements," and then published it in a volume he edited.[1] As I was then developing a course on the history of religious thought in America, I had encountered various concepts of Zion, not only in Puritanism but also in various other movements, including communitarian and African-American groups as they struggled for freedom. The invitation gave me an opportunity to investigate the meaning of the word "Zion," primarily in Protestant hymns, magazines, sermons, and books. I became increasingly aware of the longstanding fascination of the Holy Land for Christians, and my understanding of its central significance for Jews deepened. Looking back on the text of the lecture I gave more than forty years ago, I think that even a generous but honest critique of what I then did would cover more pages than the original! But it got me started, and I continued to read about and ponder the various ways that Christians of many backgrounds understood the significance of the land of the Bible in the past and present. America–Holy Land Studies illumined areas of the Christian past that were important to my daily work as a church historian. To compare and contrast that with what I was also learning about Jewish attachment to the land deepened my understanding of both faiths.

Over the next few years, especially during the joint meetings of our two seminaries, I had occasion to discuss my new interest with Davis and some of his colleagues. But when he accepted an invitation to move to Jerusalem in 1959 to teach and to found the Institute of Contemporary Jewry (ICJ) at the Hebrew University, I thought our paths would cross only on rare occasions. Happily for me, that proved not to be true, for he continued a relationship at JTS as research professor, and his new responsibilities at the Hebrew University involved travel to New York several times a year. Often at such times I'd get a friendly call, and we found time to get together for a meal and conversation. To cite just one of such contacts, in October of 1963, he wanted to see what holdings in the UTS library might relate to our mutual interest in America and the Holy Land. Under the general heading "Palestine," he was excited by finding several trays full of 3 x 5 cards (those were pre-computer times), and his request that we microfilm the cards for him was quickly granted. We were surprised by the amount of material on the historical connections between the Holy Land and the United States so readily available, and we realized that there were many neglected aspects of our project that needed investigation in depth. As Moshe Davis and his wife Lottie worked closely together on his many projects, I also had the opportunity to get to know, admire, and learn from her.

Wherever he went, however busy with other efforts, he was ready to interest individuals and groups in America–Holy Land studies and their importance. He was always alert to involve both mature and promising young scholars in our project. In various addresses and writings, he would refer to relationships between America and the Holy Land.[2] On leave from the Hebrew University in the fall of 1965, he was instrumental in planning a seminar on that theme for qualified students from both JTS and UTS—and as both seminaries had links with Columbia University, we drew a few participants from there also. Both our faculties approved, and as we met at the two seminaries alternately, increasingly finding ourselves at home in both and making use of each other's remarkable libraries, Moshe Davis's vision was spread. There were some wonderful learning experiences for all participants: we began to learn the meanings of terms as used by students of Christian, Jewish, and secular backgrounds, and found how differently a given, seemingly familiar word was often understood in varying and at times quite opposite ways, influenced by one's background. Some of the students in that seminar, and in a second one offered in 1970, were later to become active scholars in this new, slowly developing field of study. Notable among them was Esther Y. Feldblum, who completed her Ph.D. dissertation at Columbia University in 1973 on "The American Catholic Press and the Jewish State, 1917–1957."[3] It was the first of a number of dissertations undertaken in the areas of the project's concern. Throughout his career, Davis was deeply involved in reaching out to students and helping them with their studies.

In 1967 I was offered a grant by JTS to spend two weeks in Israel in December—six months after the Six-Day War. It proved to be a fascinating and rewarding trip, as I traveled literally from Dan to Beersheba and talked with persons of many backgrounds, including those of varied strands of the three faiths of the Holy Land. I had the joy of not only seeing Lottie and Moshe Davis in their home in Jerusalem, but traveling with them on their first trip to Galilee. For me, one of the most informative parts of our journey was his telling me what he was experiencing as a Jew as we saw many sites central in biblical history, and I would seek to explain my reactions as a Christian. No doubt, as do most travelers and pilgrims to the Holy Land, I saw what I came to see—but had the good fortune also of seeing it through others' eyes, too. I came away much better prepared for our second joint seminar and more richly informed on ways to help Moshe Davis and some of those attracted by his work to bring the vision into fuller realization.

    Prominent among the latter was Selig Adler, distinguished historian of American diplomatic policy, whose lecture on "Backgrounds of American Policy Toward Zion" at JTS had been published in *Israel: Its Role in Civilization*.[4] We three agreed it was time to formalize an America–Holy Land Studies project. Though Davis generously called us co-directors of the project, and consulted with us frequently, he unquestionably was both the source of inspiration and administrative leader, matching his vision with his impressive leadership and administrative skills. Efforts of mine to secure formal recognition of the project from UTS and financial support from foundations with which I had some connections failed, so sponsorship came from the American Jewish Historical Society (AJHS) and the Institute of Contemporary Jewry. Davis's gifts for raising money allowed us to plan for some scholarly meetings and publications. On April 12, 1970, a colloquium on America and the Holy Land was convened at UTS with thirty-five participants.[5] After considerable discussion, touched off by presentations by the three directors, it became increasingly clear there were many rich but widely scattered and little-known archival and bibliographical materials relevant to America–Holy Land studies. To make those more readily available could illumine the bases of many different views of the Holy Land and lead to fuller understanding of why so many varied and often conflicting views of the past were so rarely shared across the many groups concerned about the Holy Land and its relationships with America. One major consequence of the gathering was the decision by its leaders to focus on the task of selecting relevant varied resources—from manuscripts, periodicals, pamphlets, and books—and to publish or republish them, along with bibliographies to make clear where those and other materials were. Research teams in the United States and Israel were led by two librarians, Nathan M. Kaganoff of the AJHS and Yohai Goell of the ICJ. They set to work to identify and annotate relevant materials. As samples to help draw others into the work, some of the results of the early labors were published as specimen pages. Much of my role in the project was to do some lecturing and writing about what was unfolding as opportunity afforded.[6]

The project came of age with the holding of the first major Scholars Colloquium on America–Holy Land Studies at the National Archives in Washington, D.C., on September 8–9, 1975. Milton O. Gustafson, chief of the Diplomatic Branch of the National Archives and Records Service, had been at the preliminary discussion in 1970, and he was not only instrumental in helping to arrange for the significantly larger and longer colloquium to meet in the National Archives, but was also among the speakers, describing the large body of records there. The colloquium was an important milestone in the life of the project and was followed by the appearance over the next few years by a series of publications, some of which had been in the making for years. In 1977, Arno Press published seventy-two previously printed, but long out of print, works on America and the Holy Land. Davis was the advisory editor; the only "original" volume was the full report of the 1975 Scholars Colloquium, *With Eyes Toward Zion,* complete with the addresses given.[7] The other volumes of a *Guide to America–Holy Land Studies, 1620–1948,* edited by Kaganoff, were published in the early 1980s.[8]

By then, the project was widening out to include other lands, with Davis's guiding hand at the helm of the second Scholars Colloquium at the National Archives in 1983.[9] His enlarging vision had been caught by the speakers and participants, and his perseverance over three decades had led to a thriving and expanding project. Two more volumes of the *With Eyes Toward Zion* series, which reflected the wider perspective, were published.[10] Until the end of his life in 1996, Moshe Davis's vision was still fresh, and his perseverance and ability to work with scholars of varied backgrounds had resulted in the establishment of an important field of study.

## Notes

1. Moshe Davis, ed., *Israel: Its Role in Civilization* (New York, 1956), 284–97.

2. E.g., Moshe Davis, *The Emergence of Conservative Judaism: The Historical School in 19th Century America* (Philadelphia, 1963), passim; see esp. 268–74.

3. Later published as Esther Y. Feldblum, *The American Catholic Press and the Jewish State, 1917–1957* (New York, 1977).

4. Selig Adler, "Backgrounds of American Policy Toward Zion," in *Israel: Its Role in Civilization,* 251–83.

5. "America and the Holy Land: A Colloquium," *American Jewish Historical Quarterly* 72, no. 1 (September 1972): 4–62; rpt. (Jerusalem, 1972) by the Institute of Contemporary Jewry.

6. See Robert T. Handy, "Studies in the Interrelationships between America and the Holy Land: A Fruitful Field for Interdisciplinary and Interfaith Cooperation," *Journal of Church and State* 13 (1971): 283–301; rpt. in *Jewish-Christian Relations in Today's World,* ed. James E. Wood (Waco, Tex., 1971), 105–23.

7. Moshe Davis, ed., *With Eyes Toward Zion: Scholars Colloquium on America–Holy Land Studies* (New York, 1977). Gustafson's address appears on pp. 129–38.

8. Nathan M. Kaganoff, *Guide to America–Holy Land Studies, 1620–1948,* vol. 1: *American Presence* (New York, 1980; ibid., vol. 2: *Political Relations and American Zionism* (New York, 1982); ibid., vol. 3: *Economic Relations and Philanthropy* (New York, 1983).

9. Moshe Davis, ed., *With Eyes Toward Zion,* vol. 2: *Themes and Sources in the Archives of the United States, Great Britain, Turkey, and Israel* (New York, 1986). Menachem Kaufman and Mira Levine, eds., *Guide to America–Holy Land Studies, 1620–1948: Resource Material in British, Israeli, and Turkish Repositories* (New York, 1984).

10. Moshe Davis and Yehoshua Ben-Arieh, eds., *With Eyes Toward Zion,* vol. 3: *Western Societies and the Holy Land* (New York, 1991); Moshe Davis, *With Eyes Toward Zion,* vol. 4: *America and the Holy Land* (New York, 1995); this is a collection of his essays on that theme, carefully revised with considerable updated bibliographical information.

# Moshe Davis and the New Field of America–Holy Land Studies

Michael Brown
*York University*

My introduction to Moshe Davis came in a graduate seminar on America and the Holy Land offered jointly by the Jewish Theological Seminary and the (Protestant) Union Theological Seminary over three decades ago. That seminar, which Professor Davis taught together with Professor Robert T. Handy of Union, was the first attempt ever to teach America–Holy Land Studies. It was also the first time that the two seminaries had cooperated in mounting a course. The seminar had the excitement of a pioneering venture, excitement heightened by the energy, enthusiasm, and imagination that, as I was to learn, Moshe brought to everything he did. When I was a student, he took me in hand. Then, and later, he would often put that hand on my shoulder with avuncular concern and inquire: "How are you, boy?" I remained his student, and he remained my teacher until his death.

From student, I progressed to research assistant the next year as Moshe edited his collection of texts and studies on American Judaism: *Beit yisrael beamerikah: mehkarim umekorot* (Jerusalem, 1970). Later, I was a junior scholar involved in the America–Holy Land Project, and then Moshe's colleague, when we offered a seminar together at the Hebrew University's Institute of Contemporary Jewry, itself one of his creations. It was then, while we were teaching together some twenty years ago, that illness first struck. Moshe fought so valiantly for so long, most of us assumed and hoped he would continue to vanquish disease for years to come. But that was not to be.

Professor Davis leaves behind many legacies: institutions that he created, his writings and edited works, scholars whom he trained and encouraged, family, friends, and acquaintances whose lives he touched. Among the most important of the legacies is the academic field that he created: America–Holy Land Studies. Having been present at the creation, it seems fitting that I have been assigned the task of addressing that aspect of his career.

But just what are America–Holy Land Studies? What does it mean to create a new field of study? And how did Moshe Davis do it?

Davis himself defined the new area of inquiry. He noted in 1970 that "the Zion theme is part of the spiritual history of America" and serves "as an important factor in the interplay of ideas among [its] . . . religious faiths." Within "the broad field of cross-cultural and pluralistic exchange in the United States, the America-Eretz Yisrael [land of Israel] theme represents a meeting point of Jewish and American history. Even as the two elements are separately discernible," he asserted, "they nevertheless mingle and intertwine with resultant impact and illumination. [In] . . . the Zion theme . . . many diverse elements meet," he said, "sometimes antithetically, but most often cooperatively."[1]

The genesis of the field is to be sought in Moshe's biography. As a young man, he belonged to that small group of American Jews determined to keep alive the tongue of the Holy Land in the Promised Land of the New World. It was a daring idea in a determinedly monolingual country. As he well appreciated, however, from "the beginning of indigenous American culture, Hebrew was not just another 'foreign' language." To Americans of many denominations, it was the "Holy Tongue, *leshon hakodesh,* bearer of eternal values, which brought Zion close to the basic elements of American civilization."[2] As a leader of Histadrut Hano'ar Ha'ivri (the Hebrew Youth Federation) in New York, and later as a graduate student at the Hebrew University, Davis gave the concept of America–Holy Land Studies personal meaning. (Moshe was the first American to earn a doctorate at the new university of the Jewish people and one of the first Americans to be appointed to a teaching post there.) American roots were his by virtue of birth; Holy Land roots he struck early in life by design; both would nurture him to the end of his days.

Some of Davis's early scholarly research pointed the way to the new field. One of his first works, which he wrote together with his wife, Lottie, his *'ezer* (helpmate) and coworker, was a map of biblical place names in the United States.[3] Two years later came the anthology of historical essays which he edited, *Israel: Its Role in Civilization*. Published there were lectures delivered at the new Israel Institute of the Jewish Theological Seminary, the goals of which were

> to strengthen the spiritual and cultural bonds between the State of Israel and America; to offer Americans an interpretation of the spiritual and cultural values of the State of Israel; to foster an understanding of the potential role of the State of Israel as intermediary between the Orient and the Occident; and to help develop a recognition of the State of Israel as a spiritual center for Jewry everywhere.[4]

Although it was Chancellor Louis Finkelstein who was given credit for this mission statement of the Institute, Davis, who was then provost of the Seminary, undoubtedly had a hand in its formulation. Often Davis's role as provost was to coax Finkelstein along unfamiliar paths, including Zionism. By his own admission, it was Davis who gave substance to the mission statement through the volume in which it was spelled out.[5]

But the new area of study was yet to be born. In 1970, Davis remarked that "no important monograph material on the subject [of America and the Holy Land], no M.A.'s, [and] no Ph.D. dissertations" had yet appeared.[6] In the introduction to the first volume of the *Guide to America–Holy Land Studies* written ten years later, he could still say that "the theme of 'American presence in the Holy Land'" was "a relatively new subject barely touched upon in scholarly writings."[7] How different the record was only some fifteen years further in time, thanks to his work!

In his act of creation, Davis proceeded methodically in several directions. First came a number of exploratory moves, including a colloquium, "America and the Holy Land," held in 1970 on the occasion of the tenth anniversary of the Institute of Contemporary Jewry. At that colloquium, Professor Handy and Professor Selig Adler of the State University of New York at Buffalo, Davis, and the group of colleagues and students he was gathering about him began to lay their plans for the future.[8]

One of the first steps was to promote bibliographical and archival surveys. If there was to be a new field of study, its potential resources had to be assayed. First came the four-volume *Guide* edited by Menahem Kaufman, Myra Levine, and the late Nathan M. Kaganoff; then followed "America and the Holy Land: A Select Bibliography of Publications in English," by Rivka Demsky and Ora Zimmer.[9]

As the raw materials were catalogued, Davis and his coworkers began to develop a research agenda to help scholars approach these vast resources.[10] Next, some of those still little-known sources had to be made accessible to scholars. To that end, the America–Holy Land Project which was emerging at the Institute of Contemporary Jewry, now the recognized home of America–Holy Land studies, sponsored the seventy-two–volume reprint series of America–Holy Land sources. At the same time, Davis was conscious of the need, as he put it, "to amplify and deepen our understanding of the unprecedented events of our [own] time."[11] To further that goal, he initiated an oral history project to record the thoughts and recollections of the Israelis and Americans who had made history together during the period when the new state of Israel was being created and fashioned.

Professor Davis himself made a singular contribution to America–Holy Land scholarship through the volumes he edited and co-edited, including *World Jewry and the State of Israel* (New York, 1977), which assessed the Israel-Diaspora relationship in the post-Yom Kippur War era, the series, *With Eyes Toward Zion,* and others.[12] Often the work of editors is underrated. Many scholars reject the supporting role of editor and insist exclusively upon the starring role of writing monographs. Davis—like the Hebrew poet and cultural activist, Chaim Nachman Bialik two generations ago—understood the vital function of *kinus haruah,* of making broadly available not only one's own insights, but also those of others. He believed that a constellation could shed more light than a lone star, no matter how bright. To that end, through the America–Holy Land Project, he organized a series of colloquia around various aspects of the America–Holy Land relationship and edited the resulting volumes.

But researchers, however important, do not make a field of study. They must be complemented by teachers. "The role models for creative research and university instruction are the teachers,"[13] Davis wrote in 1986, and he was himself a model teacher: engaging, thoughtful, well-prepared, and always clear. But one man is not a field. Davis believed that it was "therefore a great boon, when distinguished scholars in the humanities and social sciences choose to contribute their talents to America–Holy Land Studies."[14] And that is why he anthologized the works of others and sought ways to encourage them through teaching exchanges, grants for research, publications, and the Senior Scholar Program. The Senior Scholar Program was initiated by two distinguished professors. One was Professor Aryeh (Arthur) Goren of the Hebrew University's American Studies Department, who was appointed America–Holy Land Scholar at the Institute of Contemporary Jewry in connection with his work on Judah L. Magnes, and the second was Naomi Wiener Cohen, then of Hunter College and the Graduate Center of the City University of New York, who undertook research in Israel on American Jewry and the Palestine riots of 1929.

Nurturing younger scholars was as important to Davis as attracting stars to the new field. Not one to be possessive about his area of study, he understood that its growth and development depended on fostering new generations of researchers. For that purpose, he conceived the junior scholars colloquium as a way of celebrating his eightieth birthday. And what a magnificent gesture it was! Most academicians of Davis's stature and longevity would have expected an ode to their accomplishments. Moshe refused to consider such an event. He did not want his eightieth birthday to celebrate past achievements or to spark nostalgia. He wanted it to become a milestone on the path to the scholarly future. In the colloquium, young academicians would present papers, while older colleagues would chair the sessions and respond to the papers. The colloquium was to be a forum for acquainting established scholars with the work of new researchers, thus enlarging the network of America–Holy Land Studies and ensuring its further development. Professor Davis wanted to celebrate the past and present by looking ahead. Unfortunately, the colloquium would be held not in his honor but in his memory.

There is a great deal more that could be told about Moshe Davis and America–Holy Land Studies: how he eagerly sought the "reevaluation of accepted historical positions" on contentious issues such as the Arab-Israeli conflict;[15] how he sought to expand the scope and range of the new field by fostering comparative studies of the relationship to the Holy Land of Europe, Ibero-America, Canada, and Turkey;[16] and his establishment, under the editorship of himself and Jonathan Sarna, of a new monograph series in America–Holy Land Studies, of which my own book, *The Israeli-American Connection: Its Roots in the Yishuv, 1914–1945* (Detroit, 1996), is the lead volume. Instead, however, in the space remaining, I should like to reflect upon the motivating force of Professor Davis's scholarly endeavors, because therein lies a lesson for scholars of Judaica, and perhaps for others as well.

In a 1995 review in *Hadoar*, Muki Tzur had the following to say about another contemporary historian: "He has succeeded in making of the academic study of Judaism a bridge to the struggle for the existence of the Jewish people."[17] This also applies to Moshe Davis. He was very much the academic concerned with thorough scholarship, academic integrity, and measured judgments. But these were never ends in themselves. "The overarching purpose of America–Holy Land Studies," he wrote in his introduction to volume two of *With Eyes Toward Zion*, "is to engage contemporary scholars, students, and the wider public in the rediscovery of the Holy Land. On a substantive level, this . . . project is designed to study the nature and continuity of the relationship between the American people and the Holy Land in historical context."[18] Davis noted in the Louis A. Pincus Memorial Lecture delivered at the UJA (United Jewish Appeal) National Conference in 1975, that part of the uniqueness and importance of the American-Jewish experience was that American Jews maintained their ties to the people of Israel, and especially to the Israeli center of Jewish life and experience, even as they became more rooted in the United States.[19] One could not, then, understand American Jewry without knowledge of its Holy Land connections. And at the same time, one could not properly comprehend contemporary world Jewish history or Israel without a clear perception of their American connections.

But understanding the past was never the ultimate purpose of Davis's scholarship. "Fundamentally," he asserted in the introduction to *Beit yisrael beamerikah*, "past and future suckle from the same source. . . . [My] aim in historical research is that it will not only shed light upon the past, but that it will also serve as a guiding light to future development."[20]

Davis's scholarship led not to the ivory tower, but to life—his own and that of the Jewish people. He believed that "scholarship can be very practical."[21] To borrow from Muki Tzur again, it can be said that he endeavored to ensure that "the foundations of the study of Judaism . . . will belong . . . to the . . . authentic future people of Israel."[22]

One practical result that he sought to achieve through America–Holy Land Studies was "a new union" between Christians and Jews based on each group's understanding the other. Such understanding, he expected, would emerge from the commitment of Christians and Jews to their "own tradition[s]" and, in the case of Americans, from their "involvement in Zion."[23]

But for Davis, America–Holy Land Studies had a more important purpose even than interfaith harmony. In the introduction to the oral documentary anthology, *Living UJA History,* a popular booklet intended for the general public, Davis stated his dreams without his customary academic restraint. "When a community faces a crisis in authenticity," he wrote, "as is . . . the case of our present generation—the corrective choice is not to dilute but to intensify. In our times," he went on, "such reinforcement cannot be achieved on native ground alone. To recast existing Jewish institutions in the wake of radically altered historical events requires extra-territorial qualitative connections. In the preemancipated past, Jews lived transcendentally in *Eretz Yisrael* even when they actually resided in their diasporas. The gift of our generation is that Jews who live by choice or necessity in an actual *golah* [diaspora], can be fortified by the very *real* state of Israel."[24] With America–Holy Land Studies, as with most of his life's work, Davis sought to build the whole house of Israel.

In an autobiographical note in *Siah Massad* (*Massad Reminiscences*), Moshe remarked on the idealism of his friends and himself in Histadrut Hano'ar Ha'ivri in the 1930s. "We thought," he wrote poignantly, that "we could change the world."[25] The thrust of that reflective comment was that he had been naive, that the world was not to be easily altered.

But such was not the case. In fact, Moshe Davis did change the world. He gave it a new academic field of significance: America–Holy Land Studies. And in the best Jewish tradition, he labored to ensure that Torah would lead to practice, that America–Holy Land Studies would adhere to the highest academic standards, while at the same time serving to strengthen the Jewish people.

## NOTES

1. Moshe Davis, quoted in "America and the Holy Land as a Field of Scholarly Inquiry," *American Jewish Historical Quarterly* 62 (September 1972): 5–6.

2. Moshe Davis, "The Holy Land Idea in American Spiritual History," in *With Eyes Toward Zion,* vol. 1, ed. Moshe Davis (New York, 1977), 8.

3. Lottie and Moshe Davis, *Guide to Biblical Place Names in America: Land of Our Fathers* (New York, 1954).

4. Louis Finkelstein, Chancellor of the Jewish Theological Seminary, quoted in the Introduction, *Israel: Its Role in Civilization,* ed. Moshe Davis (New York, 1956), x.

5. Davis, "Introduction," in *Israel: Its Role in Civilization,* xi.

6. Moshe Davis, "Archival Sources in the United States and Israel," *American Jewish Historical Quarterly* 62 (September 1972): 42.

7. Nathan M. Kaganoff, ed., *Guide to America–Holy Land Studies, 1620–1948,* vol. 1: *American Presence* (New York, 1980), xv.

8. See "America and the Holy Land: A Colloquium," *American Jewish Historical Quarterly* 62 (September 1972): 5–62.

9. Nathan M. Kaganoff, ed., *Guide to America–Holy Land Studies, 1620–1948,* vol. 1: *American Presence* (New York, 1980); idem, vol. 2: *Political Relations and American Zionism* (New York, 1982); idem, vol. 3: *Economic Relations and Philanthropy* (New York, 1983); Menahem Kaufman and Myra Levine, eds., *Resource Material in British, Israeli, and Turkish Repositories* (New York, 1984); Rivka Demsky and Ora Zimmer, "America and the Holy Land: A Select Bibliography of Publications in English," *Jerusalem Cathedra* 3 (1983): 327–56.

10. See Davis, "Introduction," in *With Eyes Toward Zion,* vol. 1, xix–xxii. This agenda has been regularly revised over the years.

11. Moshe Davis, "Introduction," *Living UJA History: Irving Bernstein, An Oral History Anthology* (Jerusalem, 1995), 2.

12. Moshe Davis, ed., *With Eyes Toward Zion,* vol. 1 (New York, 1977); vol. 2 (New York, 1986); Moshe Davis and Yehoshua Ben-Arieh, eds., *With Eyes Toward Zion,* vol. 3 (New York, 1991); Moshe Davis, ed., *With Eyes Toward Zion,* vol. 4 (New York, 1995).

13. Davis, "Introduction," *With Eyes Toward Zion,* vol. 2, xxiv.

14. Ibid.

15. Davis, "Introduction," *Guide,* vol. 4, xiv.

16. See, for example, *With Eyes Toward Zion,* vol. 3, which includes essays on Canada, South America, Western Europe, and Great Britain; and V. D. Lipman, *Americans and the Holy Land Through British Eyes, 1820–1917: A Documentary History* (London, 1989), published under the imprimatur of the America–Holy Land Project of the Institute of Contemporary Jewry at the Hebrew University of Jerusalem.

17. Muki Tzur, "Hochmat yisrael beyameinu" (The academic study of Judaism in our times), *Hadoar,* 21 July 1995, 17–18, tr. by the author; Tzur was referring to historian Ismar Schorsch, Chancellor of the Jewish Theological Seminary.

18. Davis, "Introduction," *With Eyes Toward Zion,* vol. 2, xxii.

19. Davis, *Meditations on the Bicentennial: America and the Holy Land, Third Annual Louis A. Pincus Memorial Lecture* (New York, 1976).

20. Davis, "Introduction," in *Beit yisrael beamerikah.*

21. Davis, quoted in "Archival Sources," 60.

22. Muki Tzur, "Hochmat yisrael," 18.

23. Davis, quoted in "Archival Sources," 60.

24. Davis, *Living UJA History,* 1.

25. Moshe Davis, in *Siah Massad—Massad Reminiscences* (Jerusalem, 1996), 5.

# II

# Historical Studies

# "Each mouldering ruin recalls a history"

## Nineteenth-Century Images of Jerusalem and the American Public

John Davis
*Smith College*

---

Much of what is said about traditional Christian faith and visual perception can be traced to the provocative passage from I Corinthians, which asserts that the faith of believers allows them to perceive things "no eye has seen and no ear has heard" (2:9). That notion, however, would not have found easy acceptance in nineteenth-century America, where the stress was often on the act of seeing rather than on the realm of the unseen. "Blind faith" is a concept that any good Protestant of the period would have condemned as papist; it was the task of each individual to come to his or her own understanding of religious truths through a process of reading, observation, and reflection. Unlike their more orthodox forebears, American Protestants left very little to the invisible. Belief owed a great deal to vision and to experience. For a rational mind of the middle decades of the nineteenth century, an experiential component was crucial to one's faith.[1]

In the last few decades, we have learned a great deal about both corporate and individual faith in the United States through the lens of the historical and textual relationships of nineteenth-century Americans to the Holy Land. We have a good idea of who went there and why they went. We have made significant progress in sifting through the monumental bibliography that resulted from their journeys, and this textual evidence has been plumbed for insight into American attitudes—religious, political, economic, literary—toward the historic lands of the Bible. Yet in large part, this scholarly project has concerned itself with an archaeology of *words*. The place of visual culture in the American construction of the Holy Land has received comparatively less attention, despite the important role, for example, of the many engravings that illustrate the standard nineteenth-century travel volumes and despite Americans' insistence on a perceptual component to their faith.[2]

That this is a distortion of the actual nineteenth-century experience is indicated by numerous texts which tell us in unambiguous terms that no book, no travel volume—no matter how many were read by a given pilgrim—was adequate preparation for the first *visual* sight of the Holy Land. This is particularly true of the city of Jerusalem, where ever since Chateaubriand at the outset of the century, travelers had thrown aside their guidebooks as they approached the final ascent to the bluff that would give them their first view of the holy city. Until they *saw*, they could not *understand*.

As just one example of the pervasive need for this visual proof, for a *personal* survey of the city, we might turn to the meticulous maps made at the end of the century by Underwood & Underwood to accompany its series of photographic stereo views of Jerusalem, marketed in advertisements as a uniquely authentic method of experiencing the holy terrain [Figure 1]. If everyone could not feel the pilgrim's rapture firsthand, stay-at-home Americans could at least attempt to replicate it through these series of stereo cards. To aid the process, the highly detailed plans were marked with numbered spots corresponding to individual stereographs. From each of these points on the diagram, two lines were drawn, forming a "V" that delimited the peripheral scope of the photographic view, a two-dimensional cone of vision showing exactly how much territory on the map was depicted by the stereo card. The crisscrossing lines provided assurance to the home viewer that the faraway landscape had indeed been subject to a rigorous visual plotting. Its surface had been regularized and triangulated, brought under control by multiple commanding perspectives, much like an anatomical specimen x-rayed from several angles. The numbered dots at the crux of these V's thus indicated visual points of great power, each governing its own significant scopic field within and without the holy city. Though the Underwood & Underwood scheme dates from the end of the nineteenth

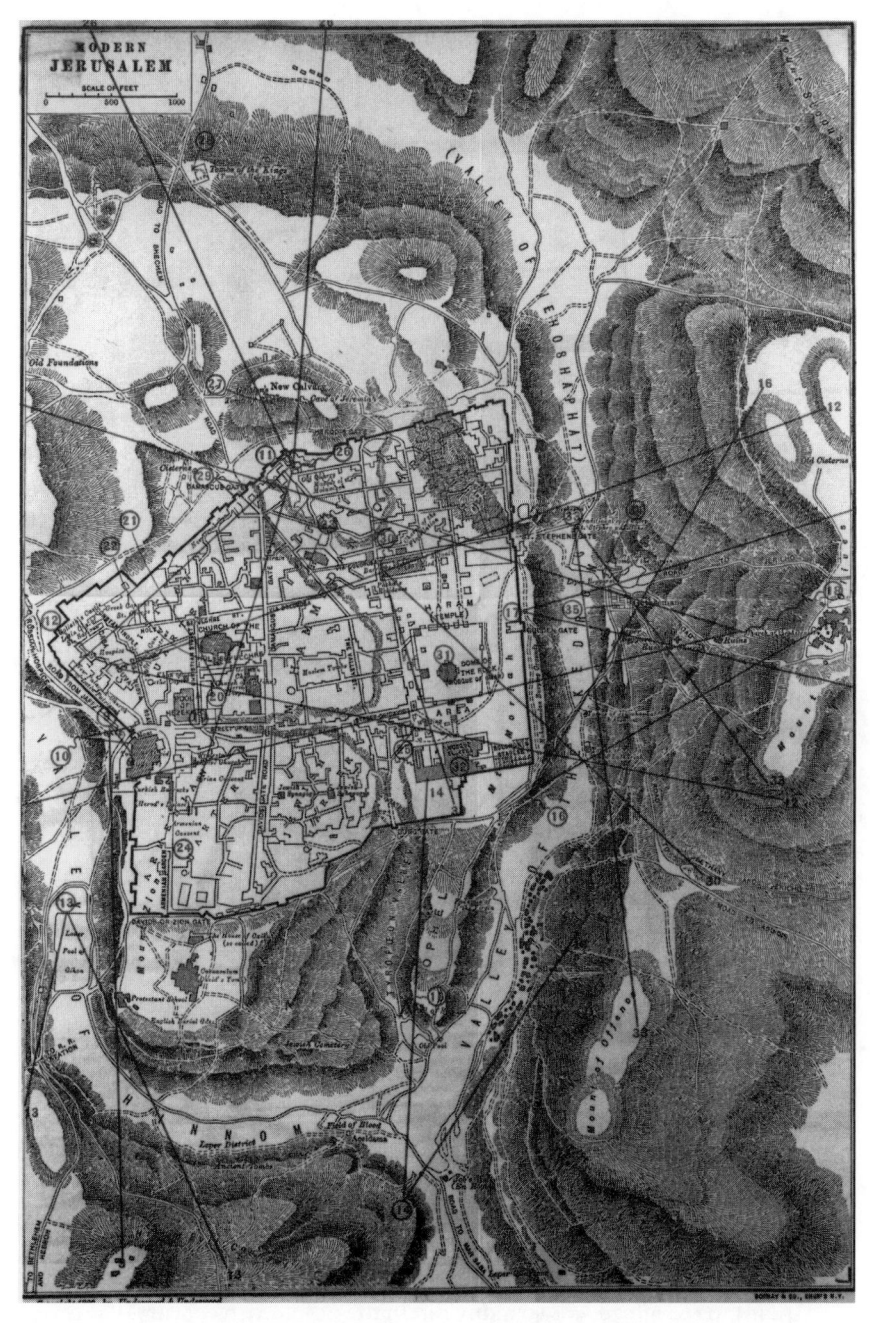

Figure 1. Map of Modern Jerusalem. From Charles Foster Kent, *Descriptions of One Hundred and Forty Places in Bible Lands.* New York: Underwood and Underwood, 1900.

century, it nicely sums up the degree to which every corner of Jerusalem was of passionate interest to Americans.

Certainly, the importance of Jerusalem to American concepts of spirituality and self needs no rehearsal here; Underwood & Underwood's map is not at all exceptional in its singular focus. Jerusalem figures prominently in the nationalistic religious topography of nearly every American Christian, from Puritan John Winthrop's seventeenth-century diary reference to "a Citty upon a hill" to Ebenezer Newhall's nineteenth-century sermon warning:

> There is, my friends, a religious patriotism, as well as a civil. You love your country. But do you love Jerusalem? Do you love its temple? Let the energies of your desires be concentrated here, imbibe deeply the sacred patriotism of our text, and your community is safe.[3]

What needs to be stressed, in addition to such textual references, is the important place that *visual* depictions of the city occupied in the vernacular culture of a surprising cross section of U.S. citizens. This essay will consider only two types of such representations—panorama paintings, especially one by Frederick Catherwood, and more conventional easel paintings by artists such as James Fairman and Frederic Church.

Long before any but a few Americans had the means to travel to Jerusalem, there existed a tradition of popular visual representations of its layout. The fascination with Bible lands encouraged a striking succession of entrepreneurial schemes that sought to bring images of the holy city—panoramas, dioramas, and models—before the eyes of the public. The emergence of these forms of entertainment and edification did more than set a precedent within the circumscribed world of the visual arts. It created the broad structure of an easily adaptable enterprise, a specific cultural "market" for knowledge that could quickly be exploited by a variety of visual artists. In fact, the practices that evolved to promote, interpret, and disseminate popular images of Jerusalem are identical with those later employed by "professional" easel painters such as Fairman and Church. Such a link underscores the virtual universality of the Holy Land as an operative symbol and metaphor, a concept important to groups of varying classes, regions, and religions. Certainly the biblical landscape meant different things to different people. Yet the important point to recognize—as so many did in the nineteenth century—was that it could mean *something* to almost anyone. This factor was crucial to the early success of those artists who employed popular methods to isolate and cultivate a public and shape its understanding of their work.

We can trace the roots of this vogue for representations of Jerusalem to mid-eighteenth-century New York. During the summer of 1764, the *Mercury* newspaper publicized a spectacle described as "Jerusalem, A View of that famous City, after the work of Seven Years. To be seen at the house of Tho. Evans, Clock and Watch-Maker. . . . An artful Piece of Statuary, in which every Thing is exhibited in the most natural manner, and worthy to be seen by the Curious."[4] Although it is difficult to know with any certainty, Evans's "Jerusalem" was likely a small, three-dimensional model of the city. According to the *Mercury*, it depicted sites contemporaneous with the passion of Christ; presumably there would have been someone on hand to point them out and relate the familiar story.

Scaled-down "sculptural" renderings of Jerusalem, while not as numerous as two-dimensional representations, are an integral part of the American visual culture surrounding the theme. They continued to be produced throughout the nineteenth century, perhaps because they responded so directly to the mapping instinct that, as we have seen, characterized American interest in the region. One of the best-known models went on view at the end of the century at Chautauqua, New York [Figure 2].[5] Even today, Chautauqua's Palestine Park is equipped with its own cast metal model of the city. Topographical accuracy, a prime concern of almost every depiction of the sacred landscape, could be expressed most clearly in these three-dimensional renderings. Additionally, the models encouraged spectators to make their own spatial connections and intellectual triangulations as they jumped between geographical points on the terrain, allowing the various paths of the eye to create narratives (inspired by Bible stories) in time and space.

By far the most conspicuous medium for the popular dissemination of views of the Holy Land, however, was the 360–degree panorama painting. At a time in the early nineteenth century when images in general were only parsimoniously available to those who were not members of the cultural elite, panoramas provided "blue-collar" viewers with a rich and comprehensive menu of visual delectation.[6] Their size and conspicuous presence in a culture where the unceasing image bombardment of the modern world was yet unknown guaranteed an experience both concentrated in content and of unusual intensity. While aspiring to "high-art" pretensions through its purported didacticism and moral

Figure 2. *Model of Jerusalem, Chautauqua,* stereo photograph, n.d. Collection of the author.

enlightenment, the panorama nevertheless remained accessible to all classes thanks to its claims of straightforward naturalism and its elaborate "packaging" of interpretive pamphlets, entertaining lectures, and, on occasion, music.

Because of its circular nature, the 360–degree panorama painting offered a unique perception of the region that was unmatched by any other experience short of actual travel abroad. Surrounding the public with a continuous horizon line, the panorama drew viewers in, testing the limits of their peripheral vision. It appeared to locate viewers within an existing space, uncompromised by an illusion-destroying, lateral frame. With the further addition of aural experiences, the totality was seen as easily surpassing a one-dimensional encounter with, for example, a travel book. A disparaging comparison with "book-learning" was often made, perhaps to emphasize the universal appeal of the panorama, regardless of intellectual preparation. Thus, when Frederick Catherwood brought his panorama of Jerusalem to New York in 1838, the *Mirror* greeted it with the following pronouncement:

> Neither the most vivid *partial* representations of foreign wonders, nor the most accurate and graphic descriptions of them can so fully bring

them before us as a well-chosen and well-painted panorama. Nothing can surpass the style in which Jerusalem—that holy city, appealing by its glorious associations to our kindled imagination, and religious interest—is brought before us.[7]

Catherwood's painting, previously exhibited in London, was the most important early panorama with a Holy Land subject in the United States. The artist had become known as an explorer and archaeological draftsman during his extended travels in Greece and Egypt. Leaving Cairo in 1833, he crossed the Sinai peninsula and established a residence in Jerusalem for several months. There, from the roof of the structure thought to be the house of Pontius Pilate, he executed a set of panoramic drawings with the aid of a camera lucida. These studies became the foundation of his large Jerusalem panorama, estimated to have been 280 feet in circumference and 36 feet high.[8] When he moved to the United States in 1836, he brought the panorama with him, exhibiting it in Boston and building a special home for it in New York, where it debuted in 1838.

Although no longer extant, Catherwood's panorama can be envisioned today through the engraving (with its seventy-one labeled points of interest) that folded out of the accompanying pamphlet selling for 12½ cents [Figure 3].[9] Guides of this type became standard for panoramas of the Holy Land. Usually, each spot marked on the engraving was laboriously described and discussed in the text, with a liberal scattering of references to Bible verses throughout. These annotated keys were important to spectators, for they allowed them to view the sometimes overwhelming painted surfaces incrementally, providing checkpoints for the eye and a program of visual paths through the complex landscape.

At the center of Catherwood's rotunda, viewers of the panorama were in a position of visual and cognitive power, experiencing what Alan Wallach has called the "panoptic sublime," an exhilarated state induced, in part, by the sensations of metaphoric dominance and control of the site.[10] Yet like all varieties of the sublime, this situation brought with it a measure of discomfort, a sense of self-loss in the face of spatial infinitude and the corresponding desire to confront that loss. Michel Foucault's celebrated "sovereign gaze" cannot be enjoyed unconditionally; it makes its own demands upon its viewer. First among these is the need for order—the space *must* be governed by an active eye. The surrounding void of the darkened panorama rotunda thus forced its viewer to make choices, to turn, pivot, and construct a narrative, to marshal the full expanse

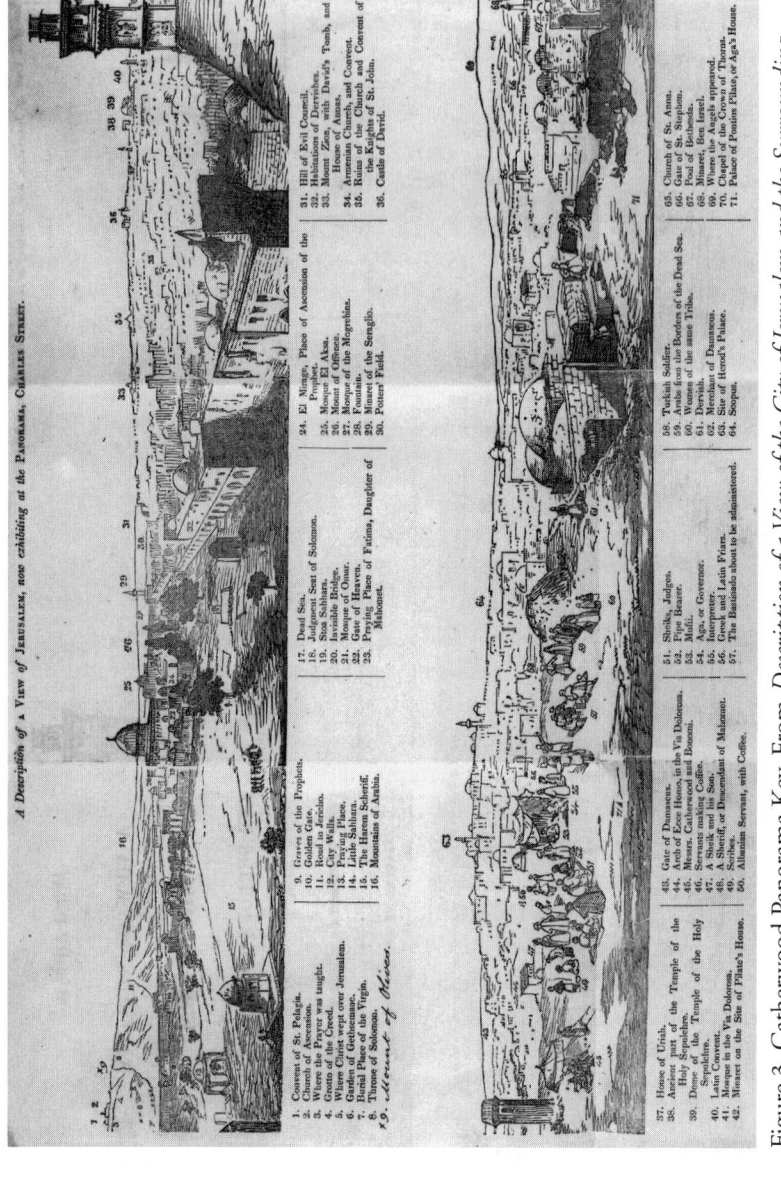

Figure 3. Catherwood Panorama Key. From *Description of a View of the City of Jerusalem and the Surrounding Country*. Boston: Perkins and Marvin, 1837.

of a 360–degree prospect. Realizing the daunting nature of this task, panoramists provided their viewers with a buffering package of texts—pamphlets, drawings, and lectures.

The pamphlet engraving reveals that Catherwood's painting gave a great deal of emphasis to the plaza of the Haram al-Sharif, with a clear view of the Dome of the Rock. This prominence undoubtedly stemmed in part from his unusually extensive researches conducted on the site, an area normally inaccessible to non-Muslims during that period.[11] Catherwood's sketching position at Pontius Pilate's former palace also placed him just off the Via Dolorosa, which he knew would be of great interest to Christians. Unfortunately, Catherwood's choice of a high, central pivot point with a close view of the Haram left many other important Christian holy places—such as the Mount of Olives and the Church of the Holy Sepulchre—in the distance.

One benefit of the "rooftop" placement of the spectator was the raised plateau of space in the foreground, where Catherwood displayed a genre-like sampling of contemporary Middle Eastern figures, each identified by religion, political position, ethnicity, gender, or trade. Included were Turks, Greeks, and Bedouins, who fulfilled their artist-assigned roles of clerics, soldiers, functionaries, and servants. Number 57 even depicted the administration of the bastinado (a method of punishment consisting of blows to the soles of the feet), which fascinated many Americans and often found its way into their travel accounts. These incidental episodes of life in the holy city, though undeveloped in the text of the pamphlet, must have provided diverting anecdotes for Catherwood's accompanying lectures. In fact, to one side of this contrived, encyclopedic figural grouping was a portrait of the artist himself, pictured under an umbrella (number 45). Panoramists frequently included depictions of themselves in their paintings. It reinforced the message of authenticity, reminding audiences of the proprietor's claims of firsthand experience of the site.

Catherwood's presence was also important in the New York rotunda itself, where the public heard his lectures and could engage him personally. The tenor of Catherwood's own lectures can be known to a degree through the text of his descriptive pamphlet. After situating the reader geographically and historically, the essay became a cautionary tale, stressing the ruinous qualities of contemporary Palestine and the lessons that could be learned from its faded past: "All is loneliness and wilderness, where once was every luxury; the glory is departed from the city, and ruin and desolation alone remain." Evoking the solid nineteenth-century belief in the sermons inherent in certain favored stones, it claimed: "Each mouldering ruin recalls a history; and every part, both within and without the walls, has been the scene of some miraculous event, associated with the great plan of human redemption."[12]

But what of the public reception of these works? There is little doubt that the panoramists significantly shaped the journalistic reviews of their paintings; in some cases, the comments appear to be little more than reprinted press releases. Yet these notices are still useful as a barometer of what their authors assumed was most important to the public. During the course of a lengthy Catherwood review in the *New York Mirror*, the concepts of "accurate information" and "glorious associations" appear in quick succession. Another article invoked romantic memories of "those places which we have been taught from our childhood to reverence as the scenes of wonders and miracles." Some adopted a rhetoric of inclusion, writing: "This admirable and correct painting should be visited by all religions and all classes"—while others employed the threat of exclusion: "We do not envy the man whose bosom does not glow with enthusiasm while he gazes upon this picture."[13]

Similar reviews accompanied the openings of other Holy Land panoramas throughout the northeast. With Catherwood's success as a catalyst, the subject became common in places of popular entertainment. Catherwood's painting, however, remained unusual in its depiction of what might be called the "inner city" of Jerusalem. Very few American paintings actually took views from *within* the walls as their subject; one of the rare exceptions is a wonderful watercolor by Miner Kellogg of 1844, an inventive, low composition of walls and domes [Figure 4]. On a sunny rooftop in the foreground, a tiny woman hanging out laundry to dry provides an element of anecdotal interest, while beyond her the crowded street grid of the walled city spreads out diagonally in patterned, squarish blocks of wash. Kellogg provides here a rare American view of Jerusalem as a contemporary, lived-in city, rather than as a fossil of the past.

In general, other American painters did not follow Kellogg in his exploration of the quotidian existence of Jerusalem residents. The preferred view was the wide-angle panorama, usually from outside the walls. These general prospects were seen as the more "Protestant" choice by artists; emphasis on specific locales within the city smacked of Catholic

"Each mouldering ruin recalls a history"

Figure 4. Miner K. Kellogg, *Jerusalem,* 1844, watercolor. Smithsonian American Art Museum, Washington, D. C. Bequest of Martha F. Butler.

worship of shrines. One of the best examples of this type of visualization of Jerusalem is the oeuvre of James Fairman, a little-known figure of crucial importance to the study of Holy Land imagery. An artist who resists categorization and easy placement in the standard narratives of nineteenth-century landscape painting, Fairman led a professional existence of extreme independence. He was a consummate outsider who desperately sought the level of acceptance and recognition accorded to the most prominent painters of his day; when it became clear that he would not get it, he spent a lifetime circumventing the barriers of an obdurate art world.

Closed out of the ranks of the academies and social clubs, Fairman responded by organizing his own extensive network of patronage and promotion—his forceful personality helped him to create a separate niche in the market. Fairman's achievement was made possible in no small part by the popular appeal of his main landscape category: views of the Holy Land. Indeed, although his repertoire of subjects varied considerably over the years, he became the preeminent painter of Jerusalem in the United States, executing, at a minimum, some twenty documented paintings of the holy city. More than any other easel painter, he took the production of Jerusalem imagery to its limits, and because of his success in taking his art directly to what he called "the great tribunal of the people," bypassing traditional intermediaries, his views of Jerusalem had an impact beyond the cosmopolitan cities of the east coast.[14]

Offering himself as a lecturer wherever he traveled, Fairman assumed the role of provincial preceptor in the arts. His career as an art lecturer can probably be traced to 1867, when he gave three discourses treating the profession of the artist at the Cooper Union, New York. To supplement these "conversazioni," as his addresses were called, he took to organizing local "art circles" which read and discussed texts of art history and aesthetics.[15] This cultivation of the layperson, he correctly surmised, would ultimately result in sales of his paintings. In cities without a developed professional tradition of art-making, his lectures and exhibitions were received as important cultural milestones. Eventually, Fairman created a network of picture-buyers stretching from Maine to California.

Before 1871, Fairman's output had consisted of American landscapes and marines, with an emphasis on views of New York Harbor and subjects from Maine and New Hampshire. In that year, he left for Europe and the Holy Land, already having secured commissions for a new range of pictures. The consular records of the United States office in Jerusalem indicate that Fairman registered there on 19 December 1871, during a period of stepped-up American travel in Palestine.[16] No other documentary evidence of his Middle-Eastern trip has surfaced, but the titles of paintings he produced suggest that he visited Jaffa, the Plains of Sharon, and the Sea of Galilee. The sheer number and variety of his views of Jerusalem make it clear, however, that the historic city held the greatest interest for him.

Fairman worked with surprising rapidity. By the summer of 1872, he was back in New York, exhibiting five Holy Land works, among which were three views of Jerusalem.[17] The titles of the Jerusalem paintings (*The Valley of Jehosaphat*, *View of Aceldama*, and *The Damascus Gate, Jerusalem*) indicate that they were taken from three different directions, respectively the east, south, and north sides of the city. Fairman made a point of changing his perspective, even if only slightly, each time he began a new Jerusalem canvas. Taken as a whole, the corpus of views forms a panoramic portrait of the city, a series of varying prospects that assigns importance to disparate topographic sites as the cone of vision pivots around the periphery of the walls.

"Each mouldering ruin recalls a history"

Figure 5. James Fairman, *Jerusalem,* n.d., oil on canvas. Courtesy Museum of Church History and Art of the Church of Jesus Christ of Latter-Day Saints, Salt Lake City, Utah.

By far his preferred view, however, was from the Mount of Olives [Figures 5–6]. Forming a cohesive series of slightly permuted images, each of these many scenes is bifurcated by the horizontal axis of the city's eastern wall, with the ponderous silhouette of the Dome of the Rock and an occasional minaret serving as its mensural coordinates. In successive canvases, the great dome shifts slightly to the left or right, reflecting the movement of the spectator's viewpoint along Olivet's ridge. Likewise, landmarks such as the walled Garden of Gethsemane or the funnel-like spire of the Tomb of Absalom reappear at various points in the middle ground of the paintings. The totality of the set of images constitutes a catalogue of discrete views, organized and unified by a sweeping field of vision and a reassuring system of fixed, signifying objects.

Despite his apparent interest in the placement and situation of the viewer, Fairman does not climb high enough on the Mount of Olives to gain the map-like command of other images of the city, such as Catherwood's. Fairman never looks over the wall, which always remains a visual

Figure 6. James Fairman, *View of Jerusalem*, n.d., oil on canvas. Private collection.

barrier, strategically placed at eye level like a narrow blindfold. Information on the layout of the city is thus withheld, making its contents appear less knowable, more difficult to explain. Fairman's Jerusalem—distant, shut up, and impenetrable—seems to exclude its audience. The glare of the sun renders its skyline darkly opaque. The light only glances off the rooftops, without revealing details. An opposition of values is set up, with the glowing disk of the sun hovering like an ever-present, divine sentinel near the shadowed blot of the Dome of the Rock. In the course of his many views from Olivet, these two orbs (light and dark, implicitly Christian and Islamic) dodge and parry like positive and negative forces, challenging one another as they shift their positions along the horizon.

Islam, or Islamic worship, takes center stage in another painting by Fairman, *The Mussulman's Call to Prayer,* in which Jerusalem is shown from the south. It is one of Fairman's most striking Middle-Eastern works [Figure 7]. Across the intervening Valley of Hinnom, the southern walls of Jerusalem are shown here to follow the gradual slope of land toward the Mount of Olives in the East. The long procession of

"Each mouldering ruin recalls a history"

Figure 7. James Fairman, *The Mussulman's Call to Prayer*, 1876, oil on canvas. Private collection.

clustered, glinting domes catches the raking afternoon light from the sun. Closer to the viewer, Fairman focuses on an unusually prominent figure perched on a projecting brow of rock.

Indeed the emphatic singularity of the lone Arab makes him the key to this work. Conspicuous in his spatial isolation, he is further highlighted by the bright sun glancing off his turbaned head, its compact, rounded form echoing the salient domes in the distance. This evocation of faith seems appropriate as the figure is actually shown engaged in an act of prayer. His shoes removed and his staff left behind, he bows his head, assuming a position identifiable as part of the devotions performed five times daily by practicing Muslims. Such prayers are inevitably directed toward the holy city of Mecca, as is every mosque, each of which has one wall oriented toward the *qibla,* the direction leading toward Mecca.

In Fairman's picture, one of the most celebrated and venerated of all mosques, al-Aqsa, is in view at the corner of the city. Its *qibla* wall, pointing south to Mecca, faces the northward-looking viewer of the painting—a simple geographical observation that would have been apparent to many of the artist's nineteenth-century spectators. Yet the praying figure is not facing south, as al-Aqsa's *qibla* indicates that he should. Instead, he is turned 90 degrees toward the east to face the Mount of Olives, the site most closely associated by Protestants with Christ's Passion (the Garden of Gethsemane can be made out at the right edge of the work). For the viewer, Fairman's figure functions as an ethnic and religious type. Through a visual telescoping from the turbaned head in the foreground to the distant rounded domes, the single Islamic believer comes to stand for the institution of his faith, a shorthand summation of a vast culture. The artist manipulates this praying manikin so that he performs theatrically, paying deference through his worship to a major landscape icon of Christianity while implicitly snubbing the holiest site of Islam. As with the deified, centrally placed "Christian" sun that repeatedly sublates the Dome of the Rock in Fairman's series of Jerusalem paintings, the natural world of *The Mussulman's Call to Prayer* is brought into complicity in a subtle act of religious degradation.

The artist's views were actually quite clear on this subject, and he made a point of calling attention to the anti-Arab and anti-Turk elements in his paintings. Fairman seems here to be in step with definite shifts in prevailing public opinion, for the decade of the 1870s saw a general reassessment of the moderately favorable American attitude toward the Ottoman empire that had hitherto prevailed. As the Turks lost a measure of their global clout (through the Balkan revolts in 1875, the internal power struggles of the Sultanate in 1876, and the Western dismemberment of the empire's outlying provinces at the Congress of Berlin in 1878), American sympathy for Islamic rule diminished considerably while concern for Christian minorities began to be expressed more openly. In this climate, Fairman was anxious to demonstrate evidence of Turkish misdeeds. Thus, in a broadside used to advertise a view of Jerusalem, he wrote (one presumes he is the author):

> The figures and accessories are careful local studies made on the spot: such as the blind man, with his hand upon the shoulder of his boy guide, a sight too sadly familiar, in a land where the mother by crude method destroys the right eye of her boy child, lest he be conscripted into the Turkish army when he became a man, frequently leading to total blindness of both.[18]

"Each mouldering ruin recalls a history"

In several Holy Land paintings, this same inter-generational pair is inserted into the foreground of each scene [see Figure 5, right]. Fairman has taken a standard Orientalist accusation—that indigenous peoples were "blind" to the historical glories that surrounded them—and made it a literal reality. Because this blindness is revealed in his broadside to be more or less self-induced, the consequent ignorance of the figures becomes willful, and thus worthy of scorn rather than pity.

The repeated inclusion of the blind man is a conscious censure of what was described in the same broadside as "the rapacity and cruelty of Turkish rule." This condemnation ended with the ominous words, "Jerusalem, the Crescent is thy Cross." Taken as a whole, Fairman's Holy Land views can be seen as a continuous effort, through structural and iconographic means, to separate the crescent from the cross, to restrict the access of indigenous Muslim figures to the topographic glories celebrated in the central territories of his canvases.

Nearly every painting operates through this centrifugal opposition of distinct sectors of landscape: an internal bowl of warm, glowing space and an elevated, peripheral rim populated with an array of notably passive figures—the profane encircling the sacred. The central areas appear devoid of inhabitants, unsullied by an infidel human presence. Like the closed-off, walled city of Jerusalem, these favored valleys become sacralized by their very status as unobtainable. Foreground figures are left to gaze into the misty center, their entrance into the scoop of space interdicted by the pronounced edge and sudden drop of their foreground perch as it pulls back from the middle ground. The bowed, "fish-eye" stretching of the landscape along the edges leaves the impression that the figures are placed as passive spectators high up in a natural amphitheater. Here, however, elevation of viewpoint does not denote visual command, but rather removal from a more privileged sphere. Fairman thus creates a field in which these human occupants are allowed to exist but with which they are not permitted a dialectical interaction. Indeed, the same might be said of the viewer of the artist's Holy Land paintings, who forever remains excluded from the precincts of the walled city.

The viewer of Frederic Church's *Jerusalem from the Mount of Olives* is subject to no such lack of connection [Figure 8]. In this, the grandest and most celebrated of all American images of Jerusalem in the nineteenth century, Church's audience found itself swept up, elevated, and encouraged to arrive at a personal union with the heavenly creator. The

Figure 8. Frederic E. Church, *Jerusalem from the Mount of Olives,* 1870, oil on canvas. The Nelson–Atkins Museum of Art, Kansas City, Missouri. Gift of the Enid and Crosby Kemper Foundation.

compositional mechanics of the image are complex and worthy of some discussion. However, some background on the artist himself is also important to any understanding of the painting.

While Frederic Church was not the first American artist to travel to the Holy Land in the nineteenth century, he was certainly the best known, a titan of the New York cosmopolitan art world. By the time he embarked on his only trip to the Old World in 1867, his American public had been conditioned to anticipate with eagerness each large new work and to flock to the exhibitions of these single canvases—which Church, the consummate businessman, promoted and staged as entertaining, educational, and devotional experiences. *Jerusalem from the Mount of Olives,* which he completed in 1870 shortly after returning from his trip, was shown privately in New York, where large crowds came for the opportunity to gaze at this dramatic, yet exacting view of the Holy City.[19]

Church traveled to the Holy Land during a period of great religious doubt. For several decades, geologists had been increasing the estimated age of the earth until it could no longer harmonize with the version of time and history given in Genesis. To this crisis of chronology, Darwin's theory of natural selection added notions that undermined the teleological concept of "good design," thus calling into question the intrinsic harmony of nature that had always been seen as reflective of God's perfect state.[20] In partial response, Church subscribed to a reactive branch of science that has been called "sacred geography," the rational study of the holy landscape with the aim of revealing the conformity of the physical and scriptural accounts. The main argument, familiar to students of nineteenth-century Holy Land literature, was that the events of the Bible, being historical, had necessarily inscribed themselves on the topography of the Holy Land. The events themselves remained invisible, but the landscape, with its unchanged rocks and natural forms, could be called upon as a witness to what had occurred in its presence. Nowhere was this a more salient issue than in the city of Jerusalem.

During his stay in the holy city in 1868, Church allowed himself ample time to survey the area. While he dutifully visited such traditional sites within the walls as the Church of the Holy Sepulchre, his Protestant bias against these Catholic-tended shrines led him to conduct his own explorations in the surrounding areas outside the city gates. In this search for "old" Jerusalem, he found himself offended by the recent erection of the Russian and Prussian pilgrim hospices, the "appearance of newness" of which had "destroyed" his first view of the city.[21]

Two days after arriving, however, Church had a rare opportunity to leave behind these modern impositions and view the most ancient parts of Jerusalem. Charles Warren, the head of the field operation of the British Palestine Exploration Fund, was in the habit of conducting visiting Westerners through his excavation shafts just outside the walls. After meeting Warren, Church was lowered into the 100–foot shaft, where he was impressed by the arched limestone passages and ashlar remains believed to be part of Herod's temple. This experience was undoubtedly the seed for his later involvement in the Fund's sibling organization in the United States, the American Palestine Exploration Society.

In the American Society, the "Members" (its board of directors) consisted of fifty distinguished American men: ministers, missionaries, industrial giants, explorers—and one artist, Frederic Church.[22] It would be difficult to overestimate the significance of Church's involvement with this organization. It is perhaps the most concrete tie that is known to exist between the Western archaeological survey teams and an American artist engaged in depicting the same local scenery.

The official rhetoric of the American Society was couched entirely in the question of faith. The chairman of the Society was unequivocal in describing its work:

> Its supreme importance is for the illustration and defense of the Bible. Modern skepticism assails the Bible at the point of reality, the question of fact. Hence whatever goes to verify the Bible history as real, in time, place, and circumstances, is a refutation of unbelief.[23]

These words were written at approximately the same time that Church's *Jerusalem* was on view in New York, and although the painting is much more than a simple answer to a call to arms against religious doubt, it is easy to imagine his meticulous canvas as just the kind of illustration of "the Bible as a Book of realities" that his Society would have welcomed.

Church's *Jerusalem* was explicitly tied to Warren's timely archaeological work in at least one review, and the connection of the painting to the contemporary Protestant surveys of Palestinian lands even seemed to affect the language used to describe it: "It is, in a certain sense, a map of Jerusalem and its suburbs," observed the *New York Tribune*. "The eye is at first confused and misled. It must go roving about and learning its lesson, like an engineer officer reconnoitering a difficult field."[24] The vast scope of the painting (itself a kind of personal expedition report) made this "reconnoitering" process a slow one; the scene was not easily comprehensible at first glance. Viewers were first required to negotiate twisting paths, a myriad of rich textures, and abrupt changes in distance before arriving at a synthetic understanding of the work. As an aid, Church provided visitors with a printed key, its numbers designating such important sites as the Holy Sepulchre and the Jewish temple platform.

The vista that the artist laid before his viewers is an impressive one. Church takes possession of the space, dominating, organizing, and clarifying it, seemingly paving the city across the measured, flat hilltop as if to display it with maximum clarity above the overly dark Valley of Jehoshaphat. The view had more than purely formal interest, however. One review of the painting drew attention to the foreground path, "down which we may well permit ourselves to fancy the Saviour passed on his first entry into Jerusalem."[25] In fact, it was often pointed out in travel volumes that Christ would have seen this exact springtime view each day near the end of his life as he rounded the ridge on his morning walk from his lodgings in the town of Bethany to Jerusalem. At the bottom of the key to *Jerusalem* was printed: "The Spectator is supposed to stand in the early spring, on the Mount of Olives, facing the West." The American viewer was thus invited to enter the painting and follow in these footsteps of Christ, beholding the "same" vision of the ancient landscape and walled city.

For viewers of *Jerusalem,* light becomes the principal effect, breaking through the great cloud mass to guide the spectator to the warmly illuminated temple platform and the spotlighted promontory of Olivet. With their surroundings remaining in shadow, these two pools of golden sunlight encourage the formation of a personal link between the viewer in the foreground and the most ancient section of the old city across the valley. An even greater bond is forged, however, when the radiance of the sun at the top of the canvas is added to this pair of highlighted areas, a dramatic, heavenly effect carefully studied in the artist's plein-air sketches. The glowing foreground is thus matched above the bisecting line of the city by a corresponding burst of warm, aerial luminescence. In the flat plane of the finished canvas, the result is read as a connecting axis of light, an *axis mundi* creating what Mircea Eliade has termed an "irruption" at the center, with its consequent aura of sacred space. Indeed, the introduction of a vertical element is crucial for Church's rapturous effect of transcendence. Its location in Jerusalem accords well with the medieval idea of the holy city as the navel of the world, and more specifically with the ninth-century theologian Rodolph of Fulda's notion of the *universalis columna,* or "column of the universe," passing through that navel.

This refulgent shaft at the center of *Jerusalem* forms a luminous "break in plane" in an otherwise uninterrupted horizon, a connecting of the celestial and the terrestrial. Viewers before the huge painting experience a lift that could almost be described as physical—the very structure of the image seems to induce an ascendant state. In this it could not be a greater contrast to James Fairman's many images of the same city, where spectators rarely find themselves swept up in such a divine and miraculous unfolding. While Fairman is fixed and controlled, Church is engaging and interactive. He gives his viewers more, but also assumes that they will be able to make more of it.

As is often the case with Church, the entire landscape is encoded with formal cues that are designed to reinforce and support the primary visual statement. Thus in the sky at left, the clouds, light breaking at their edges, appear to roll back off the city of their own volition. Like a curtain being pulled away, they help form the image of an opening, a revelation-in-process. On the opposite side of the canvas, anthropomorphized olive trees also participate in this presentation. A single smaller tree, in particular, seems to turn and regard the illuminated spectacle, its torso-like trunk bent in acknowledgement and its branches gesturing.

That Church identified with these stately, aged behemoths (the largest forms in the entire composition), rather than with the tiny Arab figures who converse among themselves and fail to exhibit the degree of awareness of their arboreal neighbors, is indicated by his signature, inscribed on the face of the hillside in the midst of the dominating grove of olives. Like the surrounding trees, the artist has become rooted in the authentic soil. Perhaps as a result of this associational communion with the Mount, its illuminated plateau of land appears to rise up assertively in the foreground, tipping toward the viewer as if to corroborate scripture solely by virtue of its material presence. Every part of the canvas, in short, performs its assigned role in bringing the viewer to a private experience of spiritual redemption.

In the end, though, despite the focus of attention on the city, Jerusalem seems strangely distant and far away. It is an effect that, to a degree, is inevitable, given the monumental scale of the work. If Jerusalem seems removed, quiet, and passive, however, it is because it is simply fulfilling its role as the physical evidence of larger phenomena—such as the heavenly proclamation of cloud and sun above it. This more elevated meteorological drama sets the composition in motion, uniting its disparate parts with strategic mounds of cumuli and shafts of light. It leaves an impression of a city and countryside being acted upon below, and there is little question of the identity of the actor.

Church was, in some respects, the last painter who was able to put forward convincingly such an unswerving belief in godly agency. By the end of the century, artists such as John Singer Sargent began painting what were essentially visual shrugs before the topography of the Holy Land, lingering stares of remarkable dispassion and ambivalence, as in Sargent's *Near the Mount of Olives* of 1905, a work whose very title, through its willful imprecision, appears to slight a scriptural landmark [Figure 9]. This is a vacant glimpse of a blanched, Eastern terrain that rejects all that his predecessors had deemed most notable in the region.

For all but a handful of faithful hangers-on, the imperatives that had structured the works of earlier generations of artists were no longer

"Each mouldering ruin recalls a history"

Figure 9. John Singer Sargent. *Near the Mount of Olives,* 1905–06, oil on canvas. Fitzwilliam Museum, Cambridge, England.

at issue when Sargent arrived in Palestine. Born at a time when they were still operative yet also a witness to their general demise, Sargent came to the Holy Land with vague expectations that could not be fulfilled through conventional religious experience. Rather, his response to the Palestinian landscape was channeled through aesthetic, formal conduits, without the programmatic biblical imperatives of a Church or Fairman. He sought art, rather than proof.

In the end, then, there is a degree of commonality between Sargent and the other artists. Though their motivations varied widely, they usually arrived in Palestine to find something in its landscape that could serve their own needs. Perhaps because it was reinvented each time a new visitor disembarked, the Holy Land could guarantee this constant supply of ideological and aesthetic sustenance. Americans departed from the biblical terrain again and again, confident that they had secured its secrets and truths. The mutability of those meanings, more than anything else, assured that no matter what had been taken away, there would always be others ready to start the process anew.

## Notes

This essay is largely adapted from my book, *The Landscape of Belief: Encountering the Holy Land in Nineteenth-Century American Art and Culture* (Princeton, 1996).

1. John Dillenberger, *The Visual Arts and Christianity in America: The Colonial Period through the Nineteenth Century* (Chico, Calif., 1984), 66. Dillenberger writes that "experiential religion was alone indigenous to America, and an expression of America's particular genius."

2. Photography is the one visual form to have received a fair amount of attention by scholars. See Eyal Onne, *Photographic Heritage of the Holy Land, 1839–1914* (Manchester, 1980); Yeshayahu Nir, *The Bible and the Image: The History of Photography in the Holy Land, 1839–1899* (Philadelphia, 1985); and Nissan N. Perez, *Focus East: Early Photography in the Near East, (1839–1885)* (New York, 1988).

3. Ebenezer Newhall, *Religious Patriotism: or, Attachment to Jerusalem* (Boston, 1830), 7. Newhall was a member of the conservative wing of the Congregationalist Church, which was intolerant of Unitarian reform. See George F. Daniels, *History of the Town of Oxford, Massachusetts* (Oxford, 1892), 66–67, 627.

4. Quoted in George C. D. Odell, *Annals of the New York Stage*, 15 vols. (New York, 1927–1949), 1:101–102.

5. For a similar model, see Ruth Kark, "Jerusalem in New England," *Ariel* 69 (1987): 52–61.

6. The entire phenomenon of panorama painting cannot be considered here. The literature on panoramas is growing, and scholars are now tracing the history of the medium as well as examining its theoretical and ideological ramifications. Of particular interest are Stephen Oettermann, *Das Panorama: Die Geschichte eines Massenmediums* (Frankfurt, 1980), and Ralph Hyde, *Panoramania!: The Art and Entertainment of the "All-Embracing" View* (London, 1988).

7. "The New Panorama," *New York Mirror*, 18 August 1838.

8. This estimate is given in Kevin J. Avery, "The Panorama and Its Manifestations in American Landscape Painting, 1795–1870" (Ph.D. diss., Columbia University, 1995), 25.

9. Most accounts of the Jerusalem panorama conclude that it was destroyed when Catherwood's rotunda in New York burned in 1842. Yet an edition of the descriptive pamphlet (with the same accompanying engravings as earlier editions) was later printed in New York in 1845. A copy is housed in the library of the National Gallery of Art, Washington, D.C.

10. Alan Wallach, "Making a Picture of the View from Mount Holyoke," *Bulletin of the Detroit Institute of Arts* 66 (1990): 38.

11. In 1843, Catherwood further displayed his knowledge of the building by exhibiting a painting entitled *A View of the Interior of the Mosque of Omar* at the annual exhibition of the National Academy of Design, New York (cat. # 285).

12. Frederick Catherwood, *Description of a View of the City of Jerusalem and the Surrounding Country* (Boston, 1837), 3.

13. *New York Mirror,* 18 August 1838; *Providence Journal, New York Evening Star,* and *New-York Christian Advocate and Journal,* all quoted in a Catherwood broadside, New York Historical Society; reproduced in Victor Wolfgang von Hagen, "Mr Catherwood's Panorama," *Magazine of Art* 40 (April 1947): 143.

14. *Biographical Sketch of Col. James Fairman, A.M.* (London, 1880), 3.

15. See "Brooklyn News," *New York Times,* 14 April 1867. One of Fairman's "art circles" in Lawrence, Massachusetts, is described in Mary Eleanor Barrows, *John Henry Barrows: A Memoir* (Chicago, 1904), 135.

16. "Travelers Register," Jerusalem Consular Post Records, RG 84, vol. C.39, National Archives, Washington, D.C. The most extensive source on American consular activity in the region is Ruth Kark, *American Consuls in the Holy Land, 1832–1914* (Jerusalem, 1994).

17. See "Art Notes," *New York Evening Post,* 8 July 1872.

18. "Jerusalem from the Mount of Olives, by James Fairman, M.A.," broadside, Carnegie Museum of Art, Pittsburgh. On American-Turkish relations of the period, see James A. Field, Jr., *America and the Mediterranean World, 1776–1882* (Princeton, 1969), 307–309.

19. Although there has been a recent explosion of publications on Frederic Church, *Jerusalem from the Mount of Olives* has received little discussion beyond the pioneering book by David Huntington, *The Landscapes of Frederic Edwin Church: Vision of an American Era* (New York, 1966), 91–101. I previously considered the painting and its place within Church's oeuvre in "Frederic Church's 'Sacred Geography,'" *Smithsonian Studies in American Art* 1 (Spring 1987): 78–96; and "Frederic Church's *Jerusalem from the Mount of Olives*: Progressive Time in Nineteenth-Century America," in *Tempus Fugit: Time Flies,* ed. Jan Schall (Kansas City, Mo.: Nelson-Atkins Museum of Art, 2000), 244–50.

20. Several authors have considered the ways in which this crisis posed a fundamental threat to Church's belief system, as well as to his art. See, most recently, Franklin Kelly et al., *Frederic Edwin Church* (Washington, D.C., 1989).

21. Frederic Church, "Petra Diary," 8 February 1868, typescript, Olana State Historic Site, Hudson, N.Y.

22. Church is also listed in the Society's statements as a contributor. Further evidence of his involvement is found at his home, Olana, where his collection of Holy Land photographs includes rare examples of prints from one of the Society's expeditions, a series issued in 1876. On the Society, see Warren J. Moulton, "The American Palestine Exploration Society," *Annual of the American Schools of Oriental Research* 8 (1928): 55–78, and Henry Innes MacAdam, *Studies in the History of the Roman Province of Arabia: The Northern Sector* (London, 1986), 234–38, 257–76.

23. Joseph P. Thompson, "Concluding Appeal," *Palestine Exploration Society,* 1 (July 1871): 34, 35.

24. "Church's Jerusalem," *New York Tribune,* 31 March 1871.

25. "'Jerusalem.' The Latest Important Work of Frederick [*sic*] E. Church," *New York Evening Mail,* 31 March 1871.

# Historical Perspective Through the Study of Ordinary People

## William H. Rudy (1845–1915), a Member of the American-Swedish Colony in Jerusalem

Ruth Kark
*Hebrew University*

> *Their estrangement hard to bear,*
> *Left alone and unprotected*
> *No man for my soul to care;*
> *Still I could be sweetly praising,*
> *On the suff'rings, borne for me,*
> *Patiently, on Calvary.*
>
> *"For the Glory Keep Me Low," from a hymn found inserted in Rudy's Bible*

### Introduction

In the summer of 1986, I set out from Jerusalem to survey nineteenth-century consular correspondence on Jerusalem, Jaffa, and Haifa at the United States National Archives in Washington, D.C., for a book I was writing on the American consuls in the Holy Land. As I pored over boxes, books, and papers—the daily bread of archival researchers—a curious container caught my eye, entitled "Personal Effects of William H. Rudy, Ca. 1895–1915."[1]

When the green container arrived in the reading room, I was surprised to find items more suited to a museum than an archive. Inside were personal belongings such as leather purses and folders of different sizes, a series of emblem pins, monocles, and a stylographic (fountain) pen, an embroidered cloth bag containing mother-of-pearl and metal buttons, a carved wooden whistle in the shape of an animal, three penknives, and eleven small envelopes that had once contained old coins, one of them a Hasmonean coin bearing the image of Yohanan Hyrcanus, son of Simon the Maccabee. Other items included prayer books and religious literature, address books, photographs of places and family members, and maps. There was also correspondence—personal, business, and official—most of it in English and some in Turkish, Arabic, and Hebrew.

Looking through this collection, many questions arose in my mind. Who was W. H. Rudy? Could anything be learned from his personal effects and papers? How had this modest estate reached the National Archives? When I returned to Jerusalem, I took some of my students to visit the small American Colony cemetery at the edge of the Hebrew University campus on Mount Scopus, where I teach. One of the tombstones was that of W. H. Rudy (Figure 1). The search for ties between America and the Holy Land, which motivated this article, had come full circle.

William H. Rudy was born in the small town of New Berlin, Union County, in central Pennsylvania on May 13, 1845.[2] From the letters and photographs, we learn that members of his family lived in Pennsylvania, Iowa, and Chicago. He kept up a correspondence with his mother; his sister, May Robinson Rudy; and his brother, J. W. Rudy, who resided in Chicago.[3]

Precisely when he moved to Chicago himself is unclear, but the documents show that he certainly lived there between 1876 and 1881. Several decades later, Rudy was described as an Easterner who had owned flour mills and had been active in real estate dealings. After a serious illness, he retired from business and began to pursue a religious life.[4]

At this time, Rudy became involved with a group of believers who had broken away from the Presbyterian church. He joined them on a pilgrimage to Jerusalem in August 1881, at the age of thirty-six. He was accompanied by his foster mother, Caroline Merriman.[5] Rudy was to remain in Jerusalem for the rest of his life, apart from two visits to Chicago and Washington, D.C., in the period between 1895 and 1898.[6]

# Historical Perspective Through the Study of Ordinary People

Figure 1. Photograph of William Rudy's tombstone (photographed by Jeremy D. Kark, 12 September 1987).

Rudy's travel papers from October 23, 1897 offer the following physical description[7]:

    Age: 52 years
    Stature: 5 feet, 7 inches
    Forehead: high
    Eyes: grey-blue
    Mouth: medium
    Chin: bearded
    Hair: brown
    Complexion: fair
    Face: oval

In mid-1898, Rudy returned to the American Colony.[8] As a bachelor, his life was devoted to religious observance, community work, and the commune. Rudy died of a stroke in Jerusalem on July 9, 1915 and was buried in the Colony's small cemetery on Mount Scopus. Otis A. Glazebrook, the United States consul in Jerusalem at the time, notified Rudy's family. In his report he added: "No further action is necessary on the part of the consular court as he left nothing but his personal effects."[9]

We know very little about the life and work of Rudy in Chicago. While he may have been the "proprietor of flour mills," the documents we found were connected with real estate, particularly a transaction with a widow, Martha P. Barrett, which involved Rudy from 1876–1895.[10]

According to Rudy (our only source), the Barrett affair began with "a note of Jos. W. Brockett in favor of Mrs. Martha P. Barrett, dated June 17, 1874, worth $7,500 with security of only $2,500." Mrs. Barrett was an elderly woman with a sick daughter who could not get Brockett and another debtor, H. S. Martin (who owed her $3,000 secured by leasehold property), to pay their debts. In need of money, Mrs. Barrett appealed to Rudy to help her. He declined at first but was later persuaded, and spent much time and labor collecting debts on the old woman's behalf.

On the one hand, Rudy's motivations were humanitarian; on the other, he recognized the financial implications of being able to acquire land in a part of the city that might one day become valuable. At some point, Rudy reached an agreement with Mrs. Barrett that certain properties would become his as payment for his efforts. According to the warranty deed, Mrs. Barrett of Cook County transferred ownership of two tracts of land to William H. Rudy on August 28, 1880 in exchange for $2,500. The property included four acres of land bordering on State Street and six acres bordering on 89th Street, Prairie Avenue, and Indiana Avenue. Appended to the deed are maps of the property drawn in black and blue ink on rag paper.[11]

Rudy's speculations proved correct. "Soon after this," he wrote, "there developed a growing demand for property in the locality where this was situated and in 10 months after I bought (June 1881) I was offered $3,000 for it. . . ."[12]

Apparently regretting her actions, Mrs. Barrett "entered a bill of complaint against me which I could not personally be present to answer to; neither had I seen a copy of this bill until June 1895, nor did I fully know the content until then." This was because Rudy had left for Jerusalem in August 1881 and did not return to Chicago for several years. Unable to defend himself, the court ruled in Barrett's favor and found Rudy "wholly in default." In 1895, he contested this ruling, citing the "great injury financially and otherwise" done to him by the elderly widow.[13]

On June 20, 1895, he requested an authorized copy of the warranty deed to present in his defense. He also wrote to V. M. Moon, asking him to look for a "tin box bearing my initials which contained papers among which were a Warranty Deed of two tracts of land from Mrs. Barrett to me. Also tax titles, abstracts of title and other papers relating to the transfer of the property to me. . . . Also a note and mortgage from Wm. P. Black to me for $1,000."[14] There is no further information about how the affair ended, or whether Rudy was able to reestablish his claim prior to returning to the Holy Land.

This episode illustrates the liquidity and chaos in the real estate market, and the spiraling of prices following the Great Chicago Fire in October 1871. Chicago lawyer Horatio Spafford and his colleagues, who had invested large sums of money in real estate (in the area that is now part of Lincoln Park in downtown Chicago, and on the northern side along the lakeshore) suffered severe losses as a result of the fire.[15] Spafford was further devastated by the loss of his four daughters in a shipwreck in 1873 and the death of his infant son in 1878. These misfortunes led Spafford and his wife Anna into a search for religious meaning and spirituality. They were joined in this search by Rudy.[16]

Rudy's preoccupation with religion, which became a central issue in his life, is hardly mentioned during his stay in Chicago. However, his leather-bound Bible, the "English Version of the Polyglot Bible containing the Old and New Testaments," published in London by Samuel Bagster and Sons, is inscribed with a handwritten message at the beginning of the book of Genesis: "1st reading through began Nov. 28, 1877." From then on, the book seems to have been in constant use. Many passages and verses are marked, especially in the Psalms.

A random examination of two such passages shows that both deal with the punishment of those who do not help or obey the Lord. Judges 5:23 reads: "Curse ye Meroz, said the angel of the LORD, curse ye bitterly the inhabitants thereof; because they came not to the help of the LORD against the mighty."

In Kings I, 13:22–27, a mark is made beside the verses describing the man of God that came from Judah in the time of King Rehoboam. A lion met him by the way and slew him "as thou hast disobeyed the mouth of the LORD, and hast not kept the commandment which the LORD thy GOD commanded thee."

Inside the Bible were two sheets of paper. One was the reprint of a hymn, "For the Glory Keep Me Low," in which the key words are meekness, humility, submission, and love, with an emphasis on devotion to God rather than human relationships.[17] The second contained portions of "an address in the tent at Keswick, on Thursday evening, July 22, 1897," expounding the importance of God's message conveyed "through the reading and the speaking about our Lord Jesus Christ." In the margins, the word "Jerusalem" appears in black ink, in Hebrew and English.[18]

Another volume in the container, also leather-bound, was a compendium of hymns and verses from the Scriptures to be read throughout the month—the *Daily Food for Christians,* published by the American Tract Society, 150 Nassau Street, New York (n.d.).

In his writings, Rudy devotes only a single line to his intentions to visit Jerusalem: "I had arranged to go to Pal. [Palestine] in Aug. 1881 with a company of others. . . ."[19] His decision to retire from what appears to have been a successful business life was motivated, according to Bertha Spafford Vester, by his recovery from a severe illness. It was at that time that he had begun his relationship with the Spaffords and some of their friends in Chicago.

In the 1870s, the Spaffords were profoundly influenced by Dwight L. Moody, a leading revivalist, and later a dispensationalist. Horatio Spafford himself devoted much of his time to evangelism, and eventually adopted dispensationalist beliefs.[20]

The bitter experiences of Horatio and Anna Spafford led them to develop religious theories that were unusual at the time—among them, "the belief in the truth of God's love and its universal triumph, and the belief in the eventual restoration of all." They held that "the blows that had been dealt them were not punishment for their sins; they did not believe in a tangible hell or a personal devil." Naturally, this doctrine was contrary to the tenets of the orthodox Presbyterian church. The Spaffords were asked to leave the Fullerton Avenue church they attended, and a number of their friends walked out at the same time in protest.[21]

This was the background for their planned pilgrimage to Jerusalem, which was widely ridiculed. According to one newspaper: "A singular sect of Christians which has recently arisen in one of the northern suburbs of Chicago is known as the 'Overcomers.' They believe in personal inspiration, in direct communication with God, and in the literal rendering of the Scriptures as applied to mundane affairs, and in the final salvation of all the universe, including the devil. A party under the leadership of Mr. Spafford is about to go to Jerusalem to build up the ruined places."[22]

The group originally intended to return to Chicago. In the end, however, they settled permanently in Jerusalem. Most of the members made their home in the American Colony and, when they died, were buried in Jerusalem.

## The American Colony in Jerusalem

On August 17, 1881, the group of sixteen Americans, among them Rudy and his foster mother, set out for Jerusalem. They arrived on September 26, settling first in a rented Arab house in the Muslim Quarter of the Old City. As the group grew larger, they rented another building in the Muslim Husseini neighborhood outside the city walls. For decades they lived together as a religious sect practicing a communal lifestyle. In this, they were no doubt influenced by post–Civil War religious movements and communes operating in North America.[23]

As with other communes, the Jerusalem group was founded on the principles of voluntarism and a shared desire to live a communal life like that of the early Christian disciples as depicted in Acts 5:42–46. They upheld separatism from the religious establishment, millenarianism, and the pursuit of a unique lifestyle that would prepare them for the coming of the Messiah. They believed in "perfectability" (the belief in man's ability to achieve moral perfection), they practiced revivalism, and aspired to establish a model society.

From its inception, the leadership of the American Colony was charismatic and authoritarian. Following Horatio Spafford's death in September 1888, Anna Spafford was the central figure until her own death in 1923. One of the cultural and religious rituals developed by the founders was the morning assembly. Most of the activities of the group revolved around religious meetings, public prayer services, music (there was an orchestra and a choir), and hymnody. The group had no bylaws or codex.[24]

The sect set its religious beliefs higher than the family. Although at the beginning they had no ascetic practices, they soon decided to adopt celibacy, disregarding former marriages and banning new ones. This was the practice until 1904. Anna Spafford was regarded as a mother substitute; the inscription on her tombstone, "Mother," shows that she was so called by her followers.[25]

In 1896, the small group was joined by a number of newcomers, most of them Swedish Americans from Chicago and fellow believers from the village of Nås in the Dalarna district of Sweden, headed by Olof Henrik Larson. There were also a few other Americans, British, converted Jews, and local Muslims who joined the community on an individual basis. During its peak period at the end of the 1890s, there were nearly 150 members.[26]

Aside from communal life, the residents of the American Colony engaged in a wide range of philanthropic, educational, and health care activities. In the process, they developed close ties with various individuals and population groups, including other Christians, Muslim Arabs from the elite and lower classes, Jews, and Samaritans. They aided Jewish immigrants from Yemen who arrived in Jerusalem totally destitute. Among the papers left by Rudy is a letter in Hebrew from a group of Yemenite families appealing for assistance prior to the holiday of Sukkot (Figure 2).[27]

Over the years, the community developed successful businesses in souvenirs, photography, and tourism. In the Colony itself were a bakery, a carpentry shop, a shoemaker, a blacksmith, and a sewing, weaving, and embroidery factory—all of them open to the wider public.[28]

The strange beliefs and lifestyle of these people, and their opposition to missionaries and conversion, drew upon them the wrath of Jerusalem's Christian religious establishment. Even some of the U.S. consuls in Jerusalem complained about their "immorality" and deceptive financial practices, and the consequent damage being done to the good name of the United States. This combination of good relations and hostility illustrates the duality in the sect's relationship with the outside world, a duality that was largely imposed by others.[29]

While the founders and Anna Spafford were alive, the group managed to abide by its principles with a minimum of controversy. Afterwards, however, the second generation of Swedes and Americans began to dispute with one another over policymaking and financial control, and eventually the group disbanded during the British Mandate (between the world wars).

William H. Rudy was one of the community's most loyal members. He is mentioned in a U.S. consular report of January 2, 1883,

# Historical Perspective Through the Study of Ordinary People

> אשרי משכיל א דל
>
> אשר נודיע למעלת אדון החכם השלם השם הטוב ד"וב ה"ין בעין צרכינו ומבקשים מפני אדון לדבר טוב בעדינו
> אצל השרים ירום הודם אולי ירחמו עלינו ויתנו לנו צרכי ימים טובים של חג הסכות כי אין לנו שום דבר
> וככל ימות השנה אנחנו מסתפקים במועט אבל ביום טוב צריך תוספת קצת כגון בגדים וכיוצא ובעבור כי גרים
> אנחנו ואין ידינו משגת הצרכנו לעשות זה הכתב ויש עוד אחרים שכאן ואין להם לא לחם ולא שמלה והמד"ך :
> מעירנו ' ואהבתם את הגר ' וברכות לראש משביר" הפבה" יאריך ימיכם בטוב ושנותיכם בנעימים אכי"ר ~

| בית מרי סעיד האמדי | בית מרי סעיד |
| בית יוסף חבשוש | בית סעיד ט'ימני |
| בית חזה ט'עדאף | בית יחיא גראזי |
| בית יוסף אישוך | בית יודא גראזי |
| בית דאוד אמלם | בית הרון חוטר |
| בית סאלם אצאדם | בית חיים אהמדי |
| בית סאלם אגמל | אמנות |

Figure 2. Photograph of letter from Yemenites asking for financial assistance. (Source: USNA, RG 84, Jerusalem, No. 27).

which lists the names of U.S. citizens registered with the consulate and residing in the American Colony in Jerusalem.[30] A report on the Spafford community in 1893 states that "of the six adult Americans—three men and three women, the three women are widows, and of the three men, one is a teacher [W. H. Rudy?], one a widower [Otis Page], and one has a wife in America whom he deserted [E. J. Baldwin]. None of these six people have passports and never have had; still I recognize them as American citizens...."[31]

Rudy's various skills made him a key figure in the American Colony. He served as its business manager, and as such conducted financial negotiations and kept a strict account of purchases. He was responsible for mail delivery, and represented the Colony in its dealings with the local authorities and the U.S. consul. At the same time, he was involved in public health and in arranging employment for the needy—evidence that he was widely connected.[32]

Little is known of his private life in Jerusalem. One of the photographs in the collection that portrays family members, the American Colony, and sites in Palestine may be of Rudy himself. In another source, we find the news that "the old dear lady Mrs. Merriman had a stroke and passed quietly away. She was buried in the cemetery of the German Templar [sic] Colony."[33] The same source tells of a birthday celebration held in Rudy's honor some time after the move outside the Old City (probably May 1897, when he was fifty-two). The party, refreshments, and gifts are vividly described. Among the gifts was a "silk scarf worn by certain Arabs and Beduins, a headdress appropriate to this country when the sun is very hot." It is said of Rudy that he was "so kind and thoughtful for us all, it was a pleasure to have a celebration for him."[34]

Rudy was extremely helpful in an incident involving the children of the Whiting family: Ruth (born in 1880) and John (born in 1882) were left a large inheritance on condition that they leave the American Colony and return to the United States. The U.S. consul, Selah Merrill, fought with the colonists in an attempt to aid David Lingle, who had come from Chicago to remove his sister, Mary E. Whiting, and her children from the "immoral" environment in which they were said to be living.[35] Rudy was assigned by the consul to serve as Mary Whiting's counsel.[36]

In December 1893 and March 1895, appeals were filed in Massachusetts and Chicago to appoint a guardian for the minors, Ruth and John Whiting, "whose mother was unfit to have such custody." The children's estate was very large: $60,000 in government bonds, drawing an annual income of $3,000 on the principal, which neither the mother nor the children were receiving.[37]

Mary attended the first trial alone. In early 1895, Rudy accompanied the children to Chicago for the second trial. An old friend of Rudy's in Chicago, Luther Laflin Mills, once State's Attorney for Illinois, agreed to represent them free of charge in order to fight religious persecution. In the public eye, it was not just Mary Whiting on trial, but the entire American Colony. The judge's decision to award custody to Mary Whiting thus represented a certain legitimization of the Colony.[38]

While in Chicago, Rudy continued to bear financial and organizational responsibility for the colonists, dozens of whom had joined them in Chicago for the trial. He arranged cheap passage for them back to Jerusalem in 1896. When they returned, a lengthy dispute ensued between the colonists and the two U.S. consuls, Edwin Wallace and Selah Merrill, over the sale of the American Presbyterian cemetery on Mount Zion and the desecration of its graves. This affair lasted from early 1897 until 1906.

It was Rudy who corresponded and negotiated with Wallace. On September 8, 1897, he left Palestine to travel to Washington, D.C., on behalf of the American Colony. Rudy's major goal was to persuade the State Department to open an investigation into the cemetery affair and into the Colony's "earlier and often repeated complaints against the two consuls." Through Rudy's efforts, the consul-general in Constantinople did investigate the issue.[39] Mementos of this second visit to the U.S. include two railway tickets—with a clergyman's discount—and an entrance permit to the U.S. Senate dated February 2, 1898.[40]

In the course of the fight against the consuls and Rudy's trip to the United States, another issue involving the Spaffords came to light. In December 1897, the Adamsons were in Chicago. This couple had joined the American Colony on April 7, 1896, and had transferred all their property to Rudy as treasurer. On April 17, 1897, they withdrew from the Colony in great bitterness, testifying against the "Spaffordites" in the presence of Consul Wallace in Jerusalem before returning to the United States. Wallace advised them to sue Rudy for the return of their money while he was still in the United States. Wallace claimed that Rudy "is after more victims who can be induced to put their money into the general fund so that the select few can live without worry."[41]

We learn about another important day in the life of Rudy and the American Colony from a pin among his personal effects. The pin, shaped in a cross in red, white, and blue, bears the inscription: "The World's Fourth Sunday School Convention 1904 Jerusalem." In April 1904, 800 American and 400 British pilgrims arrived in Jerusalem to attend this convention, whose proclaimed goals were "Education—Inspiration—Consecration." Sessions were held in a large tent erected on the road between the Damascus Gate and the American Colony (Figure 3). All the representatives of the religious and political establishment were there to welcome them, including the Ottoman district governor, the U.S. consul, and the Anglican bishop.[42]

While the convention enjoyed the avid support of the Jerusalem establishment, its leaders also promoted good relations with the American Colony. They accepted accommodations and organizational assistance from the colonists, and even invited them to sit on the platform of the convention. This constituted an important legitimization on the part of the American religious establishment, and as summed up later, "was a landmark in the history of the Colony. It was the first time Dr.

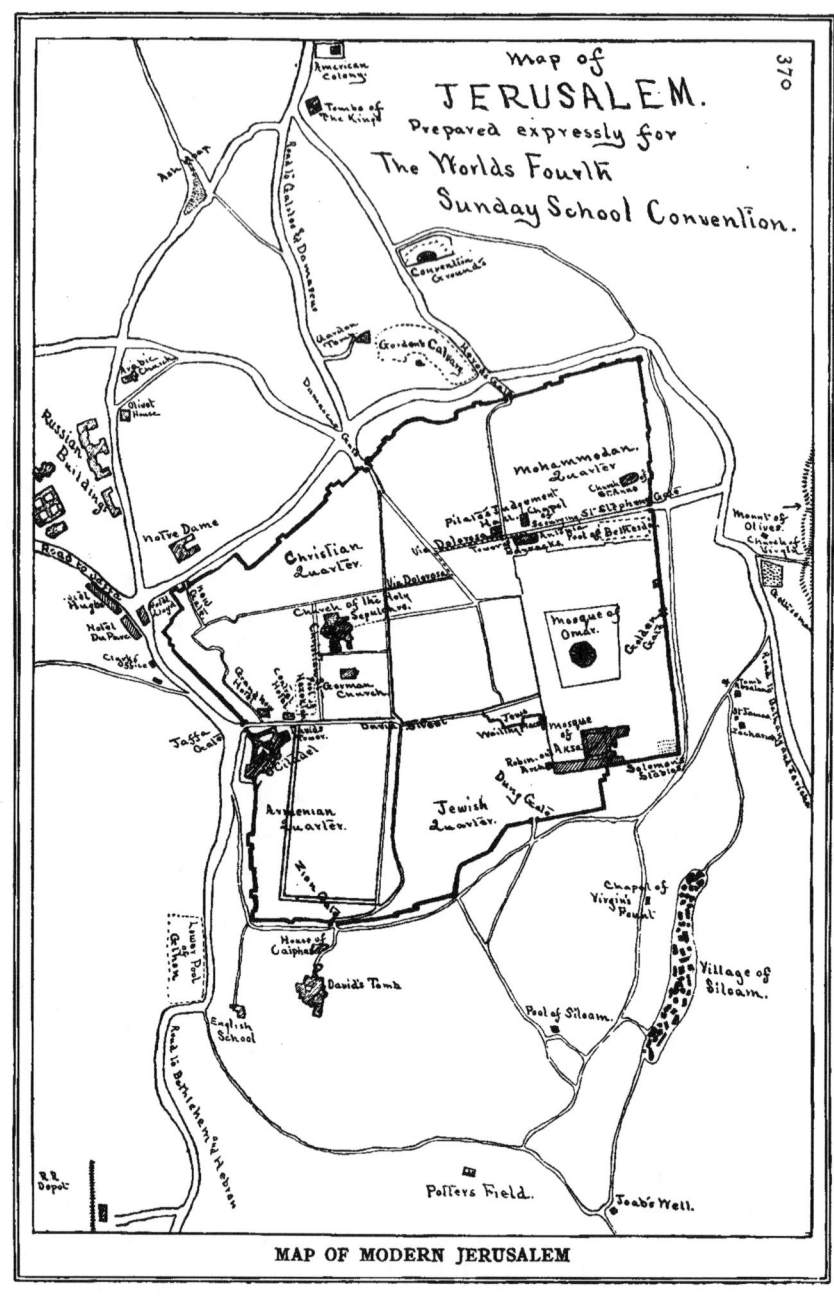

Figure 3 Map of Jerusalem published in honor of Fourth Sunday School Convention, April 1904 (Source: *The Cruise of the Eight Hundred to and through Palestine, Glimpses of Bible Lands,* New York, 1904).

Merrill [the U.S. consul] had been openly and publicly challenged and his threats ignored."[43]

A few years later, on July 7, 1915, during World War I, a box full of gold Napoleons was unearthed as a Colony member hoed a rose bush. In the commune's morning assembly, it was decided to keep it in the Colony safe until the matter was clarified. Two days later—on the day of his death, which may well have been precipitated by the incident—Rudy confessed before Anna Spafford, the "Mother" of the Colony, that he had buried the treasure. The money, he explained, had come from the sale in Chicago of the church and house owned by Olof Larson and his Swedish-American commune. One source claims that Rudy kept this sum for himself in the event of the Colony's dissolution; another possibility is that he assigned it as a resource that would be available to the community in some future time of economic hardship.[44]

By studying the items in the container of Rudy's personal effects, and using supplementary data from other sources, we have been able to shed some light on the man who owned them. However, the question of how this material came to be stored in the archives continues to elude us. It may be that his family simply did not claim his personal effects, which were eventually transferred to Washington, D.C., together with the Jerusalem consulate documents.

Through a synthesis of various types of source material, we have achieved some insight into the life of an individual who disappeared from history. To borrow an analogy from archaeology, rather than digging for palaces and temples or for kings and priests, we have been delving into the life of an ordinary citizen. In the process, we have gained a better understanding of the commercial and religious atmosphere of Chicago in the 1870s, and the reasons someone like Rudy chose to leave the city—perhaps because of the rigid Puritanism that prevailed in his church. We have also begun to scratch the surface of a unique religious sect with a longstanding attachment to the Holy Land and Jerusalem, which aroused great controversy among its contemporaries, and which founded what may have been the first "kibbutz" in Palestine.

## Notes

I would like to express my thanks to the staff of the Legislative and Diplomatic Branch of the United States National Archives, especially to its chief, Milton O.

Gustafson, to Richard Gould, and to the reading room staff, for their admirable assistance. This study was inspired by Moshe Davis and supported by the America-Holy Land Project, Institute of Contemporary Jewry, the Hebrew University.

A short version of this paper was published in Hebrew in *Ariel*, vol. 100 (1994): 40–51. I thank Ely Schiller, the publisher, for permission to include the English version in this volume.

    1. United States National Archives, Record Group 84, Jerusalem, No. 27 (henceforth: USNA-Rudy). The dating criteria used by the archivist are unclear. Some of the items in the container are from before 1895 (1887 and 1889) and the documents relate to events taking place between 1873 and 1916. For a recent general overview of the American Colony in Jerusalem see Helga Dudman and Ruth Kark, *The American Colony: Scenes from a Jerusalem Saga* (Jerusalem, 1998).

    2. Ibid., certificate of registration of American citizen, given to W. H. Rudy, Jerusalem, 11 May 1915.

    3. Ibid., J. W. Rudy, Chicago to Dear Brother, Jerusalem, 27 January [1910] and May Robinson Rudy (sister), 8 December 1907, giving particulars about family and mother.

    4. See Bertha Spafford Vester, *Our Jerusalem: An American Family in the Holy City, 1881–1949* (Garden City, N.Y., 1950). On Rudy's business in Chicago, see below.

    5. Ibid., USNA-Rudy, personal notes, warranty deed &c. &c. of W. H. Rudy (1895).

    6. Ibid. According to the personal notes, Rudy returned to Chicago only in 1895. In the container there are also two American railway tickets issued in 1897 and April 1898.

    7. Ibid., passport document No. 9215 of W. H. Rudy, issued by John Sherman, 23 October 1897 (n.p.). This document was probably applied for in Washington, D.C., after Rudy's arrival; he left Jaffa on 8 September 1897.

    8. Ibid., certificate of registration.

    9. See photograph of tombstone, Figure 1. See also the report of his death in USNA, Index Bureau, 1 October 1915, 367 m.113/74.

    10. USNA-Rudy, personal notes (Rudy's handwritten account) and blue notebook, compliments of Jas. Jay Smith and Co., Chicago.

    11. Ibid., certified copy of warranty deed, 8 August 1880, and 20 June 1895.

    12. Ibid., personal notes.

    13. Ibid.

    14. Ibid., Wm. H. Rudy, Chicago to V. M. Moon, 29 June 1895.

    15. Spafford Vester, *Our Jerusalem*, 1, 9, 27.

    16. Ibid., 44.

    17. No date or author is given. There is a note, however, stating that the hymn was translated from the Dutch by Mrs. M. Netthling.

    18. I would appreciate receiving more information from readers about this hymn and address. Rudy may have heard the address while in the United States in 1897, though according to Spafford Vester in *Our Jerusalem*, 202, he left for Washington only the following month.

19. USNA-Rudy, personal notes.
20. See Yaakov S. Ariel, *On Behalf of Israel, American Fundamentalist Attitudes Toward Jews, Judaism, and Zionism, 1865–1945* (Brooklyn, N.Y. 1991), 36–38; Ruth Kark and Yaakov S. Ariel, "Messianism, Holiness, and Community: The American-Swedish Colony in Jerusalem, 1881–1933," *Church History* 65, no. 4 (December 1996): 641–57.
21. Spafford Vester, *Our Jerusalem*, 50–61.
22. Ibid., 58. The name of the group was derived from the sect's belief that the desire to sin could be overcome by a return to the early practices of the Christian Church.
23. See Yaakov Oved, *Two Hundred Years of American Communes* (New Brunswick and Oxford, 1988), 25–42; Ruth Kark, "Post-Civil War American Communes: A Millenarian Utopian Commune Linking Chicago and Nås, Sweden to Jerusalem," *Communal Societies* 15 (1995): 75–114.
24. Alexander H. Ford, "Our American Colony in Jerusalem," *Appleton's Magazine* 8: 643–55, reprinted in *The Holy Land in American Protestant Life, 1800–1948*, edited by Robert T. Handy (New York, 1981): 164–74.
25. [Laura Petri], "Jerusalem in Prose," MS V519, Jewish National and University Library, Jerusalem (1933), 7–18.
26. Ruth Kark, "Sweden and the Holy Land: Pietistic and Communal Settlement," *Journal of Historical Geography* 22 (1996): 46–67; Aaron Yaffe, "The American Colony in Jerusalem at the End of the Ottoman Period," seminar paper, Hebrew University of Jerusalem, 1978.
27. USNA-Rudy, letter of Yemenite families (in Hebrew), n.d.
28. Lester I. Vogel, *To See A Promised Land, Americans and the Holy Land in the Nineteenth Century* (University Park, Pa., 1993), 152–59; Dov Gavish, "The American Colony and Its Photographers," in *Zev Vilnay's Jubilee Volume* (in Hebrew), edited by Ely Schiller (Jerusalem, 1984), 127–44.
29. USNA, RG84, T471, No. 84, U.S. Consul Selah Merrill, Jerusalem to Assistant Secretary of State, Washington, D.C., 19 April 1897; U.S. Consul Thomas Wallace, Jerusalem to Assistant Secretary of State, 8 October 1908; Helga Dudman, "History of the American Colony of Jerusalem" (in Hebrew) *Keshet* 12 (1976): 166–77; Gershon Greenberg, *The Holy Land in American Religious Thought, 1620–1948* (Lanham, Md., 1944), 153–59; see also Ruth Kark, *American Consuls in the Holy Land, 1832–1914* (Detroit and Jerusalem, 1994).
30. USNA RG 84, T471, No. 84, U.S. Consulate, Jerusalem to State Department, Washington, D.C., 2 January 1893.
31. Ibid., Selah Merrill, Jerusalem to the Spafford American Community in Jerusalem, 17 August 1893.
32. Spafford Vester, *Our Jerusalem*, 69, 75, 93, 105, 119, 125–26; see also USNA-Rudy, which contains letters in Turkish and Arabic (including from the *kaymakam* of Jerusalem) dealing with damage to American property and summons to court (1904, 1914).
33. USNA, RG 84, T471, No. 84; Spafford Vester, *Our Jerusalem*, 148.
34. Spafford Vester, *Our Jerusalem*, 69, which reproduces correspondence from Mrs. Gould, Jerusalem, to Aunt Rachel, Chicago, n.d.

35. Ibid., 160–73; USNA RG 84, T471, No. 84, correspondence between David Lingle and U.S. Consul Selah Merrill, including a summons to court, a warrant for the arrest of Mrs. Whiting, and a police report for 10 July–20 September 1893.

36. USNA RG 84, T471, No. 84, Selah Merrill, Jerusalem, to William B. Hess, Constantinople, 20 September 1893.

37. State of Illinois, County of Cook, application for guardianship of Regina Lingle, 3 March 1895; also court report, 17 April 1895. I wish to thank Helga Dudman for making these documents available to me.

38. Spafford Vester, *Our Jerusalem,* 69.

39. Ibid., 200–202; also USNA RG 84, T471, No. 84, correspondence on the subject, Jerusalem, 19 April, 13 September, 17 September, 7 December, 31 December 1897.

40. USNA-Rudy.

41. *Chicago Journal,* 20 December 1897; USNA RG 84, T471, No. 84, U.S. Consul Edwin S. Wallace, Jerusalem, to Assistant Secretary of State, Washington, D.C., 19 April 1897. Appended to this document is the testimony of the Adamsons, who refer to Rudy as the treasurer: "The community has all things in common, in the hand of the treasurer."

42. USNA-Rudy; *The Cruise of the Eight Hundred to and through Palestine, Glimpses of Bible Lands* (New York, 1904). Thanks are due to Nitza Rosovski, then of the Harvard Semitic Museum, who permitted me to photocopy parts of this book. It is stated (p. 369) that the Sunday Schools movement claimed a membership of 26 million in 1904.

43. Ibid., 6; Spafford Vester, *Our Jerusalem,* 192–94.

44. [Laura Petri], "Jerusalem in Prose," 8–9.

# Dedicating and Consecrating the Land

## Mormon Ritual Performance in Palestine

Steven Epperson
*South Valley Unitarian Universalist Society (Utah)*

---

On at least six separate occasions between 1841 and 1933, apostolic envoys of the Church of Jesus Christ of Latter-day Saints (Mormon) traveled to Ottoman and British Mandate Palestine to "dedicate and consecrate" the land for the "gathering together of Judah's scattered remnants" for the restoration of Jewish political autonomy within this territory, and for the renewal of the landscape sufficient to sustain a large and flourishing population.[1] These ritual benedictions, and the practices that preceded and followed them, were an expression of formative Mormon ideology regarding the centrality of covenant communities residing upon sacred territory. Moshe Davis keenly perceived the importance of the idea and reality of the scriptural Holy Land to the development of Mormon self-definitions. It is to him that this essay is dedicated.

I will argue that, consistent with recent studies of pilgrimage and sacred space, Mormon rites of dedication and consecration of the land of Israel can be best understood as prominent examples of the ways in which sacred space is socially constructed through ritualization, reinterpretation, and contestation for legitimate "ownership."[2] That is, Mormon envoys traveled to Ottoman and Mandate Palestine to ritually negate what they considered to be the negative effects of illegitimate stewardship in Palestine, thus "re-sacralizing" the land. They sought to establish a site of ingathering for the Jews—the Lord's people—in this way locating the Jewish people on territory central to Mormon eschatology. Finally, they aimed to symbolically wrest control over sacred space in the Holy Land from its historical Christian custodians.[3] By means of these rites, nineteenth-century Mormon envoys attempted to redefine the landscape of the Holy Land.

The trips to Palestine took place over a period that spanned nearly a century of the Mormon experience, and they involved the participation of more than a dozen important church representatives. If it is true, as plausibly suggested by Roger Grainger, that ritual behaviors "provide the greatest insight into the dominant *metaphors* that structure *myth* and generate *dogmas* within the religious community," and that, as Gershon Greenberg has asserted, the "religions of America projected their absolute hopes" upon and "shaped their self-definitions" in the Holy Land, then an examination of the Mormon rites of dedication and consecration will register the profound shift that took place in Mormon ideology between 1841 and 1933.[4]

The chief metaphors in nineteenth-century Mormon self-definition were "the gathering," the millennium, and the "restoration of all things." Mormons believed and preached that they were restoring saving truths and ordinances that had been lost, distorted, or neglected by the churches. The full blessings of these restored treasures could only be enjoyed by a covenant church of saints gathered out from "the world" and situated upon a prophetically designated and sanctified territory; from this site, the millennial Kingdom of God upon earth would begin to be established. Perceiving the Jewish people as another living covenant community, early Mormon leaders, including church founder Joseph Smith, preached that, like the Mormon covenant people, the Jewish people would also be gathered out from modern "Babylon" and established once again in the land of the Bible. Smith, and others, believed that there would be two eschatological "kingdoms" whose capitals would be physically situated in America and the Holy Land. A temporal, premillennial orientation informed Mormon efforts to preach and to gather out, and to urge the Jewish people to gather to Israel, with all deliberate haste. Mormonism's first generation was confident that these nation-building endeavors would furnish the most powerful proofs for the truth of the Mormon gospel. Gathering, millennium, and restoration both produced and were expressed in the rituals of consecration and dedication.[5]

## Dedicating and Consecrating the Land

By the 1920s, however, the Mormon community had undergone what Thomas Alexander has described as a paradigm shift; it had abandoned the regnant nineteenth-century metaphors of gathering, millennium, and restoration for those of universal evangelization and institutional correlation and growth.[6] Influenced by and intent upon expressing this transformed ideology, Mormon apostles traveled to British Mandate Palestine in 1927 and 1933 to "dedicate and consecrate" it primarily for missionary work. Though they ritually reconfirmed the blessings of an earlier generation on the land and summoned the Jewish people to gather to Palestine, it is certain these speech-acts were subsumed within a conversionist program. In the 1920s and 1930s, the principal signs of the efficacy of dedication and consecration shifted from Jewish national autonomy—which negated Christian hegemonic theologies of supersessionism—to hopes that Mormons would outperform their Christian rivals in effecting large-scale conversions in the Holy Land.

What Mormons meant by dedicating and consecrating the land and how that meaning changed over time will be examined in the remainder of this essay. Several ritual episodes will be presented in turn. Since Orson Hyde's pilgrimage to Ottoman Palestine in 1841 was the most important of these efforts, it will be examined at greatest length. A consideration of the Mormon envoys in 1873, 1927, and 1933 then follows.

A significant body of recent critical studies of sacred space points to the important role played by ideologies and ritual in the perception, construction, and interpretation of sacred landscapes.[7] These works revise the "essentialist" axioms of Eliade, Otto, Wach, and others, which tend to construe sacred space as removed from history, change, and context. While successful, to an extent, in replicating an insider's perceptions of certain experiential qualities of sacred space, "essentialist" accounts tend to ignore or overlook the contingencies of sacred places—that is, the way they are affected by temporal and cultural labors performed by countless individuals and institutions in contests over possession and interpretation, and the resulting significant "capital," or authority, that custodianship of holy sites confers.[8]

The revisionist studies are important for analyzing and representing the intentions and meanings of Mormon rituals of dedication and consecration. For example, Mormon writers interpret Orson Hyde's "mission to Palestine" as the prototypical expression of rituals from which successors did not vary. Typically, it is adduced as a proof-text for Mormon dispensationalist theologies or mustered as an example of unerring Mormon philosemitism. The former readings fail to situate Hyde's ministry within the historical context of Mormonism's profound struggle in the antebellum period to redefine the core of American Christianity away from ascendant Protestant evangelicalism. They also gloss over the attempts by some early Mormons who grounded the authority of their endeavor by pointing to the bankruptcy of Christian anti-Jewish supersessionism. Mormons dedicated the Holy Land as a site for an autonomous Jewish state, believing that its establishment would discredit the other churches and legitimate the Latter-day Saints. The "feel-good" philosemitic reading of Mormonism overlooks the deep theological divisions within the Mormon community over perceptions of Jews and Judaism and the historical development of normative Mormon doctrine regarding the Jewish people from an autonomous to a conversionist model.[9]

In sum, Mormon rituals of dedication and consecration can be neither fully understood nor appreciated without considering the contexts in which they were enacted. The rites were deeply entangled in a struggle over legitimation and displacement against foes outside the Mormon community. Subsequent generations of Mormon leaders have had to contend with this sectarian legacy and with the potent aura of Mormon beginnings as they assert their revisions of myth and metaphor central to the Mormon church.

## Orson Hyde's Ministry, 1840–1842

All of the key elements identified by David Chidester, Edward T. Linenthal, and others as necessary for the construction of sacred space—ritualization, reinterpretation, and contest for legitimate ownership of sacred sites—are present in Orson Hyde's account of his mission to Palestine. Hyde was thirty-five years old in April 1840 when he proposed his mission to Palestine to the Nauvoo, Illinois, conference of the Mormon church. For nine years he had served in important positions in the decade-old church: itinerant evangelist, pioneer-settlement fund-raiser, member of the church's first quorum of twelve apostles, and dramatically successful missionary to the British Isles.[10] Awaiting a divine sign directing him to the site of his missionary labors in the late winter of 1840, Hyde received what he called a "waking vision" with unusual instructions communicated by a heavenly voice. He told the Nauvoo Conference that he saw the cities of London, Amsterdam, Constantinople, and Jerusalem, and that he was commanded to travel to the Jewish communities in these cities.

Instead of preaching to the Jewish residents, Hyde said he was instructed to gather information from Jewish leaders about contemporary messianic expectations, opinions, and movements; he was to declare to these people that their "iniquity" was "pardoned"—that they had paid more than "double for their sins"[11]—and he was to urge Jewish residents of the diaspora to gather to their covenant homeland in Palestine. Hyde was assured by revelation that his undertaking would "open the eyes of many of the uncircumcized" to the fact that the "Day of the Lord" was near, and that "the Gentiles" should assist the Jewish people to gather or else they would be cursed.[12]

It is not necessary to rehearse all of the details of Hyde's mission in this essay. Rather, it is important to understand what Hyde meant to accomplish and how and to what ends his "travels and ministry" to Ottoman Palestine in 1841 were represented to the reading public. To this end, a close reading of *A Voice from Jerusalem,* an account of Hyde's mission published in 1842, is revealing.

*A Voice from Jerusalem* is a twenty-four-page pamphlet that was edited and published in Liverpool by the Mormon apostle, theologian, and then-European Mission president, Parley P. Pratt. It contains an editor's introduction, Hyde's description of travel through Europe to the Holy Land, accounts of the letters Hyde wrote to and conversations held with Jewish community leaders, a record of Hyde's encounters and disputations with Christian missionaries in Jerusalem, and a copy of the prayer written by Hyde on the Mount of Olives on October 24, 1841. An experienced polemicist for the church, Pratt most likely did not coauthor or heavily emend Hyde's text. However, he did significantly alter the arrangement of the letters for stylistic and strategic effect. For instance, Hyde's first two letters, written on October 20, 1841, and November 22, 1841 (reporting, respectively, his arrival in Jaffa and the text of his dedicatory prayer) appear only at the end of the pamphlet. Following Pratt's introduction are two other letters, lengthy reminiscences about Hyde's arrival and actions in Jerusalem, which were written in January 1842. The effect Pratt aimed for by this arrangement was first to establish Hyde's authority and the legitimacy of his mission (introduction) and then to deposit the fully empowered Hyde directly at Jaffa Gate in Jerusalem, ready to engage and displace his adversaries (letters I and II). Only after this "end" is secured is Hyde presented ritually dedicating and blessing the land (letters III and IV).

"I entered the city at the west gate, and called on Mr. Whiting, one of the American missionaries."[13] The Jerusalem encountered by Hyde was a "Christian" city where the "Latin Convent of Our Savior" extended room and board to the weary traveler. The streets and edifices named by Hyde on his initial walk into the city bear the names of holy saints and commemorate the events of Christ's passion. Nonetheless, what is most striking in this account is the presence of the American Board of Commissioners (Protestant) and Anglican missionaries virtually at Jerusalem's gates. They are the first inhabitants Hyde reported encountering, the first he identified by name, the first and most significant adversaries he would have to confront. In contrast to the Mormons who followed in 1873 and 1898, Hyde did not record visiting the Church of the Holy Sepulchre or the Temple Mount (*al-Haram al-Sharif*). Latin and Orthodox Christianities, as well as Islam, while undoubtedly present in Jerusalem, hardly merited Hyde's attention. His sights focused, instead, upon Mormonism's more immediate foe: American and British evangelical Protestants and their missionary agencies.

It is hardly necessary to restate the fact that Protestant leaders took a dim view of the claims and growth of Mormonism in the United States and Great Britain in the 1830s and 1840s. They repudiated Mormonism's extracanonical scriptures, the claims made by Mormon leaders to plenary revelation, and the Mormon witness that it, not the churches, represented an authentic, restored Christianity. The Protestants' negative appraisal was also anchored in a fundamentally different vision of sacred space. Belden Lane observed in *Landscapes of the Sacred* that one of the axioms of landscapes molded by the religious imagination is that they possess centripetal and centrifugal impulses.[14] That is, religious groups either focus immediately upon a land set apart from the world, or else they move out into the world from that site, intent upon creating a sanctified kingdom without circumference. Whereas nineteenth-century Mormonism was influenced by the first impulse, evangelical Protestantism has been propelled primarily by the second. Evangelicalism is distinctive for its universal scope and itinerancy—for the indeterminancy of its spatial center. Thus, Protestant missionaries and revivalists have always gone out to "win the world for Christ."

In the Middle East, it was clearly the intent of Protestant missionary boards in the nineteenth and early twentieth centuries to "recover the provinces wrested by Islam from the Church." Theirs was a modern crusade, to be effected by conversions of Jews and Muslims alike, and by the renovation and reform of the "Oriental" churches through gospel preaching and Protestant polity. Evangelical efforts would be crowned by control over the extensive territory of the Middle East—either administered by benevolent, Protestant imperial nations or by "enlightened" cadres of reformed/converted "native" government officials[15]—and by de facto custodianship of holy sites.

The striking success of evangelical Protestantism at home, and its extensive territorial visions for growth abroad, help explain both the presence of American and British missionaries encountered by Hyde in October 1841 and the reason why they are presented in the pages of *A Voice from Jerusalem* as the most formidable force with which he had to contend. Accordingly, the first letter of *A Voice from Jerusalem* displays Hyde in disputation with Protestant missionaries. He reports that the venue of confrontation and discussion ranged from the private residences of the Americans to the Latin Convent, and from there to the homes of Anglican missionaries and Jewish converts.

Hyde's strategy throughout was to displace and de-center his opponents. He informed his interlocutors about his ministry, the intent of which, after all, was to establish an autonomous *Jewish*, not Christian, presence in that place. He averred that Christian missionary efforts would be to "little or no purpose."[16] Hyde contrasted his authority in traveling and ministering to the Holy Land, vouchsafed by "ancient saints" and "miracles, visions, and prophecy," to the false authority of "orthodox religionists" with their missionary boards and societies, their "dogmas," and priesthood "without power and greatness."[17] It was not "modern sectarianism" (read: evangelical Protestantism) that would prove decisive in effecting significant changes in the Holy Land commensurate with the Divine will; rather, it would be "political power and influence" that would combine to gather in and build up the dispersed Jewish nation. To their faces, Hyde predicted that it would be "Israel's banner," not that of Christendom or Constantinople that would eventually flutter over the walls of the city.[18]

With this disputation over authority, the Mormon ritual process of reinterpreting and reconstructing sacred space in the Holy Land began in earnest. To Hyde and his Mormon readers, the fact that the missionaries (not surprisingly) failed to acknowledge the Mormon apostle's ministry, disputed Hyde's negative assessment of their missionary endeavors, and withheld assistance in contacting Jewish representatives in Jerusalem, combined to amply discredit their presence and authoritative claims. By way of contrast, it was a Jewish family, members of which had converted to Anglicanism, who responded positively to Hyde's account of his ministry. Indeed, Hyde reported through *A Voice from Jerusalem* that "many Jews listened," that the idea of the Jews being restored to Palestine "was gaining credibility," and that individual Jews received Hyde's message with "smiles of joy."[19]

The politics and culture of antebellum America—industrializing, evangelical, democratic—presented a landscape at odds with Mormon aspirations and self-definitions. Seemingly powerless, the Latter-Day Saints nevertheless responded to the divine injunction, "Go ye out of Babylon; gather out from among the nations," and set about establishing settlements on the American frontier. Ritually designed and sanctified, the territory of these settlements was known as "Zion."[20] Settling in compact, covenant communities, the Mormons enacted a leveling of the religious and cultural playing field in America, which was otherwise so heavily weighted in favor of commercializing and evangelical movements.

The Mormon gathering to Zion functioned in ways typical of all pilgrimages. Speaking of the latter, Alan Morinis describes pilgrimages as journeys "undertaken by a person in quest of a place or a state that he or she believes to embody a valued ideal." Pilgrimage sites are "intensified versions of the collective ideals of the culture."[21] Mormon culture-in-the-making was communitarian, liturgical, and convenantal. Mormons saw themselves as a chosen people and, according to Jan Shipps, set about "building a counterpoint of the Hebraic Kingdom with Solomon's temple at its center" in the heart of the American continent.[22] The settlement of Zion, in spite of hostility and obstructions, became an embodiment of the collective ideals of the Mormon people, the site where Mormon ideology would be validated by "facts on the ground." Similarly, the Holy Land embodied Mormon beliefs and hopes: another covenant people—the Jews, similarly marginalized and exiled in a Gentile world—would gather to this remote yet exceedingly potent pilgrimage site and "act out . . . perfectly the way things ought to be." Two peoples, marginal according to "the world's" reckoning and dispossessed of clear title to their homes, were nevertheless central to the divine drama of the last days. The success of their response to gather out from "Babylon" and to settle on ritually sanctified territory constituted a key feature in Mormon claims to authoritatively proclaim their gospel and to read the "signs of the times." However, relocating and centering Mormons and Jews in Zion and Jerusalem, respectively, entailed the de-centering of others. In Hyde's version, evangelical Protestants would clearly be the losers.

After being rejected by the representatives of Christendom and encouraged by a family of Jews, Hyde struck out on a walk "about the environs of the town."[23] It was during Hyde's perambulation round the exterior of the walled city that the third part of the ritual of dedication and consecration occurred.

Hyde's ambit took him from the Eastern (Lion's) Gate to the Mount of Olives ("that almost sacred place") to Gethsemane (where, unmediated by institutional church edifices, he felt he finally encountered the "Son of the Virgin") From there he continued on to the Tombs of the Prophets, the Pool of Siloam, Mt. Zion, and finally back to Jaffa Gate. Hyde's procession was a key part of the ritual displacement of adversaries and the restoration of the site to its "rightful" heirs. He reported that it was on this walk that he came to the conclusion that his deeds, not those of missionaries and site custodians, would "not only revolutionize this country, but . . . renovate and make it glorious."[24] With this walk, Hyde began to remap the sacred boundaries of "this country" by superimposing a blank eschatological template upon the city. His walk functioned in some ways akin to the traditional processions of rogation, which both invoked divine blessings for "the coming agricultural year" and established "the boundaries of the fields."[25] Furthermore, the walk around the city conformed to the practice of land surveys before the advent of theodolite and lasers. Hyde remeasured the landscape of the city's environs by foot, eye, and written description according to the traditional system of "metes and bounds." In this practice:

> The surveyor dedicated a piece of property by measuring a series of straight lines from one landmark to another; when these landmarks were connected on paper, the resulting irregular polygon defined . . . the limits of the property. . . . [Surveyors were] brought into intimate contact

with the land; they had to come face to face with the terrain they were mapping before they could draw lines on it.[26]

In fact, Hyde's description reads like a surveyor's notebook. He strode from landmark to landmark, carefully describing each one along with its topographical setting. He ignored the cramped and contested urban "metes and bounds" of streets, convents, churches, and shrines as if these would be of no true consequence in the messianic/millennial city-to-come. From the summit of the Mount of Olives, he gazed upon a landscape transformed though the lens of "the history of the past in connection with the prophetic future."[27] Hyde's perspective collapsed time and space; it negated the political realities of Turkish rule, European political designs, and Islamic and Christian superintendency of the holy city and its sites.

Hyde performed the fourth and climactic act of the ritual of dedication and consecration on Sunday, October 24, 1841 in the prayer he committed to writing and in raising two rock cairns, one on the flank of the Mount of Olives facing the city, and the other within the precincts of the Temple Mount. These ordinances, which followed his disputation with missionaries, the validation of his ministry by Jewish representatives, and his rogation around the city, completed Hyde's mission in Jerusalem. They also expressed, through structured gestures, the two principles of restoration and gathering that were essential to nineteenth-century Mormon ideology.

In his third letter to Pratt, Hyde reported that in obedient response to the vision of the previous year, he "offered up" a prayer "to dedicate and consecrate this land for the gathering together of Judah's scattered remnants." To that end, he prayed that Jerusalem would be built up again, that a temple would be reared "in honor of Thy Name . . . O Father," that "the kingdom" would be restored to Israel, with "Jerusalem as its capital," that the people would be constituted a "distinct nation and government," and that the land would "become abundantly fruitful when possessed by its rightful heirs."[28] In what for Mormons was a highly unusual move, Hyde wrote out and then published the text of his prayer of dedication and consecration. Few Mormon prayers are written down, most being "occasional" and extemporaneous, and the few that have been committed to print have been accorded canonical status and invariably accompany a small number of important Mormon rituals. By privileging this particular invocation, Hyde meant to raise

## Dedicating and Consecrating the Land

his speech-act above the vagaries of time and place, thus entailing his coreligionists thereafter to an authoritative reading of the Jewish people, the Holy Land of scripture, and a predictive construction of imminent "prophetic" events. Henceforth, Hyde proclaimed that this site (as he looked over Jerusalem) would now be expressly devoted to the cause of the return and restoration of the Jewish people. This is the sense of Hyde's prayer as a "dedication": his contemporaries, he believed, would live to see the end of the dispersion of the Jewish people and their subject status in the Gentile world upon their return to the Holy Land and the recreation of an autonomous nation.

After having "lavished blessings upon [the land] in the greatest prodigality in view of what is to come," Hyde "consecrated" it as well.[29] Why would Hyde set apart as sacred a land already holy in the eyes of the Jewish, Muslim, and Christian communities? From the text of Hyde's prayer, it is clear that he believed that the Holy Land had been profaned, and that its sacramental character could be restored by means of his apostolic blessing and the restoration of the land to its "rightful heirs." According to Hyde, the land was "smitten with barrenness" because it "drank from murderous hands the blood of Him who never sinned," and because it had been defiled by "the Gentiles" who had "trodden down [Jerusalem] for so long."[30] Now, however, it was prepared to reclaim its former glory.

One obstacle in realizing that end had already been removed. The divine voice of Hyde's vision had declared the land to be the site for the imminent gathering of the "children of Abraham," and that whatever role Israel's sins of the past may have played in its exile, the Jewish people had more than paid in full measure: its "iniquity" no longer constituted an obstacle to gather together in the holy land:

> "Speak ye comfortably to Jerusalem [Hyde was 'commanded' in the words of Isaiah 40:1–2], and cry unto her that her warfare is accomplished—that her iniquity is pardoned, for she has received at the Lord's hand double for all her sins."[31]

It was now *Gentile* profanation of the land that Hyde sought to overcome: first, by contesting and displacing those at the gates of the city; second, by obtaining the assent of Jewish representatives; third, by superimposing a new "map" upon the land; and finally, by effecting the transition to an eschatological, utopian landscape through the rite of dedication and consecration. Hyde was confident the "hand of Providence" was already turning the "great wheel" toward that end even as he disembarked at the port of Jaffa on his way up to Jerusalem.[32] Hyde reported to Pratt that the "Grand Sultan" had given notice to American missionaries in "Beyrout and Mount Lebanon" to leave the country; he guessed that "missionaries in Syria will have to leave" and that those in Palestine would soon follow. In all this, Hyde discerned the divine will: "God will, in due time, drive out the Canaanites [!]"[33]

However, on the day that Hyde ritually dedicated and consecrated the land, he turned to another kind of witness to vouchsafe the solemnity and efficacy of his prayer. Hyde reports that "on the top of the Mount of Olives" and "where the temple [once] stood . . . I erected a pile of stones as a witness according to the ancient custom." Hyde left behind two cairns of stones to both commemorate this crucial liturgical event and to mark the new territory he had created by apostolic authority, so as to reconfigure the landscape for its repossession by a restored Jewish people.

Finally, Hyde also informed Pratt—and those who would read his letters in *A Voice from Jerusalem*—that at the cairn constructed upon the temple site, he "used the rod according to the prediction upon my head."[34] Hyde was one of a number of early Mormon leaders who, according to D. Michael Quinn, "personally experienced and publicly endorsed folk magic belief and practices."[35] The rod to which he referred was probably a staff-like divining rod employed as an instrument of revelation. Skilled rodsmen believed that the successful use of a divining rod was a godly gift and could yield answers to yes-no questions through the "falling of the staff" in a particular direction, or the nodding or dipping movement of a forked rod.[36]

Hyde does not disclose the questions he posed, nor the answers given. But they can be inferred from the use of divining rods by some of Hyde's famed contemporaries in New England and New York, like the "Old Rodsman," also nicknamed "Commodore"; Nathaniel Wood and his "Fraternity of Rodsmen"; and Brigham Young. The Commodore once used his art to determine the identity of the builders of ancient American "monuments" (mounds), while Wood and his "fraternity" learned through "a nod of assent . . . from the rods" that "they must build a temple" near Middletown, Vermont.[37] Within days of the arrival of the first company of pioneer Mormons in the Salt Lake Valley in Utah in July 1847, Brigham Young evidently used a divining rod to point to the site where the Mormon people would build a new temple.[38] It is probable that Hyde "used the rod" to determine the site for the rebuilding of the temple in Jerusalem; he was certainly confident that a temple could be rebuilt by the Jewish people in honor of the "name" of the Father. Hyde shared this firm belief with Mormon prophet Joseph Smith, who asserted:

> Jerusalem must be rebuilt. & Judah return . . . [and] build the walls & the Temple. Yes brethren the Lord will purify the sons of Levi good or bad for it is through them that blessings flow to Israel . . . and then shall the offering of Judah & Jerusalem be pleasant unto the Lord as in days of old and as in former years.[39]

Doubtless, Smith made these bold assertions, and Hyde outlined his ministry, in near-complete ignorance of post-Temple Judaism. Their pronouncements constitute yet another episode in Christian presumption. And yet, there is a striking distinction between their "program" and the traditional supersessionist theologies and attendant practices of Christianity with regard to the Jewish people. Smith and Hyde employed the discourse available to them to assert the spiritual and territorial autonomy of the Jewish people. In contrast, according to Roger Friedland and Richard Hecht:

> The world's Christianities had long historical traditions which understood the dispersal of the Jews and the absence of Jewish sovereignty over Jerusalem as proof-texts that the Jews had been rejected by God . . . [and] that their election had passed to the Christians as a result of their rejection of Jesus."[40]

The intent of Hyde's "mission" to Palestine was to redraw the map of the Holy Land and reconfer stewardship over this territory upon those whom he considered its rightful heirs. It is also certain that this ministry entailed the displacement of those in possession of the field, who laid claim to the authority that custodianship bestowed. In the Mormon mythic imagination, the corollary of displacement was restoration, and vice-versa. Restoration to the center of those previously consigned to the margins involved a profound struggle for authority. In the mid-nineteenth century, Mormons were confident that those dispersed—both Mormon and Jew alike—would be gathered in with all their blessings, authority, and obligations restored. While it is also clear that nineteenth-century Mormons believed that they were a covenant people convoked to build the kingdom of God, theirs was not an indiscriminately exclusivist claim. *Pace* Jan Shipps, Philip Barlow, and virtually all Mormon apologetic writers, at least some prominent early Mormons perceived that their election did not entail the proclamation that "*all* existing covenants were null and void."[41] Their triumphalistic, sectarian claims extended at least as far as the congregations and boundaries of Christendom. However, it did not, in their eyes, require the subsumption of the Jewish people within the Mormon covenant. If my reading of Hyde's mission is correct, the prophetically reconfigured landscape could be a home for both Jews and Mormons.

## The "Palestine Tourists" of 1873

Two additional Mormon apostolic delegations traveled to Ottoman Palestine in the nineteenth century, the first in the spring of 1873 and the second in the spring of 1898. While the principal intent of their travels differed from that of Hyde, both groups, headed by Mormon apostles, ritually dedicated and consecrated the land in ceremonies held on the Mount of Olives. Their endeavors disclosed that gathering and restoration continued to function as the dominant metaphors of nineteenth-century Mormonism. Moreover, as with Hyde, the ritual articulation of dedication and consecration involved the assertion of authority commensurate to reorienting the landscape of the Holy Land, contesting and displacing those ensconced at holy sites as the legitimate custodians/representatives of the divine, and revising the future ideological construction of the land by placing an autonomous Jewish state on the site where Christians and Muslims asserted their supersession over the Jewish people.

By the end of the century, Mormon commentators pointed to the growing number of agricultural settlements established by Jewish Zionists as a "direct answer to the dedicatory prayer offered by Orson Hyde. . . . Indeed . . . the present condition of Palestine is almost an ocular demonstration of the truth of Mormonism." Mormons concluded that their ritual actions were contributing directly to the reconfiguration of the landscape along the lines presented by Mormon ideology and authority.[42] The structure of the ritual enacted by the 1873 and 1898 delegations was reminiscent of that first sketched by Hyde. This would not be surprising, given that the ritual was informed principally by the regnant nineteenth-century Mormon metaphors of gathering and restoration, as well as by Hyde's well-known prayer. Thus, both groups stressed that their work had been authorized by the First Presidency, the church's highest directorate; both encountered Christians in Palestine who promoted authoritative constructions of the landscape at odds with Mormon perceptions, which were contested and dismissed; Jewish residents, unlike Christian caretakers, were portrayed in essential agreement with the Mormon program of a Jewish gathering and an independent Jewish state; and finally, each group of Mormons sealed their landscape re-vision with a ritual prayer of dedication and consecration.

Because the ritual activity of the 1898 delegation did not vary significantly from that of the 1873 group, and because I have analyzed the work of the 1898 delegation elsewhere, I will focus here on the 1873 "Palestine Tourists."[43] The work and travels of the five Mormons who journeyed to Palestine in the spring of 1873 were recorded by them in correspondence to church leaders, family members, friends, and newspapers in Utah. A large portion of these letters, poems, and reports were collected and published in 1875 under the title *Correspondence of Palestine Tourists...* Part "grand tour" of sights in Europe, part apostolic journey to survey prospective fields "for the introduction of the gospel," part Holy Land pilgrimage, the *Correspondence* was the product of the aging first generation of the Mormon church elite. Unlike Hyde's ad hoc journey without purse and scrip, these later travelers—which included members of the "inner circle of Brigham Young's advisers"—voyaged, dined, and slept under the auspices of and according to the itinerary of Thomas Cook & Son.[44]

The five travelers debarked at the port of Jaffa on February 23, 1873, and left Jerusalem on March 5 bound for the Galilee and Syria. During that period, they camped just outside Jaffa Gate; visited the Church of the Holy Sepulchre twice, the Mosque of Omar and al-Aksa once, and, on the morning of March 2, 1873, went to the Mount of Olives, where "with our faces bowed toward Jerusalem, we lifted our prayers to God" to fulfill Brigham Young's injunction to dedicate and consecrate the land.[45]

None of the Palestine tourists felt compelled to describe the March 2 ritual at length; either because Orson Hyde's prayer was well enough known, and in a quasi-canonical manner determined the specific content of what was uttered more than thirty years later; or else because they felt that a newspaper column—albeit published for a Mormon readership—was not the setting for an intimate account of this sacred rite. All, however, described critically and at length their encounters with the Christian sacred sites in Jerusalem. After his first visit to the Church of the Holy Sepulchre, George A. Smith confided in a letter to a friend that "I do not wonder at Mark Twain burlesquing the ancient sites."[46] All of the Mormon correspondents catalogued at length the overwhelming testament of relics, shrines, and chapels gathered under the capacious roof of the great Christian church building. Cumulatively, the sacred objects, altars, and enclosures have functioned to validate the claims of Christendom that the very *axis mundi* had shifted west from Mount Moriah to the promontory of Golgatha. The exodus of "the center" from the Temple Mount/al-Haram al-Sharif into Christian custodianship has symbolized, to Christians, the displacement of God's first affection and his election from the Israel of old to the New—the Gentile Church. The Mormon visitors to the site, however, would have none of this.

Mormon apostle Lorenzo Snow, writing to the readers of the *Deseret News,* summed up his impressions of the Church of the Holy Sepulchre by condemning its "considerable mystery, contradictions, and disputations." In his eyes, the great edifice was symptomatic of Christianity in Jerusalem, which Snow depicted as having fallen to a "low" and "sunken condition."[47] To Paul Schettler, the story about "Adam's skull and some other legends" rehearsed for them in the "Greek chapel," beggared belief; the travelers "could not help smiling" with embarrassment and pity.[48] Snow characterized Mormonism an "enlightened Christianity" in comparison with the religion of the enthusiasts of the holy places, who practiced "deceit and imposition" and who brought Christianity into "scorn and contempt."[49]

As already observed in the account of Hyde's ministry, such contentious and dismissive language was a key element in the ritual of dedication and consecration. By heaping their own scorn upon the "titles" and "deeds" amassed in the Church of the Holy Sepulchre—its chapels, relics, and traditions—the Mormons effected a displacement of the old churches of Christendom, as Hyde had previously de-centered the evangelicals, in preparation for the restoration of the Jewish people in the Holy Land.

What did impress the Mormon travelers were the deeds and "clear titles" to real property that had been issued by the Ottoman regime to the "Portuguese" Jewish community in Jerusalem.[50] In their reckoning, reliquarian and supersessionist claims were worthless in comparison to the Jews' efforts to construct a hospital and housing for indigent members of their community in Jerusalem on land that had been bought from the "Turks."[51] They were impressed, of course, because the work to situate a Jewish population in the land of Israel coincided with and "proved" the validity of the Mormon ideology of gathering and restoration. Gathering meant the physical location and intensive settlement of Jews and Mormons in Jerusalem and "Zion" respectively; it mandated "improvements" of these places that had been dedicated and consecrated, set apart from the world. The Mormon correspondents reported that their views coincided, with little variance, with those expressed by Rabbi Abraham Ashkenazi, the leader of the Portuguese community with whom the Mormons met on two occasions—once at the Portuguese synagogue, the other in the tents of the Mormon encampment a short distance from Jaffa Gate.[52] George A. Smith related that he and the venerable Jewish leader agreed that "God would restore the land to Israel," "return . . . the ten tribes," and that "Jerusalem would again be . . . a glorious and happy city."[53] Though Ashkenazi described the Jerusalem Jews at present as "very poor," Smith repeated with approval the rabbi's claims that "if they had control, they would make great improvements," and Smith referred to their synagogue and the hospital and charity building efforts as proof.[54] In pointed contrast to these beliefs, their "pleasant and interesting" discussions, and the "intelligence" of Ashkenazi and "three of their principle [sic] men,"[55] Smith reminded his Mormon audience that he "saw many Christians of different denominations there who had no such faith."[56]

It is important here to note that, in accordance with Hyde's model, and in contrast to the labors of succeeding Mormon delegations in the 1920s and 1930s, the Mormon group in 1873 reported no efforts of any kind to proselytize Jewish leaders or individuals. Though their letter of instructions from Brigham Young directed them to observe the possibilities "for the introduction of the gospel" in "Europe and Asia Minor,"[57] their work in Ottoman Palestine was of a different nature altogether, consistent with an ideology that posited two covenant communities gathered to consecrated territories and dedicated to restoring the fallen fortunes of their respective homes to their previous glory.

Up to this point, the Palestine tourists had faithfully reenacted the first sequences of the ritual of dedication and consecration as performed by Orson Hyde. Knowing that the construction of sacred space entailed a struggle for power to "reread" the site, Mormons needed, in Joseph

Smith's words, to "employ the most efficient means in our power"; expressions of goodwill or prayers invoked in Zion were insufficient.[58] Rather, Mormon envoys had to be empowered with authority to represent the Saints, then travel to the site (like any serious land surveyor), contest the authority of those who had previously configured the landscape, seek out the approval of those "rightful heirs" whom they sought to restore to the land, and then begin to reconfigure the territory by means of their own survey.

Hyde had set new "metes-and-bounds" when he walked about the exterior of the walled city and when he erected stone cairns "as a witness according to the ancient custom" that the center of sacred power had now been resituated from the western, "Christian" city back to the Temple Mount/al-Haram al-Sharif and the Mount of Olives—the liturgical and eschatological centers, respectively.

The Palestine tourists further reconfigured the landscape to conform to Mormon ideology by dismissing the centrality and orientation claimed by the custodians of the "shrines" and "pedestals" in the Church of the Holy Sepulchre. It was when they stepped outside the eastern gates of the city that George A. Smith records viewing a scene "far more pleasing" than any they had encountered "since coming to Jerusalem"[59] It was the *land* of Israel, not its reliquary shrines and commemorative churches, that impressed the Mormon delegation. It was the news that "Turkish authorities" were "moderating the rules" and permitting Templers and Jews to "purchase and hold title to real estate," that gave them hope that their pilgrimage, their efforts to survey, and their prayers of dedication and consecration were not in vain.[60] The gently mocking irony that characterized Smith's descriptions of his visits to Christian shrines, monasteries, and churches falls away completely as he describes the terrain between Jaffa and Jerusalem and beyond. Smith's letters to Young are filled with the keen observations of a seasoned pioneer and community-builder as he takes note of the physical landscape and its potential to accommodate and support a large pioneering population.[61] True claim to the land would be validated by reclamation of the soil, the repair of an aqueduct, land irrigated and cultivated, not possession of the "skull of our father Adam" at the disputed "centre of the world."[62]

After touring and describing the countryside with the view to its imminent settlement, the Palestine tourists concluded their ritual sojourn in Jerusalem on the morning of March 2, 1873. The small Mormon group of travelers set up a tent a short distance "north and east from the church of the Ascension" on the Mount of Olives, "bowed toward Jerusalem," and dedicated and consecrated the land so that "it may be blessed with fruitfulness, preparatory to the return of the Jews in fulfillment of prophecy."[63]

## The Missions of 1927 and 1933: James Talmage and John A. Widstoe

The accounts of the Mormon apostolic missions to the land of Israel in 1927 and 1933 reveal that profound changes had taken place in Mormon ideology and experience. Whereas rites of the nineteenth century had enacted the foundational Mormon myths of gathering and restoration, Mormon apostles James Talmage and John Wistoe traveled to British Mandate Palestine to dedicate the land principally for "systematic missionary service in Palestine."[64] Earlier groups of Mormon envoys had traveled to Ottoman Palestine to re-envision the landscape of the Holy Land by carving out space for a restored and autonomous Jewish nation. In 1933, however, an official Mormon publication claimed that Orson Hyde had "predicted that it [the Holy Land of scripture] would be retaken and governed by Christian peoples."[65] Thus, the ritual efforts of earlier delegations in 1841, 1873, 1898, and 1902 were reinterpreted officially as laying the foundations for extending missionary work in the Middle East; while the great challenge "facing the mission" in 1933 was "the task of continuing the work among the native peoples [Arab, Armenian, etc.], and of presenting the gospel truths to the Jews who are returning in large numbers to their home of old."[66] As if to underline this "official" and fundamental change in orientation, both Talmage and Widstoe also reconfigured the basic ritual structure of the dedication and consecration rites established by Hyde and reconfirmed by the 1873 "correspondents." Gone are the ritualized reports of contestation with custodial Christians, and neither apostle relates encounters with representative Jewish figures who, in the past, had validated Mormon efforts to ritually re-envision and realign sacred space in favor of Jewish occupancy. The stylized rogation around the city of Jerusalem, represented most completely by Hyde and vestigially by the 1873 and 1898 groups, is missing from personal and official accounts of Talmage's and Widstoe's journeys.

Finally, both apostles shifted the principal site of their ritual efforts from the Mount of Olives in Jerusalem to Mount Carmel in Haifa. Mormon efforts to redraw the map of the sacred places in Jerusalem by constructing rock cairns to mark the new boundaries were radically modified to reflect the totalizing nature of Mormon evangelization. It is as if the apostolic envoys of the 1920s and 1930s, key apologists for Mormonism in their generation, signaled that the corollary to the rational religious doctrine they advocated was the universal and total scope of its reach; there were no exceptions, no reasonable excuses for anyone to resist the compelling logic of their faith. Accordingly, the land of Israel would now be included among the growing list of "fields" of Mormon evangelization, with the port city of Haifa, not the insular city of David, as the center of its new labors. Between 1890 and 1920, fundamental theological categories, forms of economic and social relations, and the nature of the Mormon presence upon the landscapes of the American West all underwent crucial transformations in response to the acute external and internal pressures on the Mormon people to accommodate to American cultural, political, and social norms. This period and its developments have been amply documented. For the purpose of this essay, it is sufficient to note that the formative ideologies of nineteenth-century Mormonism—physical gathering, an imminent millennium, the restoration of the powers of covenant Israel and the church of Christ by *two* distinct religious communities, Jews and Mormons—were replaced by the more "modern," rational, and unitary paradigm of a centrally and bureaucratically administered "international church."

It has been a fundamental premise of this essay that an examination of the ritual behavior of Mormons when they dedicated and consecrated the land of Israel reveals key features of Mormon ideology and the role that ideology has played in the construction of sacred space in the Holy Land. In addition, one of the principal discoveries in America-Holy Land studies is the perception of the Holy Land's crucial function in American religious history. American religious communities have projected their highest ambitions and their principal concerns onto the Holy Land, and from it they have drawn spiritual sustenance and have defined their differences. It is a landscape upon which religious communities have both embraced and excluded one another.

In the nineteenth century, Ottoman Palestine was the field upon which successive groups of Mormon leaders ritually enacted the displacement of their Christian rivals by reinterpreting the landscape as a home for an autonomous Jewish nation. This is the caveat that Joseph

Smith introduced into the otherwise totalizing nature of nineteenth-century Mormon sectarian ideology: in his words, the Jewish people "inculcate attendance in divine worship" and manifest to any "disinterested reader . . . true piety, real religion, and acts of devotion to God."[67] The implications of this outlook, for Smith and his contemporaries, were: no to Mormon missions to Jews; alongside advocacy on behalf of establishing two convenant peoples upon separate territories that would be dedicated and consecrated to their concerted, but distinct, endeavors to realize the kingdom of God on earth.

By the time James Talmage and John A. Widstoe—both of them European mission presidents and Mormon apostles—traveled to Mandate Palestine in 1927 and 1933, the rite of dedication and consecration they performed was a reflection of a transformed Mormonism. The caveat of Jewish autonomy in Mormon theology had effectively disappeared. While both apostles "confirmed" the previous "dedicatory prayers of the apostles of the land" who traveled to Palestine,[68] clearly the overriding intent of their benedictions was, in the words of James Talmage, to offer up:

> a prayer of invocation and supplication for the success of missionary labor in the Holy Land, both for the House of Judah, and for the rest of the House of Israel. This was in the nature of a dedication of the efforts of the missionaries who shall serve in the lands.[69]

And whereas official Mormon journals editorialized in favor of the reclamation work of Jewish Zionists who were "transforming the country by an application of industry and skill never excelled," a novel and intrusive contingency had been introduced: in the same editorial, the author argued that "before their venture in Palestine will be wholly accomplished . . . the Jews must acknowledge His coming, His death and resurrection, His redeeming mercy. . . . They must accept the gospel."[70]

Ninety years earlier, Joseph Smith had read selections from Michael Creizenach's Reform-oriented work on Torah and Jewish education. He was so impressed by what he read that he published those passages in the Mormon newspaper *Times and Seasons,* along with his warm endorsement of Creizenach's views. Smith's interest in contemporary Jewish developments and biblical commentary, as well as his positive assessment of Judaism and Jewish community life, stand in sharp relief to the views expressed by John A. Widstoe on May 21, 1933, on the occasion of the dedication of the new Palestine-Syrian mission headquarters in Haifa. Widstoe offered a profoundly different view when he told his audience that "the time appears to be ripe for proselytizing among the Jews. Many of the Jews are tired of the old theological systems. We must move carefully and take our time." Concurring with her husband, Leah Widstoe told missionaries in the audience: "Don't forget the Jews." Those currently in Palestine, she said, were "irreligious and looking for new truth," and "can no more than any other people succeed without a spiritual motive. Some day the Jews will see the Christian light."[71] Following the Widstoe's remarks, the land was "rededicated, as was also the mission."

Talmage and Widstoe were members of a new generation of church leaders who had to respond to the cognitive dissonance that accompanied the non-arrival of the "last days" during the lifetime of the first generation of Saints, and to the "predicament of respectability" that plagued a rapidly urbanizing, successful, and consumer-oriented Mormon population.[72] They answered the ensuing cultural crisis by systematizing doctrine, elaborating a hierarchical structure of church government, introducing rational, "result-oriented administrative procedures," and revitalizing efforts "to carry the gospel to all the world."[73] Extensive and universal missionary work effectively replaced intensive and gathered settlements as the preeminent paradigm by which Mormons confronted non-Mormon populations—including the Jewish people—in the 1920s and beyond. Mormon church President Heber J. Grant endorsed this new, fundamental orientation just months before Talmage traveled to Mandate Palestine:

> I want to emphasize that we as a people have *one supreme thing to do* and that is to call upon the world to repent of sin and to come to God. And it is *our duty above all others* to go forth and proclaim the gospel.[74]

That same year, and again in 1933, the site of dedication and consecration reflected this ascendant ideology. So central had it become as a means of internal self-definition, as well as the means by which Mormons were conceptually reconfiguring the landscape of Palestine, that an editorial commenting upon John Widstoe's travels and ritual benediction declared that henceforth, the land of Israel would "no doubt be a most interesting and profitable field in which to teach the truth of the restored gospel of the Lord Jesus Christ."[75]

Arguably no field of missionary labor has proved as intractable, mystifying, and unproductive (in terms of converts and church growth) for the Mormon church as that of the Middle East. Yet seventy years later, no compelling or realistic paradigm has replaced the universal, evangelizing orientation enjoined by church President Heber J. Grant in 1927. It must be admitted that it has served the Mormon church well in many other cultural and geographical regions. But it remains inadequate to explain and interpret the encounter between Mormons, Jews, and Christian and Muslim Palestinians in the Holy Land.

## NOTES

1. Orson Hyde, *A Voice from Jerusalem* . . . (Liverpool, 1842); for the text of Hyde's prayer, see 21–24.

2. See David Chidester and Edward T. Linenthal, "Introduction" in *American Sacred Space*, ed. by idem (Bloomington, Ind., 1995), 1, 9–16.

3. Throughout the period addressed in this essay, it is clear that Mormon envoys considered Christian churches and their representatives, both clerical and political, as possessing the strongest claims of custodianship over holy sites in Palestine.

4. Roger Grainger, *The Language of the Rite* (London, 1974), 145–46; Gershon Greenberg, *The Holy Land in American Religious Thought, 1620–1948: The Symbiosis of American Religious Approaches to Scripture's Sacred Territory* (Lanham, 1994), 9.

5. For a more complete version of the ways in which these concepts informed early Mormon doctrine and practice, especially with regard to Mormon perceptions of the Jewish people, see Steven Epperson, *Mormons and Jews: Early Mormon Theologies of Israel* (Salt Lake City, 1992).

6. Thomas Alexander, *Mormonism in Transition: A History of the Latter-day Saints, 1890–1930* (Urbana and Chicago, 1986), 4–14.

7. See Chidester and Linenthal, *American Sacred Space*; Alan R. H. Baker and Gideon Biger, eds., *Essays in the Meaning of Some Places in the Past,* Cambridge Studies in Historical Geography, vol. 18 (New York, 1992); Belden Lane, *Landscapes of the Sacred: Geography and Narrative in American Spirituality,* Isaac Hecker Studies in Religion and American Culture (New York, 1988); Alan Morinis, ed., *Sacred Journeys: The Anthropology of Pilgrimage,* Contributions to the Study of Anthropology, vol. 7 (Westport, 1992); Jamie Scott and Paul Simpson-Housley, eds., *Sacred Places and Profane Places: Essays in the Geographies of Judaism, Christianity, and Islam,* Contributions to the Study of Religion, vol. 30 (New York, 1991); Ruth Kark, "Millenarism and Agricultural Settlement in the Holy Land in the Nineteenth Century," *Journal of Historical Geography* 9 (1983): 50–59; idem, "Sweden and the Holy Land: Pietistic and Communal Settlement," *Journal of Historical Geography* 22 (1996): 46–50; Steven Olsen, "The Mormon Ideology of Place: Cosmic Symbolism of the City of Zion, 1830–1846" (Ph.D. diss., University of Chicago, 1985).

8. See Chidester and Linenthal, *American Sacred Space,* 5; Morinis, *Sacred Journeys,* 9.

9. Hyde's mission as a "sign of the times" predominates in Mormon interpretations of his 1840–1842 ministry. For example, see David Galbraith, Kelly Ogden, and Andrew Skinner, *Jerusalem: The Eternal City* (Salt Lake City, 1996).

10. See Marvin S. Hill, "A Historical Study of the Life of Orson Hyde: Early Mormon Missionary and Apostle from 1805–1852" (Master's thesis, Brigham Young University, 1955), 25–42.

11. Cf. Isaiah 40:12.

12. Hyde, *A Voice from Jerusalem,* iii., iv.

13. Ibid.

14. Lane, *Landscapes of the Sacred,* 15.

15. Julius Richter, *A History of Protestant Missions in the Near East* (New York, 1910), 14, 72; on Protestant strategy, see Henry H. Riggs, *Euphrates College and the New Era in the Ottoman Empire* (Harpoot, 1908), Archives of the World Student Christian Federation, Box 243, fd. 1991, Day Missions Library, Yale Divinity School Library; Edwin E. Bliss, *A Condensed Sketch of the Missions of the American Board in Asiatic Turkey* (Boston, 1910), 27, Special Collections, Burke Library, Union Theological Seminary; T. C. Trowbridge, "Armenia and the Armenians," offprint from *The New Englander* (January 1874), 9, Special Collections, Burke Library, Union Theological Seminary.

16. Hyde, *A Voice from Jerusalem,* 9.

17. Ibid., 10–11.

18. Ibid., 11.

19. Ibid., 10, 22–23.

20. See Olsen, "The Mormon Ideology of Place"; the quote is from *Doctrines and Covenants* 133: 4–7.

21. Morinis, *Sacred Journeys,* 4.

22. Jan Shipps, quoted in Philip Barlow, *Mormons and the Bible: The Place of the Latter-day Saints in American Religion* (New York, 1991), 121.

23. Hyde, *A Voice from Jerusalem,* 14.

24. Ibid.

25. Maurice Beresford, quoted in Kent Ryden, *Mapping the Invisible Landscape: Folklore, Writing, and the Sense of Place,* American Land and Life Series (Iowa City, 1993), 26.

26. Ibid., 27–28.

27. Hyde, *A Voice from Jerusalem,* 13.

28. For the complete text of the prayer, see ibid., 21–24.

29. Ibid., 14.

30. Ibid., 21.

31. Ibid., iii, iv.

32. Ibid., 23.

33. Ibid., 24.

34. Ibid., 22.

35. D. Michael Quinn, *Early Mormonism and the Magic World View* (Salt Lake City, 1987), 203.

36. Ibid., 30, 207.
37. Ibid., 30–31.
38. Ibid., 206.
39. Andrew F. Ehat and Lyndon W. Cook, comps. and eds., *The Words of Joseph Smith: The Contemporary Accounts of the Nauvoo Discourses of the Prophet Joseph,* Religious Studies Monograph Series, vol. 6 (Provo, Utah, 1980), 66, 180.
40. Roger Friedland and Richard Hecht, "The Politics of Sacred Place: Jerusalem's Temple Mount/ *al-haram al-sharif,*" in *Sacred Places and Profane Places,* 36.
41. For a brief overview of Shipp's reading of Mormon exclusivism, see Barlow, *Mormons and the Bible,* 118–22. A particularly arrogant version of Mormon triumphalism can be read in a book coauthored by Robert Millet and Joseph Fielding McConkie of the College of Religious Education at Brigham Young University, *Our Destiny: The Call and Election of the House of Israel* (Salt Lake City, 1993).
42. "Changes in Palestine," *Deseret News* Weekly 48 (20 January 1894), 138.
43. For an account of the work of Apostle Anthony Lund and his associates in 1898, see Steven Epperson, "'To Save Our Brethren': Mormons, Armenians, and an 'Eastern Zion' in Palestine," *Journal of Historical Geography* (forthcoming).
44. On the "inner circle," see Leonard Arrington, *Brigham Young: American Moses* (New York, 1985), 193.
45. George A. Smith, "Remarks by President George A. Smith, Delivered in the New Tabernacle . . . June 22, 1873," *Journal of Discourses . . . ,* reported by D. W. Evans, James Taylor, and J. Q. Cannon, vol. 16 (Liverpool, 1874), 102.
46. George A. Smith, in George A. Smith, Lorenzo Snow, Paul A. Schettler, and Eliza R. Snow, *Correspondence of Palestine Tourists . . .* (henceforth, *Correspondence*) (Salt Lake City, 1875, 199.
47. Ibid., 251–52.
48. Ibid., 210–11.
49. Ibid., 254.
50. Smith, Schettler, and Lorenzo Snow, who spoke approvingly of the reclamation work of the German Templers, a Pietist sect whose members had begun immigrating to Palestine to prepare it for the millennium. That Templers had secured "deed[s] of the purchase" of hundreds of acres of fine arable land in several sites, impressed Smith and Snow. See *Correspondence,* 207, 218.
51. Ibid., 225.
52. On Ashkenazi, see "Abraham Ben Jacob Ashkenazi," *Encyclopedia Judaica* (Jerusalem, 1972), 3:722–23.
53. *Correspondence,* 225; Smith, 97.
54. *Correspondence,* 225.
55. Ibid.
56. Smith, 97.
57. *Correspondence,* 1–2.
58. Hyde, iv.
59. *Correspondence,* 189–99.
60. Ibid., 248.

61. Ibid., 218, 220–21.

62. Ibid., 199.

63. Smith, 97; *Correspondence,* 2, 260.

64. James A. Talmage, *Journals, 1879–1933,* 4 November 1927, MS 12128, Library Archives of the Historical Department of the Church of Jesus Christ of Latter-day Saints (hereafter, LDS Church Archives).

65. Elder Richard S. Bennett, "The Palestine-Syrian Mission: Historical Notes," *The Latter-day Saints Millennial Star,* vol. 95, no. 31 (10 August 1933):514 (hereafter, *MS*).

66. *MS,* 526.

67. Joseph Smith, in *Times and Seasons,* vol. 3 (1 June 1842), 810.

68. *MS,* 526.

69. Talmage, *Journals,* 4 November 1927.

70. "The Return of the Jews," *MS,* 520.

71. "Minutes of the Meeting held in the Palestine-Syrian Mission," 21 May 1933, Turkish Mission Historical Records and Minutes, LDS Church Archives.

72. See Alexander, *Mormonism in Transition,* 273, 288–89; on "the predicament of respectability," see Armand L. Mauss, *The Angel and the Beehive: The Mormon Struggle with Assimilation* (Urbana and Chicago, 1994), 5, 21–31.

73. On the efforts of that generation of church leaders, see Alexander, *Mormonism in Transition*; quotes are from O. Kendall White, *Mormon Neo-Orthodoxy: A Crisis Theology* (Salt Lake City 1987), 108, and James Allen and Glen Leonard, *The Story of the Latter-day Saints,* 2nd. ed. (Salt Lake City, 1992), 442.

74. Heber J. Grant, *Ninety-Seventh Annual Conference of the Church of Jesus Christ of Latter-day Saints,* 2nd. ed. (Salt Lake City, 1992), 442.

75. "Reorganization of the Palestine-Syrian Mission," *MS,* 524–25.

# The Esco Fund Committee

## The Story of an American Jewish Foundation

Marianne Sanua
*Florida Atlantic University*

As relatively small, private family foundations achieve a new prominence in American Jewish philanthropy, and as the nature of the spiritual and financial bonds between American and Israeli Jews are undergoing close examination and reevaluation, a study of the precedent-setting Esco Foundation is of special interest. Founded in 1940 by industrialist, economist, and former Hebrew school teacher Frank Cohen (and named in honor of his wife Ethel S. Cohen, a musician and graduate of the Teachers' Institute of the Jewish Theological Seminary), the Foundation, with its board of key American Jewish teachers, thinkers, and intellectuals, over the course of forty-five years granted more than $1.5 million to small but influential projects in Great Britain, the U.S., and above all Israel. Direct human services such as rescue and relief for refugees tended to be the favored goal of most American Jewish philanthropic dollars during those years, and indeed the Esco Foundation during its beginnings in the Second World War made contributions in that area. Thereafter, however, the Foundation concentrated in the often neglected area of Jewish education. It also sponsored scholarly studies and programs to benefit the cultural—and especially musical—life of the new state of Israel, on the theory that these were not luxuries. Two of its best-known projects included an analysis of Jewish, Arab, and British policies in Palestine published in 1947, and the building of a center for classical music at Kibbutz Ein Gev, modeled after America's

Tanglewood. Among Esco's directors and advisors were major figures of the Zionist and educational elite of American Jewry, including Mordecai M. Kaplan, Rose Jacobs, Henrietta Szold, Israel Wechsler, Israel S. Chipkin, Isaac B. Berkson, and Jack J. Cohen.

Together with the Cohens, this group of friends and associates centered in New York City exhibited an unusual combination of Jewish cultural sophistication, Hebraic learning, Zionist fervor, and a deep first-hand knowledge of Israeli life as they went about making their philanthropic disbursements. The were, however, also thoroughly American in outlook. The setbacks and obstacles that the Foundation encountered while attempting to carry out its projects in Israel illustrate well some of the cultural, political, and religious clashes that adhered to the relations between the the Jewish communities of both countries. Esco's leadership was also not immune to the occasional touch of arrogance almost inherent in the relationship between wealthy philanthropists and the beneficiaries they sponsor. That all of these values and attitudes frequently contradicted one another makes Esco's many successes all the more worth examining within the annals of American Jewish and America-Israel philanthropy. At the same time, Esco's setbacks illustrate some of the cultural, political, and religious clashes that through the years characterized the relations between the Jewish communities of both countries.

## The Founders

Frank and Ethel S. Cohen's generosity did not develop with sudden wealth, but had been cultivated in them almost from birth. The home and religious upbringing of both included a strong emphasis on traditional Jewish service and philanthropy. In particular, the Orthodox parents of Ethel Silberman Cohen, who was born on the Lower East Side in 1895, took the Jewish ideals of charity with great seriousness. Amid the blessings of upward mobility, which took the family to Harlem and then to Williamsburg, the Silberman's hands and purse were continually stretched out to others. Her mother, Mrs. Cohen recalled, "was one of the most generous women . . . she was one of those who saw to it that every bride had a proper bridal outfit and wedding. *Tzedakah* was one of the major tenets of our household."[1]

Ethel Silberman graduated from Wadleigh High School and then attended the Jewish Teachers' Institute of the Jewish Theological Seminary, where one of her professors and mentors was Mordecai Kaplan, later the founder of Reconstructionism and a member of the Esco Board. It was as his student and protégé that she first became interested in Zionism. Graduating in 1915, she became a Hebrew teacher in a Brownsville (Brooklyn) Hebrew school, where she met Frank Cohen, also an avid Zionist. They were married in 1921, and the huge Star of David flag hanging on the wall, which can be seen in a photograph of their wedding reception at the Hotel Pierre, serves as testimony to the couple's inclinations.[2]

Frank Cohen, also from an Orthodox Jewish family, was born in Brownsville in 1893 and attended Townsend Harris High School, City College, and Columbia University, where he was awarded a master's degree in economics shortly before his marriage. At first he planned to go into teaching, for in his memoirs he speaks of having been part of the circle created by Samson Benderly and Judah Magnes, the American Jewish leader and later chancellor of the Hebrew University in Jerusalem. Both educators aimed to train future leaders and teachers for the New York Kehillah, a modern, experimental version of the traditional form of Jewish communal organization.[3] In 1917, Frank Cohen recalled, there were about a dozen men and women who obtained advanced degrees in various phases of communal education in order to serve the developing Jewish community. Many of these friends and associates, such as Israel Chipkin, Ben Rosen, and Isaac Berkson, were later invited to join the board of directors of Esco. Although the formal Kehillah experiment as a whole did not end in success, its educational activities bore fruit. These young people, sometimes known as the "Benderly boys," provided key leadership in Jewish education for generations of students. "If it weren't for that group of men and women," Frank Cohen recalled, "I don't think you'd have any Jewish education in the United States today."[4]

Frank Cohen was neither the first nor the last figure in the American Jewish world to realize that all the education in the world meant little unless there was control over the money needed to fund it. Consequently, he decided to leave teaching and go into business, where in a career spanning almost forty years he enjoyed considerable success. The goal was to earn a living, he later recalled, not only because it was far more lucrative than teaching Hebrew school but "because I was mad at the idea of outside people telling this group how to run education, because they had the money. So I decided to go out and make enough money so that I could sit like they did—but I'd give our fellows a free hand."[5]

Before embarking on a life of philanthropy, however, Frank and Ethel Cohen wanted to fulfill their Zionist aspirations and settle in the new British Mandate of Palestine. A solution to earning a living there quickly presented itself, one that was particularly suitable to an enterprising young American who wanted to make *aliyah* (settle in Palestine) without becoming part of the socialist framework of the collective settlements. Palestine, in 1920, had no American oil companies and electricity or gas was rare; people for the most part cooked on primus stoves. While knowing nothing about oil, Frank Cohen persuaded the Texas Oil Company to give him the job of Middle East agent in 1921.[6] It was in that year that the newlywed Cohens settled in Tel Aviv, at first living in a *pension,* and then setting up housekeeping in an apartment.

Although the couple enjoyed the company of distinguished tablemates during lunch at the *pension*—including Zionist luminaries Ahad Ha'am, Menahem Ussishkin, and Arthur Ruppin—living conditions were primitive, particularly for middle-class Jews from New York. At the *pension,* for example, the Cohens were lucky to have running water once every three days. "Today there is no recognizing the place," recalled Ethel Cohen in an interview conducted in Israel in 1952, when she marveled at the modern, bustling city that Tel Aviv had become. "Then there were only a few houses . . . and one policeman on a horse that he used to ride around the 'city' keeping order."[7] After two years, Ethel Cohen in particular could no longer tolerate the life there, and the couple returned to the United States, where Frank Cohen prospered in his many business enterprises. These included banking, oil, and insurance. Despite their decision to terminate their stay, the couple had not lost their Zionist dedication or their determination to help build the Jewish homeland.

### Esco during the War Years

Throughout the 1920s and 1930s, the Cohens were active in all manner of Jewish and Zionist affairs, but it was events in Europe that drew their sharpest attention. In the years of the Depression, as Hitler rose to power, Frank Cohen warned against the dangers of what he called "That Man" and was one of the first American Jewish philanthropists to openly support the anti-Hitler movement. In later years, Rabbi Stephen Wise, then leader and president of the American Jewish Congress, recalled the date of March 23, 1933, when the Congress, under the leadership of Bernard S. Deutsch, planned a mass rally in Madison Square Garden to protest the Nazi government that had come to power barely three months earlier. Governor Al Smith, John Hayne Holmes, Fiorello La-Guardia, Mayor O'Brien, and other prominent New York leaders and politicians were to be in attendance. However, Madison Square Garden did not permit the use of its premises for free. "We needed immediately the money with which to pay that rental," Wise recalled, "and Mr. and Mrs. Cohen gave us that money. They made it possible to begin that great work of fighting Hitlerism."[8] Frank Cohen financed this and several other demonstrations, in the meantime also paying for full-page anti-Hitler ads in the *New York Times*.

These efforts were not greeted with universal approval. Many of his fellow Jews feared "rocking the boat," and many of his fellow businessmen, who had interests in Germany, opposed such public display of the financier's sentiments. Threats were not uncommon. At one point, Frank Cohen recalled, a business associate whose firm had German interests actually visited him in his office and told him to "stop these anti-Hitler demonstrations, and so on, and attend to my insurance business. And—well, I threw him out."[9]

The approaching war decided Frank Cohen on the business activity that would both fight his personal cause and provide the financial basis for the Esco Foundation. In early 1940, more than a year and a half before the United States entered the hostilities, Cohen sold all his other business interests to organize the Empire Ordnance Corporation, whose original contracts were to manufacture war materiel for the British government. Before then, the American defense industry had attracted little or no investment. Big corporations saw no money in it, smaller ones did not know their way around the Washington bureaucracy and, most of all, there was a strong stigma attached to manufacturing or selling arms and becoming a "merchant of death." "The void ached for some self-starting, corner-cutting American enterprise," wrote *Time* in a profile of Frank Cohen published November 3, 1941, little more than a month before the U.S. formally entered the war. "It almost seemed there was none left. But there was."[10]

Under Cohen's direction, Empire Ordnance proved to be an innovative and financially successful enterprise. More important, when the U.S. finally entered the war, it was almost the only company prepared to meet the immediate challenges of rapid war production. Its activities soon expanded to include more than a half dozen operations scattered throughout the country, manufacturing such goods as 75–mm guns, recoil mechanisms, steel forgings, gun mounts, armor plates for tanks, small planes and gliders, optical instruments, and finally, ships. In addition to Empire Ordnance, his main business, Cohen organized other companies in an effort to bring Cuban manpower and Cuban natural resources to aid the U.S. war effort. These included American Steel Corporation of Cuba, which supplied fabricated steel, and other companies that manufactured foods such as dehydrated sweet potatoes and beets, tomato concentrates and juices, and guava extracts for candy and vitamin products. In this work, Frank Cohen was instrumental in reconditioning old plants rather than building new ones; in training large numbers of unemployed miners in Wilkes-Barre, Pennsylvania, for war work; and in undertaking research for less expensive and more efficient ordnance production methods, many of them subsequently adopted by the U.S. government. In all, Frank Cohen's companies at this time produced goods worth some $100 million a year.[11]

The founding of Esco, which was given a 15 percent share in all of Frank Cohen's companies, grew out of a number of factors. The first was a strong desire to perform those acts of *tzedakah,* or charity, that were within the family's capabilities and ideals. Also, as Frank Cohen recalled, there was an additional stigma and fear attached to a Jewish man accruing such large profits from the manufacture of munitions and instruments of violence at a time when organized antisemites were accusing Jews of backing and fomenting the war.[12] Furthermore, Britain was involved in a fight for its life, and to pay for military goods entailed considerable sacrifice. If the aim was ultimately to help Britain, then it did not seem fair to take so much British money at such a desperate time without putting some of it back in the form of charitable contributions.[13]

Thus Esco, as a tax-exempt, membership foundation for the purpose of disbursal of funds, was formally established as the war raged overseas. Its birth came at a delicate time when America had not yet entered the war and when the position of the entire Jewish people was in doubt. The first meetings were held in the Cohens' home in New York City in 1940. The members called upon—friends, associates, and teachers of the Cohens—included some of the most significant leaders of the American Jewish world. Many of them had also lived for extended periods in Palestine. One of the group, Leah Klepper, a classmate of Ethel Cohen's from the Teachers' Institute and a celebrated teacher of Hebrew, would emigrate to Israel in 1950 and become a tireless traveler and Israeli representative for Esco. Mordecai Kaplan, scholar and teacher, also served as a member of the board. Rose Jacobs, soon to become president of Hadassah, coordinated Esco's activities with that organization and provided priceless contacts and information when she served as Esco's first executive vice president. There were also several prominent educators, such as Isaac B. Berkson, a professor at Teachers College of Columbia University, who had served in Palestine for several years as director of Hebrew education; Leo Honor of Dropsie College (Philadelphia); Israel Chipkin of the (New York) Board of Jewish Education; Ben Rosen, director of Jewish education in Philadelphia; and Israel Wechsler, president of the board of American Friends of the Hebrew University.

The main principles of the Esco Fund Committee, in the words of its Certificate of Incorporation, were both "to assist in the advancement of the principles and practices of the democratic way of life by 1) assisting in the promotion of good will among the various faiths and 2) rendering aid and encouragement to victims of intolerance and oppression" and, concurrently, "to aid in the continued development and advancement of the Hebrew literature and arts."[14] Not long after its formation, two more organizations were added—the Esco Friends, Inc., whose function was to support educational and charitable projects in the United States, and the Esco Fund for Palestine, which, as its name stated, was devoted solely to projects in what would soon become the Jewish state. The creation of separate organizations was meant to allow for greater specialization, but by 1952 it was decided that one group could serve the tripartite Esco mission, and so all three units were merged.[15]

The funding criteria of the Esco Funds developed over time, with allowance for several exceptions. In a series of meetings, the members agreed on a number of basic principles. First, wherever possible, preference would be given to subventions that would act as a catalyst for further development, rather than providing ongoing support; ideally, the recipient would become self-sustaining. Preference would also be given to applicants who might not easily receive funds from other sources. Another criterion grew out of the unique tax laws of the United States: as a U.S.-based tax-exempt organization, Esco was forbidden to make grants to overtly political organizations or to parties that disseminated political propaganda.[16] Over time, this criterion came to symbolize the gap between the Israeli and American ways of getting things done, as most other disbursements in Israel were made on a political basis.

At its inception, Esco's aims were to help their fellow Jews in the U.S. and abroad with special attention given to the Jews of Palestine and the Zionist movement. However, it was the board members' belief—by no means shared by all their fellow Jews—that this could best be done by first helping the British in whatever way possible to defeat Hitler. The foundation's first projects were therefore calculated to relieve British suffering caused by Nazi bombing.

The idea for how best to help the British came when the Cohens took a British refugee child into their home in New York. The boy was pale and seriously undernourished, but he improved markedly when the couple supplemented his diet with vitamins. If this could be done so easily in New York, it occurred to them, why not do so for other children abroad who were suffering from the effects of the war?[17] The members of Esco agreed, in their next meeting, that any consideration for the health of British children would greatly improve the morale of the entire nation.[18] Thus the "Vitamins for Britain" project, in cooperation with the British War Relief Society and several other organizations, was born, conducting its operations between February 10, 1941 and February 28, 1942. In addition to the vitamin project, Frank Cohen made generous personal donations to the British War Relief Society for the purpose of establishing nursing shelters for British children suffering from the effects of the bombing raids.[19]

The vitamin project quickly became a nationwide affair, helping to educate and raise the consciousness of thousands of Americans, including Jewish schoolchildren in classrooms, synagogues, and community centers across the land. Its first goal, even before raising funds, was to overcome widespread resistance to the idea that Great Britain deserved any American or Jewish aid at all. A manual was composed for teachers and group leaders entitled "Why Jews Should Aid Great Britain," which included details on Jewish history in England, England's sympathetic attitude toward the Jewish state before the Balfour Declaration, and the danger of German victory to world Jewry. In addition, the Cohens sent chain letters to all their friends and associates, asking for cooperation and donations.[20]

In all, three shipments containing enough vitamins to nourish thousands of British children were sent via the American Red Cross. Smaller shipments of vitamins were also sent to children in China and Palestine. In a public presentation of the first shipment, at which many dignitaries, including Stephen S. Wise, spoke, the Cohen's eleven-year-old son, Amos, presented a symbolic box to a young British girl, declaring that the shipments came "with admiration and affection from American Jewish children to British children."[21] The response to the vitamins was deep and appreciative. English mothers and nurses caring for children evacuated to the countryside wrote letters of thanks describing how the vitamin oil helped to relieve the effects of malnutrition and the prevalent coughs and colds. One mother from Cheshire reported that her premature baby began to thrive only one month after beginning to take the vitamin oil.[22]

Despite the obvious effectiveness of the "Vitamins for Britain" project, however, Esco's campaign went decidedly against the current of American Jewish public opinion. Many Jews in the early 1940s feared that any separate Jewish organization for the war effort would play into the hands of the antisemites, who accused the Jews of backing and fomenting the war; they also felt that it impugned their status as American citizens first and Jews second. The leaders of the American Jewish Committee, among other groups, refused to have anything to do with the project, convinced that the formation of a separate organization would render a "deadly blow" to the Jews.

Displeasure with Esco's policy of aiding Great Britain did not come only from non-Zionist quarters such as the American Jewish Committee, but from fellow Zionists who understandably resented the British promulgation of the McDonald White Paper of 1939. Why should the Jews of America help the government that had almost completely repudiated the Balfour Declaration and had virtually cut off immigration to Palestine at the very moment when large numbers of European Jews were desperately attempting to escape? At the very least, it was felt, aid should not be extended to Great Britain unless accompanied by public reminders of British promises regarding the Jewish homeland. Zionist leader (and Israel's future first president) Chaim Weizmann, for his part, found it necessary to defend Jewish contributions to England despite the White Paper and to emphasize how closely the fates of the two peoples were bound together:

This is a war in which every Jew is ready to lay down his life. . . . We stand or fall by the victory or—God forbid!—the defeat of the British. . . . What we Jews ask is to be there to help meet the enemy. We have a great many accounts to square. . . . Despite our criticism of England in Palestine, there is one lodestar which no Jew forgets. It is England which has made it possible to bring five hundred thousand Jews to Palestine. She might have done more. She might have done less. Let us postpone our account until there will be less tangible anguish in the world . . . [then] England will live and we shall live![23]

Esco's activities during the Second World War were also directed toward the problems of "community relations" (frequently a euphemism for antisemitism) at home, as well as the attempt to strengthen American Jewish education and publications at the very moment that European Jewish culture was being systematically destroyed. Esco's smaller but significant projects included a donation of $1,000 to the Council Against Intolerance for a pamphlet titled "Calling All Americans," which was to be distributed among members of the armed forces. In supporting this and similar projects, the leaders of Esco accepted the common American Jewish view that prejudice and Jew-hatred were diseases of ignorance that could be banished with scientific evidence and sufficient education. Other projects included a book on home devotions published by the Reconstructionist Foundation, as well as contributions to *The Reconstructionist* magazine; grants to the Hebrew University and to the Jewish Museum of the Jewish Theological Seminary; $3,000 to the "Torah Shelemah" project, which aimed to produce an entire new edition of the Hebrew Bible and commentaries (Esco's funds enabled the publication of volume 6, *Exodus*); $2,000 to the *Menorah Journal;* $2,000 to the American Academy for Jewish Music Research in support of a massive work entitled *Cantillation of the Pentateuch;* and, in cooperation with Hadassah, a two-year scholarship for Mrs. Ethel Bloom of Palestine to study occupational therapy and rehabilitation in America so that she could carry these much-needed skills back to her own country.[24]

One of the most popular projects supported by Esco in the field of Jewish education was the Jewish Theological Seminary's Israel Friedlander Classes in Jewish Studies, named for the late scholar who had been Ethel Cohen and Leah Klepper's teacher. At one point, the Seminary offered twenty-six classes taught by eleven teachers, including Hebrew— the most sought-after subject—Jewish art (including as well dance and music), Bible, Jewish history, Palestine, literature, philosophy, and comparative religion, along with special leadership and alumni classes. The student body was drawn from Jewish men and women in all professions from the greater New York and New Jersey areas. Despite wartime pressures, their numbers doubled between 1942 and 1944.[25]

Esco's contributions between 1943 and 1945 also made possible the continued functioning of the department of Hebrew instruction at Hunter College after the Board of Higher Education of New York had eliminated it from the school's budget. As in the case of the Seminary classes in Jewish studies, the number of students studying Hebrew at Hunter College doubled during the years of Esco's support. This attracted the attention of other donors as well. The Hebrew department was able to include an especially popular course on masterpieces of Hebrew literature, given in English, as well as extracurricular activities such as a Hebrew-speaking circle and a Menorah Society. By 1947, the faculty of Hunter, convinced that the department was a valuable and vital addition to the college's curriculum, voted to establish Hebrew as a degree major, fully supported by the city's budget.[26] In addition to these projects, Esco also acted as a transfer agent for donations by Frank Cohen to the general funds of Jewish communal, philanthropic, and educational organizations, which totaled almost $90,000 between 1941 and 1945.[27]

Perhaps the most significant contribution Esco made during the war years in the field of Jewish learning was its support of the American Association for Jewish Education. This organization had been founded in 1939 on the initiative of the National Council for Jewish Education and a number of lay leaders of Jewish education in America—many of them friends and associates of Frank Cohen. Its aims and achievements were "to federate all Bureaus of Jewish Education and kindred bureaus; to serve large and small communities; to serve as a department of information and research; to create interrelationships with professionals in Jewish educational institutions."[28] However, with virtually no budget, there was very little the ambitious association could actually do. A grant-in-aid of $10,000, paid over a three-year period from 1942 to 1944, was made jointly by Esco Friends and Frank Cohen, and this was enough to plant it firmly on its feet.

The Association made noteworthy progress. By the third year of the grant, it had conducted surveys of Jewish education in more than twenty-five communities and had rendered service to more than 100 communities. It was supported by 160 members, along with seventeen affiliated bureaus of Jewish education. Moreover, a department of research and information had been initiated and a summer institute to train executive personnel was in the planning stages; a national board of license for teachers in week-day schools had been set up, nationwide publicity and student enrollment campaigns for Jewish schools were being conducted, and the Association's "Annual Review of Jewish Education" had appeared in the *American Jewish Year Book*. The Association also planned to set up local and regional bureaus of Jewish education in small communities, in pursuit of its primary goal of raising the standards of Jewish education throughout the U.S.[29] Since Jewish day schools were not yet considered a viable option, the Association's energy during those years was directed toward improving the quality of education in afternoon and weekend Hebrew schools.

Conditions governing Esco grants changed with the entry of the United States into the Second World War in December 1941. After Pearl Harbor, there could be no question of accusations that Jews were dragging the country into an unnecessary conflict. Also, with the growing awareness that Hitler planned the full destruction of the Jews—not only their persecution—considerations of the betrayal of the White Paper fell by the wayside as Jews worldwide realized to what extent their very survival depended upon an Allied victory.

Once the U.S. declared war, many accustomed avenues of action and communication were cut off. There appeared to be little that any American citizen could do while the conflict raged. The directors of Esco, however, realized the necessity for early and proper planning for the postwar future. In common with other Jewish leaders, the Cohens believed that the conclusion of the Second World War would be similar to that of the previous world war, in that nations of the world would meet around a peace table to hammer out the details of the postwar world. Obviously, Jewish interests in Palestine and elsewhere would have to be represented, backed up by facts and documentation. There existed a widely held perception among Jewish leaders that the Jews had been unprepared for the aftermath of the First World War; they did not want to be unprepared now. Therefore, philanthropy and public action became oriented toward the preparation of peacetime claims and activities. It was also obvious, as the war continued, that something would have to be done for the multitude of refugees the conflict was bound to leave in its wake. Certainly Palestine had to be built up more than ever in order to receive as many Jewish survivors as possible.

## Projects in Palestine/Israel, 1941–1951

In founding the separate Esco Foundation for Palestine, the Cohens turned their attention to an area in which they would be most active and in which its members had the most expertise and contacts. The first meeting was held at the Cohen home on November 22, 1941, with Ethel Cohen, Isaac Berkson, Rose E. Jacobs, Mordecai Kaplan, and Leah Klepper present. Frank Cohen, in response to an appeal to help save Palestine from possible invasion by the Nazis, had already personally donated $13,000 to the country (fortunately, the feared invasion never materialized).[30] With the luxury of steadily increasing funds and time to consider what was to be done, the members discussed various ways the money could be put to use, based on their own extensive knowledge and experience in Palestine and the conditions governing Esco grants. Mordecai Kaplan spoke of the problem of illiteracy among thousands of children who did not receive even an elementary education in Palestine because of the lack of public funds; Rose Jacobs spoke of the problems of delinquency and the possibilities of setting up kindergartens and nursery schools; Isaac Berkson, based on his work with Henrietta Szold in Palestine, felt that the greatest service the fund could perform would be to help organize industrial schools.[31]

The leading American authority in Palestine for social welfare projects was of course Henrietta Szold, and the foundation immediately sent her a large sum of money to dispose of as she saw fit. Afterwards, both Berkson and Jacobs conducted a steady correspondence with her, and in the early years of Esco's existence, through various grants large and small, she provided constant advice, encouragement, and information. In one letter to Jacobs, dated June 7, 1943, Szold expressed her feelings of gratitude for the formation of the foundation in the face of the greatest destruction the Jews had ever experienced:

> I wish I had the faculty of keeping steadily before my mind the fine human qualities and acts brought to the fore by a brutal war, like a rare brilliant flower springing from a swamp. There have been many such flowers. The Jews especially should recognize and treasure them. I hope

that somewhere or other is the faithful and at the same time gifted chronicler who has kept a record of the expressions of good will, the acts of compassion, the indignation at injustice and sadism, all evoked by Jewish agony alone. . . . This Esco is one of the finest war products.[32]

From the beginning, the members of the Esco Foundation for Palestine were determined to contribute in a uniquely American way, one that stressed the qualities of energy, industry, know-how, and commitment to democratic principles. As an industrialist and economist, Frank Cohen was well placed to transfer not only money, but materiel, teachers, trainers, and expertise. Also important were Esco's educational goals, as well as the foundation's desire to help facilitate children's immigration from Europe and Germany by providing accommodations and educational facilities. The Hadassah and Youth Aliyah contacts provided via Rose Jacobs appeared to improve its chances of success in this area.

In 1943, Esco's directors conceived the idea of building what they called "Freedom Village"—an industrial school and living arrangement where destitute and needy refugee youngsters could obtain gainful work and become self-supporting, thereby being able to live "in dignity and peace in Palestine."[33] The general plan, as conceived by Frank Cohen, was to create and build up an industrial village that would be started by 100 young immigrants to Palestine. The location of the village would depend upon the type of industry chosen. Through Hadassah, the necessary Jewish National Fund land and other requirements would be furnished, and Esco would maintain the students for a period of not more than two years in connection with the Youth Aliyah movement. With these ideas in place, the Foundation sent $80,000 to Hadassah in expectation of starting the project.

At first there was no indication that Freedom Village would be anything but a great success. Unfortunately, it eventually became one of Esco's greatest failures, emblematic of the huge gulf between the accepted American and Israeli methods of operation. The failure was not for lack of effort. Rose Jacobs began by visiting several American institutions, including the Brooklyn High School for Specialty Trades, to investigate how their methods might be transferred to Palestine. Henrietta Szold, when informed of the plan, called together several of her associates, including Julius Simon and Judah Magnes, and reported that "the idea aroused enthusiasm to an unusual degree."[34] Frank Cohen, in the belief that Palestine had to be industrialized in order to promote its development for immigration, began to investigate appropriate industries for the village. Ideally, the industries would not be competitive with other Near-Eastern countries and would require special skills for which Jews could be trained, producing goods that would be both non-polluting and easily transported. The optical industry, specifically, the grinding of lenses for eyeglasses and sunglasses, attracted Frank Cohen's earliest interest. In his view, Palestine might quickly become the optic center for the entire Middle East. Another possibility was sugar processing, which lent itself to a number of byproducts—especially Jordan Almonds—a delicacy that was already associated with Palestine. At one point, Frank Cohen also considered the manufacturing of tractors.[35]

Esco put years of effort and thousands of dollars into the Freedom Village project, yet the plan never came to fruition. For five years, the organizers struggled with the stream of difficulties and red tape that typify any attempt to give aid from afar. The Jewish Agency (Palestine's Jewish self-administration organization) and Youth Aliyah would not cooperate; appropriate sponsors for the project in Palestine could not be found; objections were raised to every industry that Esco proposed. At one point, for example, tractor production had to be discarded because it would have given economic opportunities to political groupings other than the Histadrut, Palestine's main labor union.[36]

A special complication confronting the Freedom Village project—and for that matter, any other Esco project in Palestine—was the existence of numerous competing political parties and ideological systems within the Zionist movement. This was a factor with which pragmatic American philanthropists were not prepared to deal. The refugee crisis in particular became highly politicized. In one case, Esco rejected a plan to build refugee children's homes in Paris after the war for the General Zionists, since there were already enough such homes being set up for Mizrachi, Labor Zionist, and Communist children. "Even our charities are now governed by Zionist party divisiveness," lamented Ethel Cohen in a letter to Israel Goldstein on June 20, 1947. "We do not recognize Histadrut, or Mizrachi, or General Zionist children. There are only Jewish children who, because they have no parents to guide or care for them, are the charges of the whole Jewish people, and not of parties among the Jewish people. What is this dreadful party-Golem we are building? We think it is scandalous that even children are not free from Zionist party indoctrination."[37]

After five years of fruitless endeavor, in a meeting held January

1, 1948, the members of the Esco Foundation for Palestine regretfully resolved to abandon all further plans to establish Freedom Village as an industrial-agricultural village in Palestine.[38] The money, however, had already been allotted; what was to be done with it? Both the board and the leaders of Hadassah believed that a substitute project along similar lines should be sought. In a series of discussions, Esco considered setting up a child guidance center in Palestine that would handle both immigrant and native youth, or a mental hygiene center.[39] Soon a suitable alternative presented itself.

In 1921, while on the boat to Palestine, the Cohens had met Tuvia Miller of Rehovot, an American immigrant to Palestine who later became an official of the Farmers' Federation—an apolitical organization representing middle-class farmers in Palestine. In 1948, Miller and two associates visited the U.S. in order to investigate mechanization of the citrus industry in the new state of Israel. Meeting with the Cohens, he told them about an agricultural school known as Pardes Hanna, located near the town of Hadera on the Tel Aviv-Haifa highway, which was sponsored and run by the Farmers' Federation. By supporting this school, Esco might be able to carry out some of the original ideas and plans of Freedom Village.[40]

In 1948, Pardes Hanna was fifteen years old and was under the direction of a graduate of the Haifa Technion. The student body consisted of 115 boys between the ages of fifteen and twenty drawn from all parts of Israel, largely from the families of the Farmers' Federation. Tuition was 300 pounds per year, with a few students on scholarships provided by the local communities or various Israeli agencies. Among the students were several Youth Aliyah members whose scholarships were paid partly by Youth Aliyah and partly by the Farmers' Federation. The school offered a five-year course, both theoretical and practical, in all branches of farming and dairying, and it had under cultivation about 500 dunams (about 274 acres) of land containing fruit orchards, vegetable gardens, and cattle. According to Rose Jacobs, the school had an excellent reputation; even the British mandatory government, which generally provided no school subsidies, approved of Pardes Hanna and provided funds for it at one time.[41]

Miller's proposal was to expand the Pardes Hanna school by the addition of a mechanical-industrial training program, to be sponsored by Esco, in areas related specifically to farming. Frank Cohen in turn proposed that a genuine assembly plant be set up where the students would both receive practical experience and earn money while they learned. Products assembled in the plant could be anything that the farming consumers of Israel might require, such as parts for tractors, plows, and other farm implements. He further suggested that the program charter would stipulate a number of spaces for Youth Aliyah (or other) immigrants, in order to fulfill one of the initial purposes of the fund; moreover, dormitories would be built for the students and faculty of the new department.[42]

After much discussion, investigation, and reflection, the members of Esco decided on March 5, 1949, to grant an initial sum of $110,000 to the Pardes Hanna Secondary Agricultural School. The money would be allotted first to establish a unit to be known as the Esco Foundation Technical Department, for the purchase of equipment necessary for technical and mechanical training of the students, and to cover costs of the assembly, modification, and repair of machinery and appliances. Upon application, forty Youth Aliyah students would be admitted to Pardes Hanna upon mutually satisfactory terms to be agreed upon by the Farmers' Federation, Youth Aliyah in Israel, and a special Israel committee appointed by Esco and chaired by Tuvia Miller. The students would be supported for two years through partial scholarships. Esco also agreed to build two dormitories for the students. The building would be made of prefabricated aluminum, in keeping with one of Frank Cohen's many industrial interests. Profits from the program would be put back into the Fund for the maintenance and continuance of the facilities.[43]

The Pardes Hanna project had its own share of problems. Once again, incomprehensible political party considerations, red tape, and the natural difficulties inherent in carrying out operations thousands of miles away intervened. The matter of finding forty appropriate Youth Aliyah students became inexplicably complicated: Youth Aliyah claimed at first that only twenty such boys could be found and supported.[44] Cost overruns were another problem: ultimately, Esco spent more than $185,000 on the Pardes Hanna school.[45] In 1952, one of the aluminum dormitories burned down, and although no one was hurt, all the children's clothes and belongings were destroyed.[46]

Nevertheless, in contrast to Freedom Village, Frank and Ethel Cohen considered the Pardes Hanna project a relative success. In the early years of the state, its agro-mechanics course provided much-needed technical training and its graduates aided in the rapid mechanization of Israeli agriculture. In addition to mechanics, the principal of the school reported in 1951, the boys were also receiving a thorough education in academic subjects, including Hebrew, mathematics, Bible, and history.[47] The dormitories drew admirers and visitors, including the Honorable and Mrs. James McDonald, U.S. Ambassador to Israel, who remarked after a 1950 stay there that the beds at Pardes Hanna were more comfortable than his own.[48]

The success of the Pardes Hanna project was furthered by the personal interest that the board, and especially Ethel Cohen, took in it. In this, Esco followed a steady pattern of never giving its money casually and without follow-up—although some of its beneficiaries might have wished it otherwise. After 1950, Mrs. Cohen visited Israel every year, usually for an extended period of six weeks, and took a direct personal role in all of the projects Esco sponsored. For example, when one of the boys lost his accordion in the dormitory fire, Ethel Cohen sent him a new one.[49] Esco scrapbooks are filled with letters and photographs that were sent to the Cohens by the Pardes Hanna students. After 1950, Esco's projects in the new Jewish state were also guided by Leah Klepper, who had moved to Israel. After one of her visits, Ethel Cohen gave the Esco board a report on Leah Klepper's activities, which included an account of her attempts to secure the desired number of forty Youth Aliyah students for the school:

> Miss Klepper, who is a wonderful representative for Esco, has been turning heaven and earth to try to find some solution to the problem. She has traveled back and forth from Tel Aviv to Jerusalem, to Pardess Hanna, to Rehovoth, to arrange meetings with the Youth Aliyah administrators and members of the Esco Committee. Those who have recently visited Israel know the almost superhuman efforts required to make telephone calls, to travel from one place to another, to arrange meetings with the constantly on-the-move government officials, and all this during the blazing heat of an Israeli summer. Yet Leah has done all this, frequently having to wait for the high moguls who do not keep their appointments, or who forget to announce holiday "office shut-downs." In one instance our friend Mr. Tuvia Miller traveled from Haifa to Jerusalem for a meeting with Mr. Rheinhold of Youth Aliyah, only to find the office closed because it was [the fast day of] Tisha B'av. Mr. Rheinhold had designated the appointment but forgot to notify Leah and Mr. Miller not to come.[50]

In addition to Pardess Hanna, other projects in Palestine supported by Esco during the 1940s were a study in vocational education by the education department of the Hebrew University,[51] a $56,000 contribution to the Working Boys' Village at Gevat,[52] and, in 1949, the establishment of a revolving loan fund for American students attending the Hebrew University.[53]

## Support for Scholarly Works

Aside from practical hands-on projects, Esco funds made a significant contribution to the preparation of several important scholarly reports, both during and after the Second World War. First and foremost were studies connected with postwar matters. Back in 1941, various Jewish research institutes, such as those of the American Jewish Congress and the American Jewish Committee, were preparing material to be used at the expected postwar peace conference. The growing controversy between Arabs, Jews, and the British in Palestine, along with Jewish hopes for founding a state there, required expert documentation and representation in international forums. Emmanuel Neumann, a Zionist leader who was then the representative of the Jewish Agency in Washington, D.C., addressed a meeting of Esco on December 12, 1942. "The Balfour Declaration [in 1917] found the Jews completely unprepared for an overall plan," he warned. "We must not be unprepared at this time when the war ceases."[54]

Consequently, Esco sponsored several noteworthy studies. Among its grants were $1,500 to the Commission for the Organization of Peace for a study to be done on regional or plural nationality by Oscar Janowsky of the City College of New York. Aside from its direct relevance in explaining the root causes of two world wars, it was hoped that this study might bear indirectly on resolving the Arab-Jewish problem in Palestine.[55] Janowsky's *Nationalities and National Minorities* was published by Macmillan in 1945. The work surveyed parallel cases of the coexistence of peoples through history and attempted to apply that knowledge to the current political situation, especially to the problem of protecting the rights of minorities and nationalities in East Central Europe.[56]

Esco also donated $2,000 to the Conference on Jewish Relations, an organization chaired by Salo Baron, director of Jewish studies at Columbia University, which published the journal *Jewish Social Studies*. Half of the money was allotted directly to the journal; the other half helped fund a scientific study on the history of antisemitism—the first such study of its kind. *Essays on Anti-Semitism,* edited by Koppel S. Pinson, was published in early January 1942. Ironically this was the very day that automobile king Henry Ford —who had filled the media with Jew-hating material throughout the 1920s and who had done nothing to prevent others from reprinting or quoting it throughout the 1930s— made his final and most decisive disavowal of antisemitism as part of a wave of patriotic fervor, tolerance, and American solidarity following the Japanese bombing of Pearl Harbor. "It was a strange coincidence," noted Ethel Cohen to the publishers, upon reading the study. "May I suggest you send him a copy with Esco's compliments? Perhaps his retraction needs the bolstering up of his opinion—and he can find it in the volume."[57] The Esco grant was also used to distribute complimentary copies of the study to editors, important Christian leaders, and other selected individuals and libraries.

Providing scholarly data on Palestine was especially important in the 1940s, since the British government and other authorities were basing their Jewish immigration projections—or lack of them—on what they saw as the limited economic absorptive capacity of the country. With enough hard evidence, the British concept of "economic absorptive capacity" could be either refuted or transformed outright. In 1943–1944, for example, the Jewish Agency began making plans for large-scale irrigation and hydroelectric development in the Jordan Valley, helped by American scientists and engineers. Such a project could transform Palestine's agricultural and industrial economy and go far to increase the country's absorptive capacity. However, the plan could not proceed without a preliminary survey and cost-benefit analysis. With the blessings of Chaim Weizmann and the various Zionist agencies, Esco members voted to sponsor the project, going so far as to set up an office and engage Emmanuel Neumann as director. It soon became apparent, however, that the intricacies of Zionist party politics were bound to intervene, a factor that not only violated Esco's criteria but endangered its tax-exempt status. After just one month, therefore, in May 1944, Esco terminated its support, and the JVA (Jordan Valley Authority) project was left to others.[58]

Esco's greatest success in the field of scholarly works related to Palestine—though not achieved without years of heartache and tens of thousands of dollars—was the classic *Palestine: A Study of Jewish, Arab, and British Policies.* The two-volume, 1,350–page study, published in 1947 by Yale University Press, took five times the time and twice the money as originally planned, and was a source of bitter dispute among the members of the board. Nevertheless, it was the most exhaustive work on that subject of its time, essential to the work of the American Zionists during the negotiations in the years immediately preceding the declaration of statehood; to this day, it is a textbook used in classes around the world.

The decision to sponsor the study was taken at a meeting of the Esco Foundation for Palestine on April 18, 1942, upon Frank Cohen's announcement that he now had an especially large sum available. There had already been discussion concerning whether Esco should undertake a study on Arab-Jewish relations to complement Janowsky's study in national pluralism. Critical events were happening in the Middle East; the fate of the British Mandate and the Jewish homeland hung in the balance, and American Zionists were gearing up for the great fight at home and abroad that would ultimately culminate in the creation of the state. Esco's contribution, they decided, could be a comprehensive study of all the problems involved in the development of a Jewish national home in Palestine, covering all historical, cultural, economic, and political aspects, supplemented by documentary materials and made available to all public bodies dealing with the problem of Palestine and postwar planning, including the UN.[59]

Isaac Berkson, a member of the Esco board, appeared to be especially qualified for the challenging task of overseeing such a study. A graduate of City College of New York and of Teachers College, Columbia, he had already served as director of the Central Jewish Institute of New York City, supervisor of school and extension activities of the Bureau of Jewish Education, and lecturer at the Jewish Institute of Religion and at City College. In 1928, he was invited to direct the Hebrew school system in Palestine, where he served until 1935. During the years 1931 to 1935, he was also a member of the Executive Committee of the Jewish Agency in Palestine, where he represented the non-Zionist faction. Finally, Berkson was the author of numerous books and articles dealing with educational philosophy, the Americanization of immigrants, and the Zionist school system.[60]

At the first meeting launching the study, the vote was unanimous that Berkson would undertake its direction and organization. A sum of $25,000 was set aside for its execution, allotted to salaries for the director, research, and office assistants, office rental, electricity, telephone, traveling, and other expenses. Other stipulations were that the study would be completed within fifteen months, and that a committee of prominent Jewish and non-Jewish leaders would be sought as sponsors.[61]

Berkson threw himself into the task with enthusiasm. "About the Study, I shall write to you in great detail later during the fall," he wrote his friend Henrietta Szold in Palestine. "The plan is to make a comprehensive study of the whole situation on the cultural, political, economic, and social side. My view is that the Arab-Jewish problem is organically related with all these other problems and while it will have full attention and in a sense is the core of the whole business, it will be discussed in the broad framework indicated. We shall have a research staff and we shall consult expert opinion in the various fields. I expect to devote a year to the project."[62]

The year turned into five, however, as new developments, unforeseen difficulties, and the sheer complexity of the subject matter hindered the study's publication. There was Berkson's insistence, against the wishes of the Esco board and the publisher (who saw it as an anthological work), that he be named its editor; there were interpersonal conflicts; fears that the material would be out of date by the time the book came out; and questions of what form the final study should take, and whether it should offer any conclusions.[63]

Even as these disputes continued, however, the study proved its direct and practical usefulness when Berkson assumed the position in 1943 of research director for the American Zionist Emergency Council (AZEC). In 1943–1944, the material that had already been gathered was transferred to the AZEC. Despite the resulting conflict between Esco and AZEC over ownership of the manuscript, the study became a crucial source for the Zionists during the hearings in Washington on the question of Palestine.[64] Abba Hillel Silver, head of the AZEC, wrote to the Cohens on May 23, 1944 to describe how indispensable the Esco material had been to AZEC and how much time and money it had saved the Zionists at this crucial juncture in history:

> We feel greatly indebted to the Esco Foundation, which your donation has made possible, for the considerable amount of material supplied by our Research Department in connection with the hearings. . . . It was possible to prepare [our] documents in short order only because of the availability of the reports and catalogued material which Esco prepared during the last year. Moreover, in numerous requests that have been received, week in and week out, for information and material, we have

constantly drawn on the Esco material and the final report which Dr. Berkson is preparing for you. . . . Apart from the fact that we should have been put to great expense to gather this material anew . . . we could never have had the material in time for our current activities if the ground had not been prepared in the course of the Esco Study during the last year.[65]

Despite doubts on the part of the Cohens and some members of the Esco boards, there was unanimous agreement among the consultants who read the manuscript that the Esco study should be formally published. "It is my considered opinion that Esco had rendered a signal service to the Zionist cause in making it possible for Berkson to prepare this work," wrote Janowsky on August 26, 1944:

> It [is] addressed to the serious-minded and intelligent reader who is handicapped by the lack of authoritative and documented information on Palestine . . . Dr. Berkson's study is the most thorough and comprehensive survey of the Palestine question that I have ever seen. It examines the Arab as well as the Jewish case, and relates both to the broader problems of Jewish homelessness and Near Eastern politics. . . . If published, the Study will become a work of reference for scholars, teachers, ministers, political leaders, and molders of public opinion. It should be placed on the shelves of every important library in the country.[66]

*Palestine: A Study of Jewish, Arab, and British Policies* was finally published in the spring of 1947, although, at Berkson's request, his name was not included as author. The final cost to Esco was $50,000, a considerable sum of money at the time.[67] Containing essays by contributing scholars from the United States and abroad, both Jewish and non-Jewish, the work included a complete history of the first 100 years of Zionism; the events of the First World War and the background to the Balfour Declaration; complete coverage of the post-Second World War peace conferences, the British Mandate, the various White Papers, and the conflicting promises and claims made by both Arabs and Jews. It also included a detailed three-section color map of Palestine, scaled 1:250,000 and executed by Palestine Surveys. Providing information with great detail and clarity, this was among the best and most complete maps of Palestine in existence up to that time.[68]

The study received ample notice in the press and, when distributed among key people involved in the Palestine negotiations, immediately fulfilled its goal of serving as a source for policy-making bodies. "You must be pleased that [the volumes of the Esco study] have received such extensive notice in the press and that they were available for the use of the United Nations and its fact-finding committee," wrote James McDonald, the U.S. ambassador to Palestine, to Ethel Cohen. "This service alone would more than justify all the expense and labor which you and your colleagues have put into the work."[69] In the stores, the speed of the sales proved gratifying to the Esco Board. "The copies are selling very well," reported Ethel Cohen to the AZEC on May 16, 1947, "and, as the *New York Times* will review it May 18 and Scribners and Doubleday will both display it in their Fifth Avenue shops beginning next Tuesday, the copies will undoubtedly sell even more rapidly."[70] Reviews of the study, carefully clipped by Ethel Cohen, were for the most part positive and gratifying. "Unquestionably factual, the Study is comprehensive and [as] objective as can be achieved by an exhaustive use of documents, and will doubtless remain for some time to come the definitive source book in the field of Palestinian affairs," wrote the *New York Times* on May 18. "Britain receives far more charitable understanding than one is accustomed to expect from a Zionist publication."[71] The Jewish press also acknowledged the value and innovation of Esco's sponsorship. Writing in the *Jewish Frontier* in March 1948, scholar Abraham Duker wrote: "This pioneer experiment of the Esco Foundation, launched by Mr. and Mrs. Frank Cohen . . . should point the way to other philanthropists whose horizon extends a bit beyond the customary charity concepts."[72]

The long-standing value of the Esco study was attested to by its use in classrooms and the calls for reprints that ensued throughout the years. Yale University Press printed two editions. In 1964, the American representative of the Jewish Agency in Israel and a lecturer in sociology at the Hebrew University urged that the study be reprinted, saying that it was "the best, definitive book on Palestine concerned with the last 100 years of Zionist history" and that it was being used in many classes at the university and elsewhere.[73] In 1968, the Kraus Reprint Company, one of the largest in the world, requested and received exclusive rights to the two volumes, stating that in its opinion, "it is one of the best surveys of the subject." The volumes were eventually reprinted by Kraus in 1980.[74]

## "Operation Sweetheart"

Education, international affairs, agro-mechanics, and politics were not the sum total of Esco's ambitions either in the U.S. or in Israel. Another goal was enriching and beautifying Jewish life. In one instance in the early 1950s, the directors became concerned that citizens under the Israeli austerity regime were in danger of nutritional deprivation. The country was reeling under the losses of the War of Independence, and the infrastructure buckled when it had to absorb hundreds of thousands of new immigrants, most of them living in transit camps—*ma'abarot*—in shacks and in tents. Food was strictly rationed, and sweets in particular were a luxury. Candy and chocolate were simply not to be had in the entire country. To help remedy this situation, the board of Esco voted to send fifty tons of fruit sugar paste loaf to the children of the ma'abarot, at the cost of approximately $25,000. This was a donation from Frank Cohen, who was in the candy manufacturing business at the time. The shipments were sent to the Israel Department of Labor (then headed by Golda Meyerson, later Golda Meir), and the distribution of the candy took place on the eve of the holiday of Sukkot, 1952. Ethel Cohen, who was in Israel at the time, as were some other members of Esco, visited three *ma'abarot*—in Petach Tikva, Pardes Hanna, and Rosh Ha'ayin—and participated in the distribution of the candy, dubbed "Operation Sweetheart," to kindergarten and primary school children.[75] From the current perspective of a society in which sugar is overabundant and the resulting health hazard of tooth decay is well known, it may be hard to appreciate the success of this one-time campaign. But children in the *ma'abarot* had not seen candy, or indeed anything sweet, from one year to the next. Ethel Cohen wrote of the joy of observing each child's delight as he or she received a half-pound of sweets. In all, 70,000 *ma'abarot* children received candy. The treat was especially appreciated since not long before, torrential fall rains and flooding had combined to make life in the camps even more unpleasant than usual.[76]

As evidence of the impact that the small gift of candy had on the children, Mrs. Cohen received a letter from Matilda J. Greenburg, originally of Briarwood, Queens, who resided in Israel and had witnessed its distribution:

> On the subject of the fruit paste sent by your Foundation for the children in the camps in Israel, I would like you to know what a really wonderful and valuable contribution this was. I went around with one of the supervisors of the Children's Feeding Dept. of the Israel Government Social Welfare Dept . . . to visit the camps, and in each and every camp I spoke with the woman in charge of this department, and received a universal comment—"It is just wonderful. Please tell the donors they have done a

great mitzvah, and also please tell them to send us some more." On the last round I made I saw how this fruit product played a part in making the children forget their discomforts when the floods played such havoc with the camps . . . [In one camp] the cook made a sort of jelly roll by making a thin pancake from powdered milk and powdered egg, and on this she spread delicious red jam (made from the fruit paste by adding water and boiling it) and then rolled up the pancake and cut slices which looked like jelly roll.[77]

According to Mrs. Greenburg, the children stood in line over and over again to partake of this delicacy, and enjoyed the paste in other forms as well:

> Besides using it in the manner above mentioned, they also used it in making puddings, as spreads on bread, and as just a sweet or candy. From my observation this product supplied a very great need not only for relieving the shortage of sugar in the diet, but also for adding zest and color to otherwise drab and monotonous menus. If it were at all possible to get more of this, it would be a great help for the children and a real "mitzvah" on your part. . . . as a resident of Israel interested in all that is done by friends abroad for the benefit of the inhabitants, I want to convey my deep appreciation of your gift, and may you get your reward in the knowledge of the good you do.[78]

## Musical Life

In a more intangible sense, music was another means to sweeten life and help raise Israelis above their all-too-drab surroundings. Indeed, the funding of musical projects in Israel became one of Esco's specialties, largely because of Ethel Cohen.

A skilled pianist, teacher, and accompanist, Mrs. Cohen had received her M.A. with honors in musicology from New York University—a distinction that merited a story in the *New York Times,* since she had returned to school after many years and was one of only four mothers among several thousand graduates.[79] Her master's thesis, unusual in that it dealt in the area of non-Western music, was entitled "The Wedding Songs of the Babylonian Jews," and was prepared with the assistance of a cantor who had immigrated from Iraq. Close to 300 pages were filled with transcriptions of the music and translations of the text.[80] Ethel Cohen also coauthored the book *Fifty Yiddish Folk Songs* (1922) and wrote a wide variety of articles, interviews, and critiques in the field of classical and Jewish music. She headed the Jewish Music Council of the Jewish Welfare Board from its inception in 1943 until 1950 and was a member of the Board of Directors of the America-Israel Cultural Foundation.[81]

As Frank Cohen utilized his expertise in economics and industry, so too did his wife make use of her musical talents in order to enrich Jewish musical life both in Israel and America. Israel had many classical music afficionados who desperately missed the high culture they had been accustomed to in prewar years. Ethel Cohen shared the view that the creation of a strong cultural life in Israel was not a luxury, but rather a central part of the Zionist ideal. The fact that Israel was still struggling to find enough food to feed its population, and could not yet provide permanent housing to a substantial portion of its population, did not obviate the need to develop cultural institutions; it only meant that others would have to help out. Music-lovers such as Ethel Cohen, along with many musicians living in Israel, yearned to prove that Jews in their own state were as capable as the most sophisticated Western Europeans of both composing and performing top-notch European-style classical music.

One of Esco's first projects, accordingly, was a program supporting young Israeli composers who wished to study in the United States. In late 1947 the Esco Foundation for Palestine voted to allot a preliminary $2,500 for a competition whose winner would attend the Berkshire Music Center in Tanglewood, Massachusetts. A U.S. committee for the competition was formed, which included such figures as acting chairman Leonard Bernstein and Stefan Wolpe.[82] Even as the War of Independence raged in Palestine, concern with musical life continued. Letters to the Cohens from music teachers in Palestine wrote of students feverishly working on their scores in order to participate in the competition (tragically, one student who hoped to take part in the competition was killed).[83]

Throughout the years, several of Israel's finest young musicians had their careers advanced and aided through Esco's sponsorship. For example, when Herbert Brun, one of the Tanglewood Scholarship winners and a protégé of both Aaron Copland and Henry Cowell, won a scholarship in 1948 to study at the Julliard School, Esco gave him a grant to cover his living expenses.[84] Another Esco scholarship winner, Yehoshua Lakner, heard two of his compositions performed at Tanglewood in 1951 before returning to Israel, where he assumed a post teaching at the Tel Aviv Conservatory of Music.[85] Two musicians, Elyakum Shapira and Robert Starer, studied at the Julliard School. Ben-Zion Orgad, also one of the early winners of the Tanglewood scholarship, received both personal and financial support from Esco throughout the 1950s and into the 1960s, including supplemental support for a year of advanced study at Brandeis University in 1960–1961. During that year, in addition to his studies, he found time to compose several works, lecture on the development of art music in Israel, participate in the summer session of the Berkshire Music School at Tanglewood, and observe the teaching of music in New York City public schools and at Teachers College. Orgad eventually returned to Israel to assume the post of associate director of the music department at the Israel Ministry of Education, from which he retired in 1988.[86]

Another of Esco's small-scale but fruitful musical projects was its sponsorship of Johanna Spector, an ethnomusicologist and Jewish music researcher who played a major role in rescuing from oblivion the music of Israel's non-Western immigrants. Spector had been born and raised in Latvia, where her husband, Robert Spector, was killed by the Nazis in 1941. Surviving the war, she arrived in the U.S. in 1947, where she met Ethel Cohen. Beginning in October 1950 and throughout that decade, Spector received financial aid from Esco as she traveled throughout Israel to research, tape, and catalogue Oriental Jewish biblical chants and prayers. "She is an indefatigable, conscientious worker," noted Ethel Cohen in a description of these activities, "thinking little, for instance, of spending a whole night recording a synagogue service, or seeking out synagogues or cantors in the most remote, and oft-times dangerous neighborhoods in Israel."[87] During her first year in Israel, Spector recorded more than 1,500 Sabbath, holiday, and secular melodies. On a return trip to New York, she enthralled the Cohens and their friends with an evening presentation of excerpts from her recorded collection of prayers and cantillations of Yemenite, Iraqi, and Samaritan Jews. From 1951 to 1953, aided by a grant of three thousand Israel pounds from Esco, she was a research fellow in musicology at the Hebrew University;[88] in 1954, she returned to New York to join the Jewish Theological Seminary, becoming associate professor in 1966. The greater part of Spector's music collection was eventually deposited at the Archives of the Hebrew University and National Library of Jerusalem.[89]

The largest music project sponsored by Esco—which also became its most renowned achievement—was the Esco Music Center at Kibbutz

Ein Gev. Situated on the eastern shore of the Sea of Galilee, the 2,500-seat auditorium and music center, modeled after the Music Shed in Tanglewood, attracted hundreds of thousands of concertgoers. Following the Six-Day War, Ein Gev became a geographically secure, thriving tourist center, and most of the functions of the old Esco Music Center were taken over by the Israeli government. In the early years of the state, however, when the Syrian border was a few dozen yards from the kibbutz, the Cohens demonstrated faith and foresight in recognizing Ein Gev's great musical potential.

Established in 1937 by Jewish refugees from Central Europe—many of them musicians—Ein Gev had quickly become known as a site of musical culture. Annual Sukkot and Passover concerts had begun in the early 1940s, held at first in the communal dining room. Soon the dining hall became too small for the crowds, and the settlement began to consider how an adequate-sized music center and auditorium could be built.[90] The opportunity to begin such an ambitious project first presented itself in the form of a small compensation subsidy granted by the Israeli government in the wake of the 1948 War of Independence, during which Ein Gev had been attacked by the Syrians and had lost six of its members. The kibbutz decided to erect a music center as a memorial to these fallen comrades. Early in 1950, Serge Koussevitzky, then conductor of the Boston Symphony, visited the kibbutz and suggested that a music "shed" similar to that of Tanglewood could be built. Tanglewood's architectural plans were made available and construction of an outdoor auditorium was begun.

At this point, Ethel Cohen, an inveterate concertgoer, attended the Passover Festival at Ein Gev and became interested both in assisting Ein Gev to complete its building and in helping the area become a major musical center.[91] When Yaakov Steinberger, one of Ein Gev's directors, came to the U.S. seeking funds to complete the auditorium, he spoke to the Esco board on March 5, 1951. Steinberger underscored the great need for a regional cultural center in an area that included twenty-five rural settlements—rural life in Israel, though rooted in the soil, must be combined with a highly developed cultural standard—and emphasized Israel's position as a bastion of Western culture in the Middle East. Finally, he spoke of the desire to provide gifted children of the area with an education in music and the fine arts.[92] After discussing the matter with members of the board, Frank Cohen announced that Esco would supply the funds necessary to complete the music center. He declared it a gift to his wife in recognition of her love for music and in honor of their thirtieth wedding anniversary.[93]

At a preliminary cost of $150,000, the Esco Music Center was the most expensive and ambitious project the foundation had ever undertaken. Some feared that it was also a fool's errand. It was hard to believe that an outpost on the edge of the Syrian border could ever amount to a major cultural center, that a festival first held in a dining hall with orange crates for chairs could ever evolve into an internationally acclaimed concert event. In March 1951, for instance, the Rev. Dr. David de Sola Pool (rabbi of the Spanish and Portuguese synagogue, Shearith Israel, of New York), together with his wife, themselves active in Zionist affairs, wrote to the Cohens expressing their delight at the announcement of a gift to build an Esco Music Center in Israel. They doubted, however, that Ein Gev was the best site that could be chosen as it was "not in a district with Jewish settlements within easy range. . . . It is accessible only by boat. Should you not look for somewhere like Tanglewood which is readily accessible by all kinds of arterial roads and which has a very large population to draw on within a radius of fifty miles?"[94]

In reply, Ethel Cohen pointed out that Ein Gev had sponsored two annual spring music festivals for several years that had attracted a number of famous visiting musicians; that the Tanglewood-style music shed was already partially erected; that a new road had been built the previous year, and that more than 2,500 people had attended the last concert, apparently undeterred by orange crates. Moreover, despite Ein Gev's present relative desolation, it was necessary to look to Israel's future. "The Lake area is expanding," she wrote. "There are already about twenty-five settlements there. After all, Israel will hardly be static in population, and in ten years the attractive Lake area will undoubtedly be heavily populated. The Center isn't contemplated for the present only. . . . I trust our faith in the future development of the Lake Galilee area will be justified."[95] Following a five-week visit to Israel in 1952, where she witnessed the renewed construction effort, Ethel Cohen once again defended the choice of Ein Gev before members of the Esco board. If proper facilities were built, she insisted, then the Ein Gev Center could be turned into a fine concert hall.[96]

Under the original letter of agreement between Esco and Kibbutz Ein Gev, dated March 4, 1951, Esco agreed to supply building materials and equipment with the approximate value of $150,000 for the purpose of erecting a music and cultural center. Conditions, at least on paper, were made as firm as possible. The Center was to be used primarily for performances of music, drama, and dance, and secondarily for such other cultural purposes as lectures, festival and holiday celebrations, and sports. The Center would be available to all inhabitants of Israel without discrimination. It would include a music school for the gifted children of the Lake Galilee area, and it would conduct a music festival and music institute at least once a year, affording gifted young people in Israel, teachers, and other specialists the opportunity for advanced study in the field of music. The actual physical plant would consist of an outdoor auditorium seating 2,500, as well as a guest house for visiting artists. The Center would be landscaped and would contain statuary, footpaths, parking space for vehicles, washrooms, and other facilities "as are necessary to its proper functioning. . . . The physical structure and surroundings of the Center shall be worthy of its historic background on Lake Galilee and a credit to Israel, Ein Gev, and Esco."[97] The Center would be governed by a board of directors and an executive director in Israel, along with an advisory planning committee in New York that would include prominent musicians and leaders interested in arts and in Israel. Finally, in view of the political disputes in Israel at the time (particularly the Mapai-Mapam conflict between different factions in the Israeli Labor bloc) the Cohens insisted on legal safeguards that the Center would remain autonomous and not be tied to any political movement. "The Center or its facilities," declared the letter of agreement, "may at no time be used for political or partisan activities, directly or indirectly, in part or in whole."[98]

Given the chaotic conditions existing in Israel in the 1950s, the music center experienced extensive problems in its construction, operation, financing, labor, schedules, and management. More than once, Esco threatened to cut off its funding, on the grounds that certain conditions of the original letter of agreement had not been met. Even after the original building had begun, the sponsors objected that the site of the auditorium remained unlandscaped and primitive. After three members of the Esco board, including Mordecai Kaplan, visited the Center in the spring of 1951, they reported that the auditorium was finally roofed and that the guest house had been built. But there had been no other improvements—no landscaping, lighting, roads, or walks, with the result that knee-deep mud often cut off access to various parts of the kibbutz. There had been only one event that year, the Passover Festival, which unfortunately had been a financial failure because of bad weather. "Heavy rains poured through the roof, causing cancellation of several concerts," the visitors reported. "The thick mud on unpaved walks caused one serious accident and profits from the Festival had to be drawn upon for compensation to the injured person."[99] Moreover, there was the ever-present Syrian threat: soldiers had to be stationed on all the surrounding roads, and members of the kibbutz frequently approached the concert stage bleary-eyed from having stayed up all night doing guard duty.

The transfer of equipment from the U.S. to Israel was an especially complicated affair. Everything, including construction materials, seats, the guest house and garage, cafeteria, storage bins, drink-dispensing machines, and furnishings for the guest house, had to be shipped to Israel. Yaakov Steinberger, the director of the Center, reported that the Israeli government was charging excessive import duty, even though these items were essentially gifts. Construction costs computed while he had been in the U.S. had almost doubled by the time the structures were erected.[100] The promised music school never materialized, and the Esco Center's unique status was challenged when a rival amphitheater was built at a nearby kibbutz. There were problems caused by massive Israeli inflation, the devaluation of currency, enforced bank loans, delays, and charges of inefficiency and inferior workmanship on the part of Solel Boneh construction firms which enjoyed a virtual monopoly on such enterprises.[101] Kibbutzniks did not take well to Esco's American ethos, which prized efficiency and accurate accounting. Even the Center's future programming became a matter of dispute: should it copy the great musical festivals of Europe, or else attempt to produce a festival that was indigenously Israeli?[102] What were the Center's ultimate goals?

Notwithstanding all of these obstacles, both the Cohens and other members of the Esco board agreed to forge ahead with their project. Precisely because of Ein Gev's precarious geographical position, they felt it was important to cast their lot with the area's inhabitants in order to help raise the general morale.[103] In its efforts, Esco was helped considerably by prominent members of its advisory board, including Leonard Bernstein, Teddy Kollek (a member of Ein Gev and later mayor of Jerusalem), Aaron Copland, and Yehudi Menuhin, who in April 1951 recalled the times that he and his sister had played together at Ein Gev during the period when there was only a bare stage.[104]

The inaugural concert of the new Esco Music Center was scheduled for Sukkot in the fall of 1952, although the structure was not yet finished. In an especially appropriate touch, two of the pieces were composed by Israelis whom Esco had supported: Herbert Brun, who contributed a fanfare; and Ben-Zion Orgad, who composed a Psalm set to chorus and a small chamber orchestra.[105] The Passover Festival of 1952 was the first to be held in the outdoor auditorium. Ethel Cohen was among those in attendance. The week-long festival, she reported, had included performances of new works performed by the Haifa Orchestra (conducted by Yehudi Menuhin) and the Israel Ballet Theatre. More than 20,000 visitors had attended the concerts, with hundreds turned away each evening for lack of seating accommodations. At the Menuhin performances alone—which had to be repeated afternoon and evening—there were more than six thousand people in attendance. Visitors had come from as far south as the Negev, from the city of Tiberias across Lake Galilee, and from all the neighboring settlements and towns. Finally, thanks in part to the generosity of two of the artists, who had donated their performance fees to the Center, the festival had turned a sizable profit, which could be used to complete the structure.[106]

The festival also attracted international attention. Peter Gradenwitz, an Israeli music critic, writer, and composer, wrote a review that was published in the music section of the *New York Times* on Sunday, May 4, 1952:

> The general success of the Ein Gev Festival was remarkable: the pillars and walls stand, the chairs nicely arranged, the stage looks beautiful, the terrain is even, rising slowly, so that the view (over Lake Galilee and the hills) is good everywhere, acoustics at the moment are good in about 80 percent of the space. . . . There were great masses of people, much excitement . . . and a very many-sided audience.[107]

Throughout the 1950s and the 1960s, the annual concerts at the Esco Music Center—faithfully attended by Ethel Cohen each spring—continued to flourish as Israeli and international composers, orchestras, choruses, singers, and dance groups came to perform at the auditorium beside the lake. The looming danger of the Syrian-dominated hills never led to the cancellation of a concert, although during the Passover Festival of 1967, there was a military skirmish in which six Syrian MiG's were shot down over the area. At this time, the new roof was repeatedly hit by Syrian gunfire and was pitted with more than 100 holes. However, the center itself survived intact.[108]

Certain friends and relatives, however, still questioned the wisdom of spending so much time and energy at Ein Gev, and indeed in visiting Israel generally. During one of her annual six-week visits, Mrs. Cohen replied to these questions in a letter written in April 1956 not long before the Suez Campaign, a war that was fought in part in order to stop the scourge of seemingly endless terrorist attacks:

> I have been asked whether it was dangerous in Israel during my sojourn. It is always dangerous there these days. Look at your map and see how close the Arab borders are. In Jerusalem, from the balcony of the King David Hotel, one looks across into the old walled city to Jordan, and on a clear day one sees Mt. Scopus and the old University buildings, silent and unused, mute testimony to stupidity and hostility. . . . At Kibbutz Ein Gev on Lake Galilee where 3,000 men, women, and youth attended the Passover festival at the Esco Music Center to hear a wonderful performance by the Robert Shaw Chorale, there were armed soldiers guarding all roads, the auditorium and the surroundings against possible incidents by the Syrians who encompass the kibbutz at a distance of a short stroll. No matter where one happens to be in Israel there is danger from enemy sniping and worse.[109]

Eventually, Ein Gev and the Esco Music Center would attain both financial and physical security following Israel's capture of the Golan Heights in 1967, which eliminated the continual threat of Syrian guns overlooking the kibbutz.

## The Twilight of Esco

By 1958, the activities of the Esco Foundation were winding down. Many of the older board members had died or were no longer able to attend meetings. It was not easy to replace a group of people who had been among the giants in their fields. Frank Cohen's only son, Amos, who as an eleven-year-old during the Second World War had been photographed presenting a shipment of vitamins to British children, now took his place as the youngest member of the board. However, as a member of the new generation he could not be automatically expected to demonstrate the same drive and interest in Jewish philanthropy that his parents did. Frank Cohen, for his part, suffered from an increasingly serious heart condition that curtailed his activities. On May 2, 1959 he suffered a fatal heart attack in Jerusalem. Even knowing that his health might be endangered, he had gone to Israel with the strong desire to see

## The Esco Fund Committee

the country once again.[110] At the annual meeting of the Esco board of directors on July 15, 1959, Frank Cohen was eulogized:

> None of his numerous and varied achievements during his lifetime gave him greater pleasure or made him more proud than the benefits made possible through Esco. Though there were disappointments when anticipated results were not achieved, Frank Cohen was never discouraged and never withheld assistance when he and the . . . Board of Directors . . . agreed that the project under consideration warranted support. Esco was as a beloved child to him.[111]

After Frank Cohen's death, the Esco Fund Committee became a residuary legatee under his will, with his widow named as the executrix of the estate. Ethel Cohen was determined to continue the activities of the foundation, both to support those programs that Esco had already started and to find ways to memorialize her husband, especially since the board could expect a large sum of money once the estate was settled. This would be a finite amount, however, and she realized that the days of the foundation were numbered. She and the remaining members of the board thus turned their attention to a search for appropriate memorials for Frank Cohen—both in the U.S. and in Israel.[112]

In her annual visits to Israel each spring, which she continued faithfully as long as she was physically able to do so, Ethel Cohen saw how her husband's memory was enshrined in the projects he had helped to sponsor. In June 1960, she reported at an Esco meeting that Kibbutz Ein Gev had set aside an area near the auditorium, overlooking Lake Galilee through a grove of palms, for a memorial garden to her late husband. The planting ceremony, held during the intermediate days of Passover, she wrote at this time, "was a moving event, one which is indelibly inscribed in my memory." Approximately thirty friends from various places in Israel had attended the ceremony. The plan for the garden included a shelter of trees and a circular bench set in a flower garden for the purpose of rest and contemplation of the lake. "Frank loved to sit and look out over the water and it seemed fitting that others should enjoy this pleasure as well," she observed. A tablet with an inscription dedicated to Frank Cohen was placed in the garden.[113] A plaque in his memory was also erected at the Pardes Hanna Secondary Agricultural School, and Esco donated the funds for an annual scholarship to be granted in his name.[114]

The City College of New York, Frank Cohen's alma mater, seemed a particularly suitable institution in which to set up a memorial project. Thus in 1963, Esco gave a grant of $5,000 to CCNY for the purpose of establishing the Frank Cohen Memorial Scholarships to graduate students in the field of economics.[115] It also established the annual Frank Cohen Memorial Lectures in Judaic affairs, to be given each year by a prominent scholar.

Another memorial project was the establishment, under the National Jewish Book Council of the Jewish Welfare Board, of the Frank and Ethel Cohen Jewish Book Award for the best book on Jewish thought. This award was given annually from 1963 until 1986, the first book honored being Moses Rischin's *The Promised City*.[116]

Mordecai Kaplan and the Reconstructionist movement he had founded played an important role in the lives of both Frank and Ethel Cohen. For Frank Cohen especially, Reconstructionism represented an alternative to Orthodoxy and a guarantee of religious freedom. Accordingly, several of Ethel's new projects in the 1960s and 1970s were designed to support and expand the movement both in the U.S. and in Israel. Grantees during that period included the *Reconstructionist* magazine, the Reconstructionist rabbinical seminary in Philadelphia, established in 1968 by Kaplan; the newly established Mevakshei Derech ("seekers of the way") congregation in Jerusalem, which was led by Dr. Jack Cohen (a new member of the Esco Board); and finally, *Petachim*, the Hebrew journal under the editorship of Joseph Salomon Bentwich.[117] "Petachim," meaning "gates," was taken from the saying, "there are many gates to God." The journal, which received grants each year from 1967 until 1984, came to play an important role in Israel's intellectual life by providing a forum for alternate religious opinion and advocates of religious toleration. This was one of the last major projects that Esco sponsored.[118]

The Israeli music world also continued to be the recipient of Esco's largesse, both through its projects already established and through the support of new ones. In 1964, Esco gave an endowment of $10,000 to the Jewish Music Research Center at the library of the Hebrew University of Jerusalem. The Ethel S. Cohen Music Collection Fund, as it was called, supported the purchase of books, music, and recordings in the fields of Far and Middle Eastern music.[119] Among the tape collections the library acquired were those of Johanna Spector; Leo Levi's collection of Italian liturgical music; and the collection of the late Robert Lachmann, an important German Jewish musicologist who was one of the

## The Esco Fund Committee

first to collect the music of the Jews of Djerba and of the Oriental communities in Israel. Half of the funds were kept in reserve for the periodic purchase of rare and exceptional books and music; the grant agreement stipulated that preference was to be given to music from Middle and Far Eastern countries.[120] In 1969, Ethel Cohen established another music library in Israel with a grant of $2,000 to the Music Center in Ein Kerem, Jerusalem. In this instance, she stipulated that the tapes were meant to be used for educational purposes for youth and adults, teachers and lecturers.[121]

The crowning glory of Esco's music projects remained the Esco Music Center at Ein Gev, which the foundation helped maintain throughout the years by means of grants for new curtains, chairs, a parking lot, instruments, repairs, and refurbishing the guest house. As observed by Ethel Cohen in her annual visits, conditions at Ein Gev had improved considerably. The early days of knee-high mud and open shower stalls, of gusts of wind that blew musical scores into the lake, were over. At the same time, the concerts themselves no longer attracted the same audiences or performers. By the late 1960s, the auditorium at Ein Gev competed with numerous fine auditoriums built throughout Israel. And by the 1980s, musical tastes had changed, leaning more to pop rather than classical music. Moreover, members of the kibbutzim and other settlements of the area, once the mainstay of Esco's audiences, now had their own auditoriums as well as being able to view television broadcasts of musical events.[122]

Notwithstanding, there was still a place for the Esco Music Center at Ein Gev, albeit in a somewhat different guise. In 1965, a picnic and camping area along the lake was built, and by 1969, Ein Gev was a flourishing and secure part of the national Israeli tourist network.[123] Younger kibbutz members were taking over the operation of the Center and were eager to plan new and exciting programming. The 1970 Festival in particular was a huge success, with performers including the Israel Philharmonic Orchestra, the Israel Chamber Orchestra, Theodore Bikel, and performance troupes of the kibbutzim and the Israeli army. In 1972, the Passover Festival program was incorporated into the national Israel Festival Program and thus financed and promoted by the Israel Festival Committee of the Ministry of Tourism. "Each year that I return to the Center," wrote Ethel Cohen in one of her annual reports, "I am more and more convinced that we have made a very valuable cultural contribution to Israel. Despite setbacks, disappointments, heartache, and disillusion, I believe Esco may take pride in the Center. . . . Now that the Golan Heights are no longer menacing—may that be the case forever!—the Center may have an even greater future."[124]

One testimony to the impact of the Esco Center throughout the years is its guest book, which has been maintained since 1950 and which was photocopied by the kibbutz as a gift to Ethel Cohen in 1986. Thousands of signatures, messages, and drawings expressing visitors' appreciation and enjoyment, are written in numerous languages (including English, Hebrew, French, German, Spanish, and Japanese). Many of the musicians and composers have signed their names and messages with bars of music. One French musician wrote, quite simply, "Ein Gev—un rêve!" Ethel Cohen, expressing her thanks for the gift of the photocopies, sent a letter to the kibbutz, dated May 11, 1986:

> Dear Yaakov and all my other good friends at Ein Gev: This has been one of my happiest visits to Ein Gev. Among other reasons, the fact that the young generation here has the vision, determination, faith and dedication to continue realizing our dream—my late husband Frank's and mine, as well as the Esco founders of Kinneroth, has uplifted my spirits. I thank you all from the bottom of my heart for this gift. May your efforts succeed; and may your rewards be a cultural center here on beautiful Lake Kinneret of which you, the kibbutz, and Israel, may be proud. With all my love, Ethel S. Cohen.[125]

Among Esco's last large grants were those made to the America-Israel Cultural Foundation and to the National Foundation of Jewish Culture. By 1976, the Fund—which through its existence had granted close to a million and a half dollars—had dwindled to the point where it was donating only $4,000 a year.[126] Rosalie Cohen, Ethel Cohen's sister-in-law and a member of the last board of directors, comforted Ethel Cohen upon her announcement that the Fund would soon have to be terminated:

> Not unlike the nurturing of children, the anxieties always seemed to be more numerous; yet in perspective, the satisfactions should give you reasons to rejoice. To have had a part in shaping the cultural character and image of the Yishuv in the days when cultural resources were few and meager in Israel should be deeply rewarding to you now, when Israel's cultural life is a national pride and a light unto all the nations.[127]

On August 6, 1986, with funds no longer available, the decision was made to terminate the Esco Fund Committee, Inc.[128] Ethel Cohen lived on to see the start of another decade, continuing her many activities almost until her death in November 1990 at the age of 95.

In the forty-five years of Esco's existence, Frank and Ethel Cohen enjoyed the rare privilege of acting publicly in harmony with their private convictions and aspirations, using their wealth to support first the great effort of the Allies during the Second World War and later supporting numerous cultural and educational projects both in the U.S. and in Israel. The history of Esco reflects the rise, maturity, and eventual passing away of a dedicated American Jewish couple and its circle of friends. As a group, the leaders of Esco had demonstrated a rare combination of the values of Jewish charity, American philanthropy, a love for Jewish education, cultural sophistication, and Zionist commitment. The conflicts and contradictions inherent in this combination, as well as the inevitable tensions between granter and grantee, did not prevent Esco from creating a valuable precedent for family foundations that followed it.

Though the history of Esco, it is also possible to view in microcosm the birth, growth, and maturity of Israel, as well as aspects of the changing philanthropic roles that American Jews were asked to play. Esco's criteria had always included a desire to act as a catalyst to projects that would ultimately become self-sustaining. In the days of an embattled Jewish community and the desperate years of early statehood, Israel's economic and cultural life might not have survived intact without the enormous contributions made by supporters outside its borders. However, as with the music center at Ein Gev, the passage of the years helped to bring on a financial and cultural independence to match the political independence that Israel had won in 1948. There could be no greater tribute to the legacy of Esco, or to the benefactors of any Jewish charity, than the fact that, through their help, they were able to bring about the day when help was no longer needed.

## NOTES

The files of the Esco Fund Committee, Inc., and its related Esco Foundation for Palestine and Esco Friends, Inc., all charitable organizations, were donated by Ethel Cohen to the Rare Book and Manuscript Library of Columbia University in November 1986. Its sixty-seven boxes contain correspondence, reports, clippings, Esco board minute books, photographs, and Esco publications. The collection also includes papers relating to Ethel and Frank Cohen's personal (non-Esco) Zionist and Jewish interests. The collection also includes four bundles of scrapbooks and memorabilia. The author wishes to thank the staff of the Rare Book and Manuscript Library, Columbia University, for their help and cooperation in the preparation of this work.

Abbreviations:
EFC Esco Fund Committee, Inc.
EFP Esco Foundation for Palestine
AZEC American Zionist Emergency Council

1. Ethel S. Cohen, interview by author, New York, 7 June 1988.
2. Scrapbooks and memorabilia.
3. For information on the New York Kehillah experiment and some of the Jewish leaders who later served on Esco's board, see Arthur Goren, *New York Jews and the Quest for Community: The Kehillah Experiment, 1908–1922* (New York, 1970).
4. Frank Cohen, memoirs, box 4, folder: "Frank Cohen, personal," undated.
5. Ibid.
6. Interview with Ethel Cohen, 7 June 1988.
7. Interview in *Haishah,* September 1952, scrapbooks and memorabilia.
8. Address of Stephen S. Wise at luncheon in honor of Frederick W. Gehle, 9 April 1941, box 42, folder: "Interfaith Committee, 1940–1941."
9. Frank Cohen, memoirs, box 4, folder: "Frank Cohen, personal," undated.
10. *Time,* 3 November 1941, 75.
11. *National Cyclopedia of American Biography,* photocopy of entry for Frank Cohen, box 4, folder: "Frank Cohen, personal."
12. Frank Cohen, memoirs, box 4, folder: "Frank Cohen, personal." Undated.
13. Minutes, EFC, 22 November 1941, box 37.
14. Certificate of Incorporation, EFC, 1 July 1940, box 39, vol. 1.
15. Letter from Ethel Cohen to Esco Board members, 7 Jan. 1952; Minutes, EFP, box 38, vol. 5.
16. Minutes, EFC, 11 Feb. 1943, box 39, vol. 2.
17. "Vitamin Shipments Started by Cohen," *Savannah Evening Press,* 3 April 1941, scrapbooks and memorabilia.
18. Minutes, EFC, 22 Dec. 1940, box 39, vol. 1.
19. Minutes, EFC, 16 June 1941, box 39, vol. 1.
20. "Report on Project to Raise Funds from among Children for Vitamin Aid to British Children," presented by the EFC Board to the National Council of Jewish Education, 31 December 1940, box 39, vol. 1.
21. Minutes, EFC, 20 February 1941, box 39, vol. 1.
22. Box 44, folder: "Letters of Acknowledgement, Vitamins for Britain, Inc."
23. Ibid.
24. EFC Annual Report, March 1944–April 1945; including a list of Grants-in-Aid, 1941–1945, box 37, vol. 2.

The Esco Fund Committee

25. Minutes, Joint Meeting, 9 May 1944, box 37, vol. 2.
26. Israel S. Chipkin to Frank and Ethel Cohen, 15 May 1947, box 20, folder: "Hebrew classes, Hunter College."
27. EFC Annual Report, March 1944–April 1945, box 37, vol. 2.
28. Esco Friends, Inc. Grants-in-Aid, April 1943–April 1944, box 37, vol. 2.
29. Esco Friends, Inc. Annual Report, 1944–1945, box 37, vol. 2.
30. Chaim Weizmann to Frank Cohen, 10 Aug. 1942, box 1, folder: "Chaim Weizmann"; see also Gisela Warburg to Ethel Cohen, 20 March 1943, box 18, folder: "AZEC."
31. Minutes, EFP, 22 Nov. 1941, box 37, vol. 1.
32. Henrietta Szold to Rose Jacobs, 7 June 1943, box 1, folder: "Henrietta Szold."
33. Minutes, EFP, 14 February 1946, box 37, vol. 3.
34. Rose Jacobs to Henrietta Szold, 26 Mar. 1943, box 22, folder: "Henrietta Szold."
35. Ibid.
36. Ethel Cohen to Rose Halprin, 19 April 1948, box 15, folder: "Board Members, Esco Fund Committee."
37. Ethel Cohen to Israel Goldstein, 20 June 1947, box 43, folder: "Grants rejected."
38. Minutes, EFP, 1 January 1948, box 38, vol. 4.
39. Minutes, EFP, 1 November 1948, box 38, vol. 4.
40. Ibid.
41. Ibid.
42. Ibid.
43. Letter of Agreement with the Farmers' Federation, 5 March 1949, box 31, folder: "Farmers' Federation."
44. Minutes, EFP, 6 October 1950, box 38, vol. 4
45. Box 32, folder: "Pardess Hanna."
46. Box 32, folder: "Fire dormitory 1952."
47. Progress report sent by Dr. Rosenberg, principal, Pardes Hanna; Minutes, EFP, 6 September 1951, box 38, vol. 5.
48. Minutes, EFP, 6 October 1950, box 38, vol. 4.
49. Box 32, folder: "Fire dormitory 1952"; see also photographs of Pardes Hanna in scrapbooks and memorabilia.
50. Ethel Cohen to EFC Board Members, 6 September 1951, box 38, vol. 5.
51. Minutes, EFP, 22 November 1941, box 37, vol. 1.
52. Grants-in-Aid prior to April 1943, box. 37, vol. 1.
53. Minutes, EFP, 19 Sept. 1949, box 38, vol. 4.
54. Minutes, Joint Meeting EFC and EFP, 12 December 1942, box 37, vol. 1.
55. Report: Subventions granted by EFC January 1, 1941–June 30, 1942, box 39, vol. 1.

157

56. Box 33, folder: "Books and Publications."
57. Ethel Cohen to Joshua Starr, 13 January 1942, box 18, folder: "Conference on Jewish Relations."
58. Ethel Cohen to Esco Board Members, 23 May 1944, box 31, folder: "Jordan Valley Authority."
59. Minutes, EFP, 18 April 1942, box 37, vol. 1.
60. Curriculum vitae of I. B. Berkson, May 1942, box 55, folder: "I. B. Berkson."
61. Minutes, EFP, 18 April 1942, box 37, vol. 1; see also contract letter, Ethel Cohen to I. B. Berkson, 29 May 1942, box 55, folder: "I. B. Berkson."
62. I. B. Berkson to Henrietta Szold, 12 August 1942, box 22, folder: "Henrietta Szold."
63. See correspondence, 1942–1947, boxes 55–58. In particular, see Ethel Cohen to I. B. Berkson, 12 March 1946, box 55, folder: "I. B. Berkson."
64. Report: EFP Grants-in-Aid, April 1943–1944, box 37, vol. 2.
65. Abba Hillel Silver to Frank and Ethel Cohen, 23 May 1944, box 55, folder: "AZEC."
66. Oscar Janowsky to Leah Klepper, 26 August 1944, box 58, folder: "Readers of Manuscript."
67. Interview with Ethel Cohen, 7 June 1988; see also Ethel Cohen to Rose Jacobs, 12 May 1946, box 56, and Minutes, Joint meeting EFC and EFP, 5 June 1947, box 37, vol. 3.
68. Memo on progress of publication from Yale University Press, box 55, folder: "Yale University Press."
69. James McDonald to Ethel Cohen, 9 June 1947, box 55, folder: "James G. McDonald."
70. Ethel Cohen to Harry Shapiro, 16 May 1947, box 55, folder: "AZEC 1943–1947."
71. Book review, *New York Times,* 18 May 1947, box 55, folder: "Reviews."
72. Box 55, folder: "Reviews."
73. Report to the Board of Directors of EFC, 25 June 1965, by Ethel Cohen, box 41, vol. 12.
74. Kraus Reprint Co. to Ethel Cohen, 11 November 1968, box 57, folder: "Reprints."
75. Minutes, EFC, 5 November 1952, box 40, vol. 5; "Mivtza Motek," *Davar,* 28 September 1952, scrapbooks and memorabilia.
76. Minutes, EFC 5 November 1952, box 40, vol. 5.
77. Matilda J. Greenburg to Ethel Cohen, 26 May 1952, box 40, vol. 5.
78. *New York Times,* scrapbooks and memorabilia.
79. Master's Thesis, box 2, folder: "Ethel Cohen, personal."
80. Box 3, folder: "Ethel Cohen, personal publications."
81. Box 42, folder: "EFP Composition Scholarship."
82. Ed Poznanski to Erminie Kahn, 19 January 1948, box 42, folder: "Berkshire Music School Scholarships."
83. Box 42, folder: "Herbert Brun, 1948–1951."

84. Minutes, EFC, 5 November 1952, box 40, vol. 5.
85. Ethel Cohen to Esco Board Members, 7 June 1961, box 18, folder: "Brandeis University Scholarships."
86. Minutes EFC, 5 November 1952, box 40, vol. 5.
87. Minutes, EFP, 26 March 1952, box 38, vol. 5.
88. Other music projects sponsored by Esco were Albert Sendry's *Bibliography of Jewish Music* (1951), which covered the period from biblical times to the present, and Solomon Roswasky's *The Cantillation of the Bible* (1946); box 34, folder: "Books and Publications."
89. Address of Yaakov Steinberger to Esco meeting, 5 March 1951, box 39, vol. 4.
90. Ethel Cohen to Clarence Berger, Creative Arts Dept., Brandeis University (containing capsule summary of Esco Music Center history), 20 September 1957, box 23.
91. Address of Yaakov Steinberger, 5 March 1951.
92. Ibid.
93. Minutes, Joint meeting EFC and EFP, 5 March 1951, box 38, vol. 4.
94. David de Sola Pool to Ethel Cohen, 26 March 1951, box 24, folder: "Letters of Commendation."
95. Ethel Cohen to David and Mrs. de Sola Pool, 29 March 1951, box 24, folder: "Letters of Commendation."
96. Minutes, EFC, 5 November 1952, vol. 5.
97. Letter of Agreement on Esco Music Center at Ein Gev, Israel, 4 March 1951, box 23.
98. Ibid.
99. Report of Mordecai Kaplan to Esco Board, Minutes, 6 September 1953, box 40, vol. 5.
100. Ethel Cohen to Esco Board, 6 September 1951, box 38, folder 5.
101. Ethel Cohen to Israel Chipkin, 27 April 1954, box 23, folder: "Dr. Israel Chipkin, 1952–1955."
102. Ethel Cohen to Esco Board, 6 September 1951, box 38, vol. 5.
103. Minutes, joint meeting EFC and EFP, 14 June 1954, box 40, vol. 5.
104. Yehudi Menuhin to Ethel Cohen, 18 April 1951, box 1, folder: "Yehudi Menuhin."
105. Box 23, folder: "Commission to Composers, 1951."
106. Ethel Cohen to members of the American Advisory Planning Committee, 9 May 1952, box 23, folder: "American Advisory Planning Committee 1951–1952."
107. Ibid.; *New York Times,* 4 May 1952 (clipping).
108. Report to the Board of Esco from Ethel Cohen, August 1967, box 41, vol. 16.
109. Ethel Cohen to family (mimeograph), April 1956, Box 9A.
110. Interview with Ethel Cohen, 7 June 1988.
111. Minutes, EFC, 15 July 1959, box 40, vol. 6.
112. Minutes, EFC, 2 July 1962, box 41, vol. 7.

113. Report on Esco's projects in Israel by Ethel Cohen, 10 July 1963, box 41, vol. 7.
114. Ibid.
115. Minutes, EFC, 25 March 1963, box 41, vol. 7.
116. Minutes, EFC, 22 December 1962, box 41, vol. 7.
117. Minutes, EFC, 15 August 1967, box 41, vol. 14.
118. The journal ceased publication shortly after the death of Joseph Salomon Bentwich. See box 64, folder: "Petachim, Correspondence," including a clipping of Bentwich's obituary, *Jerusalem Post,* 12 July 1982.
119. Report to the Board of Esco from Ethel Cohen, 20 June, 1964, box 41, vol. 7.
120. Report to the Board of Esco from Ethel Cohen, 20 June 1964, box 41, vol. 12.
121. Ethel Cohen to Brach Eden and Alexander Tamir, 5 February 1969; Bracha Eden to Ethel Cohen, 9 September 1969, box 20, folder: "Ein Kerem Music Center."
122. EFC Annual Report, 1982–83, box 16, folder: "Board of Directors."
123. Report to the Board of Esco from Ethel Cohen, August 1967, box 41, vol. 16.
124. Report to the Board of Esco from Ethel Cohen, July 1970, box 41, folder: "Minutes 1970–1977."
125. Ethel Cohen to Kibbutz Ein Gev, 11 May 1986, plus photocopies, box 23, folder: "Guest Book."
126. Minutes EFC, 10 May 1976, uncatalogued.
127. Rosalie Cohen to Ethel Cohen, 10 September 1967, uncatalogued correspondence.
128. Minutes EFC, 6 August 1986, uncatalogued.

# A Cultural Model for America–Holy Land Studies

## One Early Example

Matthew Silver
*Emek Yezreel College*

### Introduction: An Ongoing Dialogue between Two Jewish Cultures

Studies of American Zionism during the Mandatory period (1918–1948) often substantiate a downgraded view of the subject. They assess Zionist activity in America, not in terms of what it did to build up the Jewish community in Palestine—the Yishuv—but, instead, as a barometer of broad sociological processes that molded particular American Jewish leaders, or entire subsections of the American Jewish population. Thus, American Zionist activity after 1917 provided opportunities for "Russian Jews" to mobilize in power struggles against the "German" Jewish establishment in America; or, for talented individuals unhappy with their position on the periphery of the American elite, Zionism might have served passing tactical needs.[1] Otherwise, the standard of reference appears to be lobbying and ethnic agendas pursued by other minority groups in the United States.[2] In other words, the scholarly and popular literature rates pre-1948 American Zionism as being relevant only inasmuch as it functioned as a gateway to something else, to power realignments among Jewish immigrant subgroups in America, or to new forms of ethnic politics in America. The main theater is domestic, meaning American Zionism *in America*. Since, it is assumed, actual American

Zionist activity *in Palestine* throughout the 1918–1948 period was sporadic and limited, the whole phenomenon ought to be read historically as a domestic issue. American Zionism before 1948 was a fulcrum for internal American Jewish individual and community development.

Israel's subsequent emergence as a much admired and much disputed country had done surprisingly little to alter the American focus of discussions of Zionism and American Jewry after 1948. Prominent on the scholarly agenda is the study of pro-Israel activity as a transformative ethnic factor in America.[3]

According to the "civil religion" theory, Israel has since 1948 assumed a quasi-sacrosanct position in American Jewish life.[4] Nonetheless, analysis of the American Jewry-Zionism connection after 1948 has retained much of its unidirectional, land-locked character. As they remark upon how the philanthropic desire to provide for Israel's needs is a defining characteristic of American Jewish identity, researchers seem to be saying that the important thing is what Zionism has done for American Jews, not what American Jews have done for Zionism.

What rationale can be adduced for reexamining that point of view, along with associated ideas about when, where, and how American Zionism has been significant? One reason to favor such a revision is factual. American Zionism has been an oscillating phenomenon in whose peak periods (usually connected to wartime mobilization and crises in both Mandatory Palestine and Israel) the character of American Zionist commitment appears to move from a passive to a more active mode. In fact, the period chosen as a case study in this paper, several months in 1919, is particularly important for reassessing the image of American Jewish philanthropists casually detached from the agonies of nationalist strife or from the burdens involved in defending, governing, and building a new Jewish society.

However, the case for a reexamination of American Zionism does not hinge upon one scholar's assessment of how representative the data from any particular period might be. The problem with the perceptions of American Jews as far-off philanthropists, and Yishuv pioneers and their Israeli descendants as the bona fide Zionist redeemers, is that it does not adequately capture the ways in which members of these groups really think about themselves—not then, and not now. This is a cultural relationship whose protean capacity for tension and creativity should not be underestimated. Episodes in this relationship need not be studied exclusively for the concrete results tolled by a particular American

Zionist endeavor. They can be analyzed instead as moments expressive of cultural identities that are always in flux, and whose reshaping depends symbiotically upon periodic encounter, dialogue, detachment, conflict, and partnership.

The dichotomy of passive American Jewish philanthropists and activist Yishuv (Israeli) pioneers could never go uncontested. By choosing to work for Zionism, American Jews were often defying inherited norms and carving out a public space in which they sought to promote and satisfy idealistic impulses. From their point of view, debunking them as mere charity dispensers was bound to be resented, for the allegations applied to a realm of their lives in which they had chosen to work actively and make sacrifices for a far-off Jewish community.

Similarly, in the perspective of the Yishuv *halutz* (pioneer), an attitude of proud socialist detachment from the tainted capitalist philanthropy of the Americans could not be honestly maintained for long. As in the example of the protracted discussions in the 1920s about the inclusion of American "non-Zionist" philanthropists on the expanded Jewish Agency, the Zionist establishment was always debating how actively involved American capital should be in the Yishuv-building process.[5] In this connection, leaders of the growing Labor Zionist movement like Ben-Gurion and Berl Katznelson were forced continually to weigh the merits of nationalist goals as opposed to socialist ones. Choices made in this process were influential in the realm of Zionist politics and ideology, as recent research suggests, and they could be a factor in a reevaluation of cultural identities in the dialogue between offshore American Jewish supporters and on-site Zionist state-builders.[6] How long could rigid boundaries in a dichotomy between capitalist philanthropy and halutz *hagshama* (Zionist pioneering) be maintained, when even the most hardened Yishuv Zionists were noticing that without infusions of American Jewish capital, the enterprise of the "state in the making" would be lost?

Tensions attendant upon any patron-client relationship can be found repeatedly in the Yishuv period, and they are the cultural ancestors of many highly charged expressions in the American Jewish-Israeli relationship today, such as the outburst of an Israeli journalist who complains polemically about how his countrymen shed their blood for Israel's survival, while American UJA donors pay their debts to Jewish identity in dollars.[7] For their part, Zionist-oriented American Jews have been forced to consider the contrast between two political solutions of the Arab-Israeli conflict: a liberal conception based on principles of self-determination and minority rights, and a Jewish nationalist formula with a more rigorously ethnocentric agenda. Under the force of actual circumstances, some American Jews regularly came to believe that these two political formulas are not complementary. The political choice which they felt compelled to make—as Jews and as Americans—has figured as a consistent source of tension in the American–Israel nexus.[8]

Yet, some overlap of identity components based on experiment and encounter can be found. What is striking is how consistently such compromise formulations arose in creative response to the two identified problem areas—patron-client relations, and the liberalism versus nationalism dilemma. Indeed, the precedents for these compromise formulations date back to the earliest days of the Zionist enterprise. With the British conquest of Palestine and the Balfour Declaration, sanctioning Jewish settlement and development in the framework of the Jewish "national home," cultural and political parameters that subsequently defined the challenges and dilemmas of American Zionism were already coming into place.

## American Zionist Activity, 1919

Weeks after the promulgation of the November 1917 Balfour Declaration, the British authorized the formation of a "Zionist Commission" for supervising Jewish settlement work in Palestine. The new body was authorized to act as a liaison between the new military government and the Yishuv to organize the Jewish population in the country in a general fashion, to supervise welfare work, and to collect data pertinent to future Jewish settlement.[9] The Commission's powers were circumscribed not only by these formal guidelines: its authority to promote Zionist development was also hampered by the temporary British military administration. Formally committed to preserving the status quo (pending the international approval of the Palestine Mandate), the new military government was widely suspected in the Yishuv of harboring anti-Jewish sentiment.[10] Working originally under Chaim Weizmann's on-site tutelage, the Zionist Commission members were drawn from Diaspora communities, reflecting a tacit assumption in the world Zionist movement regarding the dearth of public culture and self-governing skills within the Yishuv. In practice, Weizmann's early Zionist Commission associates, such as Englishman David Montague Eder, brought to Palestine social and scientific prestige acquired by work in modern fields like psychoanalysis, albeit precious little experience in Zionist affairs.[11]

The participation of American Jews on the Zionist Commission was natural. During the late throes of the Ottoman period, American Jews had been involved in important charity and rescue work on behalf of the depleted and beleaguered wartime Yishuv.[12] The world Zionist movement had been headquartered temporarily in the United States during the First World War. Under the leadership of Louis Brandeis, membership in the reorganized American Zionist movement—called the Zionist Organization of America (ZOA)—soared to unheard-of levels, numbering around 176,000 by the end of the war.[13] Discussions about American Jewish involvement on the new Zionist Commission started as early as January 1918, but core members of the Brandeis ZOA leadership, distracted by personal or professional commitments in America or by dramatic global events as the war drew to a close, declined offers to serve on the Zionist Commission in Palestine.[14] It was not until a year later, on January 23, 1919, when Dr. Harry Friedenwald, a prominent American Zionist, left for Palestine to serve for several months as the acting chairman of the Zionist Commission. Despite frustrating delays and complications connected to this appointment, it appeared that the ZOA had selected an eminently qualified delegate. In contrast to Jews from other countries who had been improvising as Zionist Commission officials, Dr. Friedenwald arrived in Palestine with an impressive Zionist curriculum vitae.

For years, in the prewar period preceding Brandeis's ascension, Friedenwald was nominally head of the Federation of American Zionists. Characterizations of his prewar leadership differ. One account stresses the lucidity of Friedenwald's ideological formulations, arguing that they foreshadowed and encapsulated many of Brandeis's well-known positions and slogans.[15] Another depicts Friedenwald as a poor organizer, noting that the Baltimore ophthalmologist presided over a movement that was negligible in number and in constant administrative disarray.[16]

Whatever his liabilities as an organizational leader, Friedenwald was not vulnerable to the sort of allegations that would subsequently dog the members of the Brandeis clique. Brandeis himself, as well as jurist protégés Felix Frankfurter and Julian Mack, were recent Zionist recruits whose enthusiasm for the cause could not always camouflage the fact that they were newcomers to Jewish matters whose numerous professional and daily engagements in the American elite left little time to catch up on internal Zionist nuances. As was also the case with his Baltimore friend, Henrietta Szold, Friedenwald's orientation was a rarity in America's "German" Jewish establishment, in the sense that his Zionist allegiances were well-rooted, and not the fruits of a latter-day enlistment.[17] Jewish sensibilities in his family had been nurtured scrupulously by his grandfather Jonas, who had in the 1870s helped establish a traditionally spirited synagogue. *Chizuk Amuno* was known around Baltimore as the "Friedenwald Schul," and it was a symbol of Harry's firm footing in a growing American Jewish community. With Szold, he founded a Zionist group in Baltimore in 1893. Four years later, his parents toured the Holy Land. Later, "Dr. Harry" followed their trail, and before the 1919 assignment he had twice toured Palestine and worked there in health care. At the start of 1919, it would have been difficult to find an American Jew with credentials more apposite for constructive work on the Zionist Commission.

On April 24, 1919, weeks after the start of his work as Commission Chairman, Friedenwald delivered to a temporary Yishuv body (the "Vaad Hazmani") a political address. It was hardly a portentous appearance, given the difficulties he had with the language barrier; his Hebrew was not up to snuff and he relied upon an interpreter. Nonetheless, in the context of public discourse in the Yishuv, the rarity of the subject matter Friedenwald chose to discuss should not be overlooked. Friedenwald declared that the Yishuv had a duty to improve its relations with its Arab neighbors, "as far as we can." Speaking with an air of urgency, he regretted that "time had been lost" with respect to building bridges. He concluded: "We shall have to live with them and among them and we must establish relations as neighbors and friends."[18] Here was an American Zionist preaching a liberal message of reconciliation, and referring to an issue which nobody else in the Yishuv seemed to want to talk about. Indeed, Neil Caplan, a scholar who has researched early Zionist discussions about the Arab question finds that Friedenwald's message of rapprochement delivered to the fourth assembly of the Vaad Hazmani was almost entirely distinctive in this period. Caplan concludes that in this postwar period, only Chaim Kalvarisky, formerly a land agent with the Jewish Colonization Association who was to become during the Mandate an indefatigable crusader for Jewish–Arab cooperation, struck the

## A Cultural Model for America–Holy Land Studies

same chord in public.[19] It is probably no coincidence that Friedenwald's private journals refer to his meeting with Kalvarisky around the time of his late April address.[20]

Friedenwald did not observe affairs in Palestine as a professional politician or polished ideologist, and his views on the Arab question were bound to fluctuate. During his months-long term with the Zionist Commission, pan-Syrian sentiment gravitated around the figure of Emir Feisal, and Arab nationalism was fanned by rumors that the Allied powers would be sending a "Syrian Commission" to the region to conduct a plebiscite and monitor public will.[21] For decades, publicists and scholars have been debating the extent to which events in this period were milestones in the mobilization of Palestinian nationalism—in some measure, their implications at the time would have been beyond the ken of any imported American Zionist official.[22] Nonetheless, the wild gyrations in the Zionist Commission Chairman's daily grappling with an evolving political problem cannot be explained solely in terms of these broad retrospective considerations. In his April address, he chided Zionists for pretending that economic prosperity in Palestine wrought by the energetic Yishuv could ever allay Arab anxieties. It would, he preached, be a "grave mistake" to suppose that economic gain could be transferred to neighbors in the absence of meaningful contact and cooperation. Yet, several weeks later, by the end of his term as a Zionist official in Palestine, Friedenwald was turning somersaults on the Arab question, advocating precisely the paternalistic approach of "noblesse oblige" which he had previously lambasted.[23] What had really happened to change his mind?

For one thing, his composure and idealism had been jarred by ominous developments in the incipient nationalist conflict. Some of the sentiments expressed by Friedenwald and colleagues in this early armistice period evinced real fright and also culture shock.

As a Mandate charter for Palestine was being drafted for possible inclusion in the peace treaties, Zionist diplomats scored propaganda points in Paris by declaring emphatically that there could never be Jewish–Arab fighting in Palestine. Taking a cue from earlier meetings which Balfour Declaration architect Chaim Weizmann had conducted with Emir Feisal, Felix Frankfurter initiated a public exchange with that same Arab prince at the Versailles peace conference at the beginning of March 1919. Texts of the Frankfurter–Feisal correspondence (which was facilitated by T. E. Lawrence), and subsequent explications portray Brandeis's representative in Paris as an American Zionist underwriter guaranteeing Arab–Jewish harmony in Palestine. With astonishing certitude, the Harvard law professor, whose sole visit to Palestine was not to come for another fifteen years, described Arabs and Jews as "friends who are animated by similar purposes." The last sentence of his letter to Feisal evoked a utopian Semitic teleology: "the Arabs and Jews are neighbors in territory; we cannot but live side by side as friends."[24]

Anyone active in Palestine in this period was bound to discover that its realities hardly conformed to the springtime images of Arab–Jewish friendship articulated by the diplomats and propagandists at the Hotel Meurice in Paris. In fact, a thought-provoking assessment of the asymmetry in the relationship surfaced in the operations of the 39th Royal Fusiliers, the battalion in the Jewish Legion which deployed most of the hundreds of American Jews who enlisted in this First World War Jewish fighting force.[25] On March 9, the 39th's Regimental Medical Officer, Dr. Redcliffe Salaman, recorded that a week earlier an Arab village near the Jewish settlement at Rishon Le'Zion had been "destroyed" with "its active members removed," in reprisal for "an outrage which had been committed."[26] Subsequent accounts confirm that virtually on the day when Frankfurter, Feisal, and "Lawrence of Arabia" swore solemnly that Jews and Arabs would "continue to have the closest friendly relations," Americans and other Jewish soldiers in the 39th engaged in a fierce raid to avenge the stabbing of one of their mates.[27]

A reality gap yawned between events in the field and promises disseminated overseas. Trying to bridge this formidable distance between dreams and realities, the American chairman of the Zionist Commission confronted a genuine dilemma. His job description stated that he was there to accumulate objective data to be shared with the new governing power in the country. At the same time, Friedenwald had considerable incentive not to circulate bad news that might discredit assurances utilized in sensitive Zionist diplomacy abroad. Also, though the Commission had no real executive authority, it could not always stave off expectations that it was there to ensure the Yishuv's welfare. These express directives and implicit demands and responsibilities were not inherently consistent and so, by the end of April, Dr. Friedenwald was hard-pressed to find an intelligible way of articulating his fear that the worst was about to happen.

In late March, a spine-chilling Zionist Commission intelligence report provided evidence of Arab nationalist preparations to attack the Yishuv. Citing names and figures, the report described individuals and secret societies that were organizing to undertake "small massacres" against Jews in Palestine, to "intimidate Jews abroad," and to forestall Zionist immigration. Though disclaimers were inserted concerning the reliability of some of the information ("the material is submitted without guarantee"), the report had an authoritative air. It surveyed militant nationalist agitation in Arab villages around Jerusalem, Tiberias, Ramleh, and elsewhere; and, as in the case of a Gaza secret society said to be wielding "18 rifles and 15 bombs," the report's documentation of Arab firepower looked systematic.[28]

The Commission sent this document abroad to the Zionist Inner Actions Committee, and it also used the report to buttress an urgent request to the Chief Administrator of the British military government, Major General Money. Demanding that Money garrison British troops near Yishuv settlements, censor Arab periodicals and implement other deterrent or repressive measures to preempt an Arab uprising expected to break out around the time of the Nebi Mousa holiday (April 11), the Commission added that it had sponsored precautionary measures of its own in the Yishuv. It had instructed Jews not to sing Hatikvah in public or give any other "grounds for provocation." This cover letter and related documents bespoke panic in the Commission.[29] Some overseas members of the body, including the Italian Commandante A. L. Bianchini, were considering evacuating.[30] An American colleague of Friedenwald, Robert Szold, who had grave doubts about British intentions in the country, contemplated traveling to Paris to deliver the alarming information by hand and disabuse his Anglophile mentor, Felix Frankfurter, of utopian illusions.

The diplomatic necessity of not being too grim about Palestine's future caused him to put some retrospective spin on public summaries of his activities during this period, but the intelligence concerning imminent physical threats clearly influenced Friedenwald's own shifting private views on the Arab question. Though Muslim Nebi Mousa observances came and went without the much-feared outbreak of violence, Friedenwald remained on edge through the end of April. Coeval with his Vaad Hazmani exhortation about Arab–Jewish cooperation, Friedenwald uncorked his fears in letters dispatched home to Baltimore.[31] Gripped by panic, he went so far as to beseech his son Jonas to seek out "Uncle Louis" Brandeis, "to indicate how very anxious I am, and how far he is from estimating the possible danger." Finally, in May, the commission chairman managed to put a lid on fears whose dissemination could have damaged Zionist lobbying abroad, in Paris and elsewhere. In a "strictly confidential" memorandum he composed on May 2 for the Zionist Inner Actions Committee, Friedenwald opined that "there probably never was a great danger of a general uprising."[32] Though he and his Commission comrades had been chilled to the core, Friedenwald intimated that his earlier concerns had been about public relations, not safety. The Jewish national home's destiny was being decided by diplomats like Frankfurter abroad, and the ranking official on-site in Palestine was supposed to keep things quiet for them. "A loss of life or two would not have been welcome news to you in Palestine," Friedenwald averred.

The acting Commission chairman took some credit for this success in image control. As he told the Inner Actions group, the pressure he had imposed on General Money resulted in the British military government's taking effective deterrent measures. On the Nebi Mousa holiday, airplanes flew over from Egypt and special detachments were deployed to prevent "Bedouin groups" from crossing the Jordan. Had peace really been kept by the British affirmative response to the American Zionist's urgent pleading? In this connection, the praise lavished on Friedenwald by his biographer is speculative—to be sure, violent events that ensued a year later in Palestine on Nebi Mousa mitigate the impression that Commission intelligence and activity in spring 1919 was unduly alarmist.[33]

In any case, the specific contents and immediate results of the Commission chairman's negotiations with the temporary British military administration do not constitute the most intriguing aspect of his experience. Friedenwald's term with the commission can be seen historically as a revealing, spontaneous effort to adapt American liberal sentiment to bewildering, inauspicious developments in Palestine. He wrestled with tensions and possibilities that seemed very urgent and alive to him—it is not entirely clear that hindsight knowledge concerning the fate of Wilsonian diplomacy and the rise of isolationism in the 1920s renders concepts contemplated by him and other Americans on the Commission in 1919 as being unduly quaint, or precociously ahead of their time.

Even as British troops consolidated the empire's conquest, American Zionists on the scene ruminated about how only their home country could defuse Palestine's evidently combustible situation. In part, this vision of political Americanization was a reflex response taken after exhausting, disappointing negotiations with the new British administration. On April 23, a day before his public address, Friedenwald confided privately to some Yishuv notables (Dr. Yitzhak Levy and Yosef Meyuchas) that the British administration was ignoring the Balfour Declaration as being "either indifferent or inimical to our aims." On May 1, in a candid assessment prepared for Brandeis, Friedenwald complained that the new British authorities were "playing with us as a cat plays with a mouse," and he protested that "we are sold to them [the British], body and soul."[34] Such comments contained cryptic hints that the British had squeezed from the Zionist Commission scarcely palatable concessions. Indeed, Friedenwald's negotiation leverage had been compromised not only by the Nebi Mousa security scare, but also by peremptory orders he received from the Zionist Organization in London (on April 8) to do whatever was necessary to prevent the British from allowing land transfers in Jerusalem to the Muslim Waqf.[35] Badly discouraged after such dealings, Friedenwald doubted that the British would really promote the Yishuv's development. "I fear that after the Mandate has been given to Great Britain she will continue to allow some officials to hinder us in our work," Friedenwald prognosticated in his letter to Brandeis. "I fear that they will exploit us and the country for the British."[36] Friedenwald now disavowed his original idea that Great Britain was the best government to which the Mandate could be trusted. Two weeks earlier, in a frantic cable to Frankfurter, Robert Szold, Friedenwald's young colleague on the commission, had been explicit as to what this disavowal entailed.[37] If not Britain, then the United States was the country best suited to steward the development of the Jewish national home. With Szold, Friedenwald championed an American mandate.

In Paris, Frankfurter rejected the anti-British data and the radical conclusion proffered by the Americans on the Zionist Commission. His estimates and biases are worth investigating briefly, because they serve as an analytic foil to the attitudes and circumstances of the Zionist Commission officials. The exchanges between Paris and Palestine illustrate how on-site duty in the Yishuv might enhance or strain the perceptions of committed Zionists like Friedenwald or Szold. Conversely, they underscore how estimates and prognostications of overseas colleagues could stem from sociological circumstances or great power diplomacy not immediately connected to Palestine's vexing realities.

Sometimes showing disdain, other times using cajolery and ingenuity, Frankfurter wrote a series of letters back to Szold and Friedenwald. The Anglophile Frankfurter claimed to have learned from "high diplomatic circles" that the British military officers in Palestine were antisemitic types redeployed from Sudan or Egypt, who "treated the Jewish population as though they [sic] were the ignorant felaheen." The army officers, Frankfurter promised, would be replaced by an enlightened civilian regime which would redeem the spirit of the Balfour Declaration.[38]

Frankfurter had little practical advice to give his frightened colleagues in Palestine for the interim period. Artlessly, the Paris diplomat coached Friedenwald to use his own and Weizmann's exchanges with Feisal as a kind of trump card any time trouble came up on the Arab front. Not more helpfully, he preached to Szold that "the world is young," as though the Wilsonian commitment to a new democratic world order would magically alleviate any passing tensions in Palestine.[39] In truth, Frankfurter's solution to the Arab problem was to pretend that it wasn't there, until the British got around to doing something about it. In a secret cable to Brandeis, Frankfurter instructed that "there should be as little talk as possible [about the Arabs], and all of it moderately pitched."[40]

Dismissing evidence of British malfeasance in Palestine, Frankfurter was drawing upon experiential and psychological components that not many Americans, or American Jews, shared. His optimism soared at the Paris peace conference (one biography marks Frankfurter's ebullient mood as a psychological turning point in his impressive career[41]), and this self-confidence was sustained by his solid connections with the British peacemakers. The diplomats there were, as Frankfurter recalled years later, a "swirling crowd of familiars"—Frankfurter had in fact lived with two of the English officials (Eustace Percy and Loring Christie) in a Washington residence before the war.[42]

Such friendships with articulate, influential Englishmen probably served psychological purposes. As a Jew and an immigrant with boundless ambitions in the United States, Frankfurter's relations with New England's Brahmins were often ambiguous and strained, as shown by his difficult courtship before the war with a gentile woman, Marion Denman, and then in the 1920s by his no-holds-barred confrontations with the Lowell establishment at Harvard over admission quota disputes and in the Sacco and Vanzetti affair. Excluded at times by Anglo-Saxons in America, Frankfurter might have cherished relations with Englishmen to show the American Brahmins how he was valued by the real thing. Another probable source of his Anglophile outlook was his legal training. At Harvard, Frankfurter was taught by professors like James Bradley Thayer to assess the virtues of the U.S. Constitution in terms of precedents in English law.[43]

The impact of Frankfurter's Anglophile orientation on Zionist diplomacy can be evaluated both for its short-term effects, and in terms of the long haul. In the spring of 1919, his connections with Allied policy makers were indeed unsurpassed; several weeks later some of the assurances he offered to his beleaguered American Zionist associates in Palestine on the basis of this insider knowledge were vindicated. Partly as a result of lobbying undertaken in Europe and Palestine by Justice Brandeis toward the end of the summer, the English administration eased its hostile posture toward the Yishuv.[44] In terms of the broader record of the Mandate in the ensuing three decades, no consensus has emerged as to whether Szold and Friedenwald's evolving anti-British orientation, or Frankfurter's Anglophilia, was a better remedy for the Yishuv, though a recent reexamination of the Mandate period has argued that British policy toward the national home was never guided by colonial self-interest, and was in important senses indispensable to the Yishuv's survival and growth.[45] In any case, this passing debate in 1919 about the merits of a British, as opposed to an American, Mandate is interesting not so much for its forecast of possible future realities, but rather as a measure of how the encounter with Palestine's challenging circumstances might compel American Jews to revise self-perceptions and fundamental political outlooks.

American Jews in 1919 who did not share the psychological derivatives and social connections that informed Frankfurter's unswerving pro-English stance, could nevertheless find virtue in the English Mandate formula. The English initiative relieved them of burdens and responsibilities that might have been incurred had America assumed a more direct role in the dispensation of the former Ottoman territory. Notions of an American protectorate for Palestine were floated occasionally during World War I; for the most part these ideas were regarded as exotic and tentative, both by the U.S. administration and Jewish leaders.[46] The on-site American Zionist officials in Palestine had a directly engaged perspective, however. They were drawn to the American solution due to palpable concerns for the Yishuv's safety and well-being, and by an unusually intensive process of learning by doing. While the "American Mandate" idea was, of course, a quixotic diplomatic notion in 1919, their effort to sort out the normative implications of the formula—what sort of "America" should come to Palestine, and how were Wilsonian standards of self-rule and democratic development to be applied—was in fact a precursor of debates about the "Americanization" of Zionism that continue between American Jews and Israelis today.

Friedenwald's reflections concerning normative and practical aspects of U.S. involvement in Palestine meandered. In the April 1919 period when he prescribed grass-roots Arab–Jewish cooperative ventures, he was logically disposed to minimize the necessity of outside, great power intervention. These creeping doubts about Americanization coincided with reports about Allied power-mongering and hypocrisy at Versailles which filtered into the Yishuv. On April 24, the commission chairman wrote in a private letter to his son Jonas that "human progress will not depend on America or England or France alone."[47]

He rejected the crusading idealism in Wilson's foreign policy, saying that he was "skeptical" when "they speak of Americanism as though it was the last word in human progress." Perhaps the future of civilization belonged to the "small peoples," the American Zionist official reflected. As a native of a border state that had not been spared dilemmas and agonies of racial strife (loyalties in Friedenwald's own family had split during the Civil War), he knew that America's track record when it came to resolving conflicts between majorities and minorities was far from perfect.[48] "How can we raise our heads in the world and speak of Americanism when we treat the Negroes as we do," he wondered.

That was a legitimate query, but the most apposite problem posed by the fleeting post-armistice burst of Wilsonian idealism involved the application of the Fourteen Point program in Palestine. The platform's twelfth point promised "an absolutely unmolested opportunity of autonomous development" to non-Turkish peoples in the liberated Ottoman regions, and the "interallied Syrian Commission" mechanism was devised at the Versailles meetings to redeem this guarantee. In the end, a scaled-down body, the American King–Crane Commission, arrived in Palestine in early June to probe Arab popular will.[49] This group's wherewithal to do real polling or to support its policy recommendations were severely circumscribed due to many factors, including Frankfurter's aggressive and shrewd lobbying in Paris, Wilson's subsequent incapacitation, and probably also the headlong behavior of the group's leader in the field.

In fact, judging the historical impact of the King–Crane Commission's anti-Zionist report has proven to be a complicated task. George Antonius, who regarded the Versailles discussions of plebiscites in Syria and the King–Crane mission as a catalyzing process for Palestinian nationalism, admits that the final mission report was "totally disregarded"[50]—but in a sense this evaluation is misleading, because for decades the document furnished putative empirical evidence for State Department officials who supported policies unsympathetic to Yishuv needs or other Jewish interests.[51] Combining missionary commitments, Progressive interest in social engineering, and antisemitism, the King–Crane Commission was not exactly neutral, and one key figure's mixed record as a partner with Louis Brandeis on some reform projects,[52] and then later in his career as a "hysterical antisemite,"[53] encapsulates this contradictory amalgam of motivation. For all its failings, the King–Crane episode constituted, according to one researcher's reckoning, the most significant anti-Zionist maneuver of the interwar decades.[54] It compelled American Zionists to ponder how loose ends could be tied as attempts were made to fit together Wilson's new democratic world order and the Zionist political program. As long as the Yishuv's residents remained a small minority of the population of Palestine, how could any proposed application of the principle of self-determination not be a threat to Zionist interests?

Zionist theoreticians would subsequently oppose a mechanical application of the self-determination rule in Palestine, basing a special-case theory for Jewish prerogatives in the country on historical arguments and on appeals to the crisis situation in Europe.[55] Though lugubrious reports of the disastrous postwar Jewish conditions in Eastern Europe reached Frankfurter in Paris and Friedenwald in Palestine, the American Zionists in 1919 did not frame their opposition to the self-determination rule in terms of this "special case" appeal of Jewish need. Instead, they argued aggressively that Palestinian Arabs were not ready for democratic self-government.

In Frankfurter's case, this position was no curiosity. His support of the nascent mandate system of enlightened colonial control derived not only from his Anglophilia, but also from a consistent position on regional development. Frankfurter never believed that democracy could work among non-modern, non-industrial peoples.[56] Both in his capacity as a Law Officer in the Bureau of Insular Affairs before the war, and as a guiding influence shaping the editorials of the influential liberal journal *The New Republic* during the war, Frankfurter had expressed reservations about popular democratic reforms involving new citizenship or independence criteria in cases such as Puerto Rico or the Philippines.[57] Thus it is no surprise that when recalling his opposition to the King–Crane Syria plebiscite idea, Frankfurter was blunt, calling it "a crazy idea" to propose polling "degraded" and "ignorant" Palestine Arabs.[58]

The American chairman of the Zionist Commission reached the same conclusion concerning the King–Crane plebiscite initiative, yet it was not a theory of political development which led him to his overwrought exclamation that bestowing franchise rights on Palestinian Arabs would be a "calamity for the world."[59] Instead, the upheavals in Friedenwald's position poignantly demonstrated how direct confrontation with Palestine's political and social realities might transmogrify the political judgments of an American Jew. At a time when Jewish–Arab separation theories were becoming Zionist doctrine, Friedenwald had defied convention and boldly called for real cooperation with the Arabs. At the same moment, however, the prospect of Arab violence had terrified him; and when the British appeared not to offer adequate protections, he groped for a different mandate plan involving American stewardship. Then this Americanization program appeared to come with too many strings attached; and, with histrionic excess, he feared that Wilsonian idealism in Palestine could wreak havoc, for Zionists and others. On June 10, dreadfully anxious about the pending arrival of the King–Crane group, he turned another circle, opting for a rather doleful strain of neo-colonialism. "I think that on the whole, these people [Palestine's Arabs] do not know what they want," Friedenwald wrote to his son. "What they need is a good power like Great Britain to rule over here for a few years and train them." Frustration over his seeming inability to articulate norms and procedures for Americanization, rather than newfound illusions concerning the character of Palestine's British military administration, dictated this ad hoc resuscitation of the British Mandate formula.

Squeezed by unexpected or mutually incompatible realities, the eye doctor gazed distortedly at the new representation of American power and interest in the region. Friedenwald clashed clumsily with two relatively sympathetic American officials. On June 15, as the King–Crane surveyors combed Arab opinion, the Zionist Commission chairman complained to the American consul, Otis Glazebrook, that "fanatical and false speeches were inflaming the Arab." This interview achieved nothing. Friedenwald had still more exasperating dealings with Captain William Yale, a trained engineer and former State Department envoy who had been assigned to the King–Crane group as a technical advisor. Friedenwald accused Yale of gerrymandering testimony given to the King–Crane panel, and accused him and other American officials of concocting a "deep laid plot" to subvert Zionist needs. He wrote privately to his family on June 17 that the American visitors and diplomatic officials in Palestine were perpetrating the "most consummate bit of hypocritical rascality that ever was"; a toned-down version of the same complaint dominated his official record of events that was sent to the Zionist Inner Actions Committee a few days later.[60] The jaded characterizations of these particular American officials betrayed ironic shortsightedness. A careful study of American consul Glazebrook's responses to crisis situations in Palestine has revealed that he was far more sympathetic to Yishuv needs than his State Department colleagues, or his successor in Jerusalem.[61] Yale's behavior on the King–Crane expedition proved to be judicious. Appalled when the group's leaders cabled to Wilson a partisan, anti-Zionist report just forty-eight hours after their arrival in Palestine, Yale set about compiling a kind of dissenting minority report. His polished product incisively propounded the Zionist special-case objection to the original inter-Allied commission plebiscite program.[62]

As the King–Crane survey wound down, the normally cordial Dr. Friedenwald came across as a terribly embittered individual. Far from the proud leader of a Zionist proto-government that might be setting a political precedent vital for the "state in the making," he acted like an isolated American Jewish exile in Zion. The main impetus for his sudden, almost apocalyptic sense of alienation involved the political challenges followed in this article. Yet these inconclusive dealings with the Arab question had been trailed throughout by testy relations between the Zionst Commission and the Yishuv in social welfare spheres.

Naturally, Friedenwald had a keen interest in health matters, and he collaborated closely with the American Zionist Medical Unit's talented director, Dr. I. M. Rubinow. Mostly, however, the commission's programs for the provision of much-needed relief to the war-stricken

Yishuv were enacted by colleagues, like the energetic young rabbi from New York's Shearith Israel congregation, Dr. David de Sola Pool. As Pool and others were finding out, relief work in this period was a thankless task. War-time deprivation lingered cruelly and there were ceaseless cries for assistance. Undaunted, activists in the Yishuv press chided Americans and others on the Zionist Commission for catering to "schnorrers."[63] As their ranking superior, Friedenwald sometimes could not escape serving as the butt of such criticism. Writing home to his daughter, Friedenwald retained a humorous veneer when he cited "stupid and ridiculous newspaper reports" that "say all sorts of things about us, short of our absconding with public money and taking graft." Jokingly, he said he was saving some clippings to "illustrate the splendid revival of Hebrew and how wonderfully it can be used for all purposes." Privately, Friedenwald and his American Zionist associates could only have been hurt by the vituperative Yishuv polemics.

Friedenwald symbolically marked his alienation from an unreceptive Yishuv on June 18, when he chose to miss the main part of a memorial service conducted in Jerusalem at the Western Wall in honor of the Jewish victims of recent ordeals in Eastern Europe. Instead of standing in solemn communion with his national brothers at the holy spot, the Zionist Commission chairman had a "really delightful lunch" with the chief British military administrator, General Money. Perusing Friedenwald's private reflections about the memorial service, it is hard not to suspect that he projected onto the Jewish situation at large his own personal disappointment and the sense of futility as an imported Zionist official in the Holy Land.[64] He wrote that he had turned away from the Wall because the mourners appeared to him as an abject "crowd of beggars." The scene was a depressing display of Jewish weakness. He summarized: "Today the fervent prayers of pious people which otherwise and at all times impresses me deeply, struck me as being hollow." For Friedenwald, his months-long work in a capacity which, albeit after innumerable transformations, would someday belong to the prime minister of Israel, was anything but an empowering experience. He was leaving Palestine believing that active American Zionist work there could do little to protect the Jewish future. He prophesied darkly: "Doesn't it sometimes look as though the future were only the great cavern of a violent volcano just before an eruption, with all of us heading into it?"

## Conclusion

Liaison work with the new British administrators engaged in by Americans on the Zionist Commission had some utility, and Friedenwald and his colleagues provided vital assistance to American Zionist projects like the medical unit. Dr. Friedenwald's bleak, self-negating mood at the Western Wall thus reflected neither his affable personality nor the sum total of the American Zionist enterprise in this period. Nonetheless, his acute isolation from the Yishuv during a hopeful moment of national rebirth portended key problematics in a dialogue between two historically ascendent Jewish cultures.

Positive renderings of the American Zionist Commission appear in documents from the period, yet at least one perspicacious commentator grasped that the Friedenwald team's endeavor had some makings of a cautionary tale. For two decades as an immigrant in the Yishuv, Jesse Sampter, an enigmatic, ailing Hadassah intellectual, worked on drafts of a novel entitled *In the Beginning*.[65] A flawed yet fascinating unpublished manuscript, the text embraces the romantic, chalutz-pioneering ethos and rejects the dispassionate, disciplined, scientific expertise attributed to the imported, Brandeis-affiliated, American Zionist officials. Her main American Zionist official is a composite of professional, real-life counterparts like Friedenwald and Szold. With a satiric bite, Sampter calls this character Mr. Gross, and is generally cool to his overweening rationalism, to his "wisdom of multiplication tables, of shadowless diagrams."

Sampter meticulously analyzes the sources of Gross's emotional woes in Palestine. She finds two. First, not unlike Friedenwald, the character is continually uneasy about the Arab question. He tosses around tentative hypotheses to account for mounting signs of Arab nationalism, and is periodically incapacitated by mortal fear. Frantically, at one climactic juncture, he forecasts that "a massacre of all the Jews here" could transpire. Second, Gross is infuriated by Yishuv objections to the way he has handled American Jewish philanthropy. The criticism strikes him as rank ingratitude, and as an insufferably arrogant attempt to dictate procedures to benefactors. In Sampter's rendering, the brand of Americanization offered by the Brandeis-led Zionists was mechanical, unfeeling, and ill-fitted for the stormy passions and unpredictable circumstances of life in the Holy Land. Gross and other expert technicians on the commission become marginalized and embittered, as the Yishuv clamps an ideological embargo on their efficient, modern methods. Gross's alienation derives from his "inability to work in the smooth, machine-made American fashion." Not pulling punches, he projects his frustrations upon the Yishuv, castigating the pioneers for not appreciating American Jewish largesse.

Insightfully, the author observes that Zionist nation-building rhetoric might serve as a substitute for genuine dialogue between two Jewish cultures. "Do you know how many Jews there are in Palestine?" Gross asks. "Fifty thousand," he answers, and then prophesies that the country will some day be home to five million Jews. He concludes scornfully: "These that are here don't count, they are rotten." When the obstacles separating Yishuv pioneers and American patrons in this Armistice period became insurmountable, figures like "Gross" ignored the present and looked ahead to a utopian future. By the mid 1930s, Sampter must have had an inkling that this orientation was sadly ironic. The circumstances of American Jewish life would rarely again be as propitious for active Zionist commitment as they were in 1919. It remained to be seen whether other forms of individual involvement, and other visions of American contributions to the Holy Land, would shape the terms of a productive dialogue between what had become world Jewry's main two communities.

## NOTES

1. With differing emphasis and formulation, this approach can be found in Yonatan Shapiro, *Leadership of the American Zionist Organization, 1897–1930* (Urbana, Ill., 1971); Alon Gal, *Brandeis of Boston* (Cambridge, Mass., 1980); Ben Halpern, "The Americanization of Zionism, 1880–1930," *American Jewish History* 69 (1979): 15–33; Arthur Herzberg, *The Jews in America* (New York, 1989), 217–36. A standard work on American Zionism also emphasizes "offshore" developments: Melvin Urofsky, *American Zionism from Herzl to the Holocaust* (Garden City, N.J., 1975).

2. Samuel Halpern, *The Political World of American Zionism* (Detroit, 1961).

3. Peter Y. Medding, "Segmented Ethnicity and the New Jewish Politics," *Studies in Contemporary Jewry* 3 (1987): 26–48.

4. Jonathan Woocher, *Sacred Survival* (London, 1984).

5. Yigal Elam, *The Jewish Agency: The First Years* (in Hebrew; Jerusalem, 1990).

6. Zeev Sternhell, *Nation Building or a New Society?* (in Hebrew; Tel Aviv, 1995).

7. Matti Golan, *With Friends Like You* (in Hebrew; Tel Aviv, 1992).

8. A third area of cultural conflict in the American Jewish-Israel relationship involves contested versions of Judaism. However, relevant historical processes, especially the Reform movement's rapprochement with Zionism in the 1930s and 1940s, were largely America-bound affairs and did not result from the sort of cultural encounter with which the model proposed above is concerned. Recent discussions attest to the highly contentious and (from the American Jewish perspective) demoralizing character of religious conflict, which dates from the original incarnation of the "who is a Jew" dispute in 1988. (See J. J. Goldberg, *Jewish Power* (Reading, Mass., 1996), 337–67.) Arguably, these recent religious disputes are derivatives of the main causal determinants of tension in American-Israeli affairs. Their cyclic character has thus far coincided with phases when empowered, liberal-minded elements of American Jewry have been especially alienated with the policies (on settlements and other political issues) enacted by right-wing Israeli governments. Also, mutual resentments fostered by the vagaries of patron-client relations must have played some part in the failure of Reform and Conservative American Jews to build bridges with the non-Orthodox majority in Israel and thereby protect progressive Judaism interests through Knesset legislation. One analysis of the contemporary situation is Charles S. Liebman and Steven M. Cohen, *Two Worlds of Judaism: The Israeli and American Experiences* (New Haven, 1990).

9. Hagit Lavsky, *Budget Foundations for the Zionist Enterprise: Zionist Commission, 1918–1921* (in Hebrew; Jerusalem, 1980), 40.

10. Evyatar Friesel, *Zionist Politics After the Balfour Declaration* (in Hebrew; Tel Aviv, 1977), 98.

11. Tom Segev, *Palestine under the British* (in Hebrew; Jerusalem, 1999), 61–62.

12. Nathan Efrati, *The Jewish Community in Eretz-Israel During World War I* (in Hebrew; Jerusalem, 1991), 88–115, 136–42.

13. Urofsky, *American Zionism,* 134.

14. Central Zionist Archives (CZA), A264/26. Originally there was interest in having Aaron Aaronsohn, a Yishuv rugged individualist who was the famed discoverer of "wild wheat" and who was admired by the Brandeis group, serve as a surrogate for the American Zionists on the Commission.

15. Evyatar Friesel, *The Zionist Movement in the United States, 1897–1914* (in Hebrew; Tel Aviv, 1970), 82–84.

16. Urofsky, *American Zionism,* 98–99.

17. Biographical information summarized here relies on Alexandra Lee Levin, *Vision: A Biography of Harry Friedenwald* (Philadelphia, 1964).

18. CZA A181/13.

19. Neil Caplan, *Palestine Jewry and the Arab Question 1917–1925* (London, 1978), 39; idem, *Futile Diplomacy,* vol. 1 (London, 1983), 13, 234. Besides Kalvarisky and Friedenwald, one other name, that of Yitzhak Epstein, crops up in these allusions to pronouncements about the need for Arab–Jewish cooperation.

20. CZA A181/13.

21. Harry Howard, *The King–Crane Commission* (Beirut, 1963).

22. Yehoshua Porath, *The Emergence of the Palestinian-Arab Nationalist Movement, 1918–1929* (in Hebrew; Tel Aviv, 1976); George Antonius, *The Arab Awakening* (London, 1938); Baruch Kimmerling and Joel Migdal, *Palestinians: The Making of a People* (New York, 1993); Rashid Khalidi, *Palestinian Identity* (New York, 1997).

23. Rafael Medoff, "American Zionist Leaders and the Palestinian Arabs, 1898–1949" (Ph.D. dissertation, Yeshiva University, 1991), 77.

24. CZA A264/10; Simcha Berkowitz, "Felix Frankfurter's Zoinist Activities" (Ph.D. dissertation, Jewish Theological Seminary, 1971), 114–15; Harlan Phillips, *Felix Frankfurter Reminisces* (New York, 1960), 155–56; Esco Foundation, *Palestine: A Study of Jewish, Arab and British Policies,* vol. 1 (New Haven, Conn. 1947), 143.

25. See Yigal Elam, *The Jewish Legion in World War I* (in Hebrew; Tel Aviv, 1973); Vladimir Jabotinsky, *The Story of the Jewish Legion* (New York, 1945).

26. Redcliffe Salaman, *Palestine Reclaimed* (London, 1920), 208.

27. One source, printed by the Herzl Press and friendly to the Jewish Legion, describes an atrocity: "The soldiers grabbed all the men they could get hold of, and began to beat them. The young Bedouin women picked up their children and disappeared. . . . Now the soldiers started their systematic work of destruction. . . . In less than an hour the camp was flattened, and only rubbish remained in its place." Roman Freulich, *Soldiers in Judea* (New York, 1964), 161–65.

28. CZA A264/9.

29. See, for instance, the Szold-Frankfurter correspondence from April, CZA A264/7.

30. With tragic irony, several months later, Bianchini was killed in the region by Arab attackers.

31. CZA A181/13.

32. Ibid.

33. Levin, 253–62. The British "Palin Report" on the April 1920 events equivocated about the possibility that the Nebi Mousa pilgrimage to the Jericho area (where Moses is buried, according to Muslim tradition) was a factor. Other accounts point to Feisal's 1920 coronation in Syria as the main determinant of violence. See Porath, *Emergence,* 79–81; Esco, *Palestine, A Study,* 132–33; Segev, *Palestine under the British,* 108–21.

34. CZA A181/13.

35. CZA A264/30; Kenneth Stein, *The Land Question in Palestine, 1917–1939* (London, 1984), 41.

36. CZA A181/13.

37. CZA A164/7.

38. CZA A264/30, A264/32.

39. Ibid.

40. CZA A264/30.

41. H. N. Hirsch, *The Enigma of Felix Frankfurter* (New York, 1981), 64.

42. Phillips, *Felix Frankfurter Reminisces,* 160–61.

43. Leonard Baker, *Brandeis and Frankfurter* (New York, 1984), 24.

44. Friesel, *Zionist Politics,* 107.
45. This argument is made in Segev, *Palestine under the British.*
46. One example, from May 1917, is discussed in Frank Manauel, *The Realities of American-Palestine Relations* (Washington, D.C., 1949), 178.
47. CZA A181/13.
48. Levin, *Vision,* 20.
49. See Howard, *The King–Crane Commission.*
50. Antonius, *Arab Awakening,* 294–98.
51. Peter Grose, *Israel in the Mind of America* (New York, 1983), 89.
52. On Crane as a progressive figure, see Jacob Sulzbach, *Woodrow Wilson & Progressive Reform* (unpublished dissertation, 1994), and Ben Halpern, *A Clash of Heroes* (New York, 1987), 237.
53. Manuel, *Realities,* 237.
54. Stuart Eugene Knee, *The Concept of Zionist Dissent in the American Mind, 1917–1941* (New York, 1979).
55. By this theory, the needs and desires of persecuted European Jews—future Yishuv residents—were to be incorporated in a plebiscite head-count in Palestine. Any contemporary demographic imbalance in Palestine unfavorable to the Yishuv would be rectified by such inclusion of future residents. See Halpern, *Clash of Heroes,* 181–96.
56. In this connection, one perceptive commentator labels Frankfurter's position as "realism" and notes that it did "not display much of the anti-imperialist perception that powerfully excited liberal thought" by the twentieth century. Joseph P. Lash, introduction, *The Diaries of Felix Frankfurter: With a Biographical Essay and Notes.* (New York, 1975), 7.
57. Lash, *Diaries,* 108–109; Phillips, *Felix Frankfurter Reminisces,* 64; *New Republic,* 13 May 1916.
58. Phillips, *Felix Frankfurter Reminisces,* 150.
59. Harry Friedenwald to Jonas Friedenwald, 10 June 1919, CZA A181/13.
60. CZA A181/13.
61. Gideon Biger, "The American Consul in Jerusalem and the Events of 1920–1921" (in Hebrew), *Cathedra* 49 (September 1988): 133–59.
62. Appealing to the same extraterritorial calculations that figured in Zionist treatments of the self-determination issue, Yale insisted that "the wishes and desires of 14,000,000 Jews who have a national history, national traditions and a strong national feeling must be taken into consideration." Manuel, *Realities,* 250.
63. Hagit Lavsky, *Budget Foundations,* 133–36.
64. CZA A181/13.
65. CZA A219/8. On Sampter, see Bertha Badt Straus, *White Fire: The Life & Works of Jesse Sampter* (New York, 1956); Joyce Antler, *The Journey Home: Jewish Women and the American Century* (London, 1997), 109–21.

# The Ambiguous Missionary

Robert Lindsey in Israel, 1948–1970

Yaakov Ariel
*University of North Carolina at Chapel Hill*

In the fall of 1961, Israeli newspapers published a series of articles on Robert Lindsey, the head of the Baptist mission in Israel, in which the missionary was described as a hero. This was not the only time in Lindsey's long career in Israel that he had enjoyed a favorable press, although his interaction with the public was marked by ambiguity. In the course of his missionary activities, Lindsey established some amazing friendships and alliances with Israeli groups and officials, in defiance of all expectations. In part, Lindsey's unusual standing in Israeli society reflected the complicated relationship between evangelical missionaries and the newly born Jewish country, as well as the sometimes paradoxical realities of Israeli life during the 1950s and 1960s. But it was also due to the Baptist leader's independent and daring personality, and to a personal agenda that was not always in line with that of his church.

Robert Lindsey was born in 1917 in Norman, Oklahoma, the only son of a top official at the University of Oklahoma. As an undergraduate student, he majored in classical languages, a knowledge that later provided him with a solid basis for the study of the New Testament in the original Greek. It was while he was a student in the late 1930s that Lindsey became interested in the Jewish people, the Land of Israel, and the Yishuv—the pre-1948 Jewish settlement in Palestine. In 1937, he came to Jerusalem and took courses at the Hebrew University. Inspired by a biblical messianic understanding of the Jews and their role in history,

Lindsey saw more than incidental historical facts in the Jewish national movement and the resettlement of Palestine. For him, as well as for many in his church, events unfolding in Palestine represented the fulfillment of ancient prophecies, stirrings of the End Times, and the groundwork for the messianic age.

Lindsey made a special point of learning modern, spoken Hebrew and becoming acquainted with the new, Zionist-oriented Jewish culture of the day. When World War II broke out, he went back to America to pursue his studies, eventually receiving a doctoral degree from the Baptist Theological Seminary in Louisville, Kentucky. At war's end, he and his wife returned to Israel to head Baptist missionary efforts in the country.

The Baptist mission in Israel dates back to the beginning of the twentieth century when Palestine was under Ottoman Turkish rule. The mission's work was interrupted by World War I, but during the subsequent period of British rule, the Baptists resumed their work in the country on a more permanent basis, as did other Protestant groups, taking advantage of the hospitable and welcoming British policy toward missionaries.

The establishment of the State of Israel in 1948 changed the political reality and opened new avenues for Baptist work in the country. As with other evangelical groups, the Baptists found new meaning and interest in Israel. Evangelicals viewed the creation of an independent, internationally recognized Jewish state, and its somewhat surprising survival and victory over its Arab neighbors as "signs of the times," an indication that history was unfolding according to plan and that the eschatological drama was soon to begin.[1] As a result, Israel was a particularly desirable site for missionary activity.

"Suddenly everybody seems to be 'called of God' to go to Jerusalem as a missionary!" wrote the director of the American Board of Missions to the Jews, one of the larger missions to the Jews in America at that time.[2] George T. B. Davis, the director of the Million Testaments Campaign, a mission headquartered in Philadelphia, wrote even more enthusiastically:

> We desired to have further personal part in sowing the good seed throughout the length and breadth of that Land that has become one of the strategic mission fields of the world. Long centuries ago God chose that Land and that People to be His own, and we believe this is His appointment time to plant His Word there.[3]

## The Ambiguous Missionary

To the surprise of many, Israeli leaders chose to keep the status quo in religious matters, which meant that Christian missionary activity work was allowed to continue unabated.[4] Since Jews had traditionally viewed attempts to evangelize them as humiliating and hostile, both missionaries and Orthodox activists had expected the Jewish state to limit or even ban missionary activity. Christian opponents of Zionism had argued since the late nineteenth century that a Jewish state in Palestine would act against Christian interests.[5] The issue of protecting Christian rights and privileges had often arisen in the discussions that preceded the establishment of the state of Israel. From its inception, Israeli leaders decided therefore to make it clear that their government would protect Christian rights and institutions, not only with regard to freedom of worship, but also in the matter of guaranteeing property rights, tax exemptions, and the freedom to evangelize.[6] Allowing Christian missionaries to propagate the Gospel in Israel was, they believed—a small price to pay for establishing Israel's record as a free, democratic country.[7]

Thus, the Southern Baptists were free to pursue their work in Israel. However, from their point of view, there was a catch in the generally tolerant and protective government policy. In committing itself to maintaining the status quo, the government did just that: old, established missions could carry on their work freely, but work permits were restricted to the number of missionaries employed by each mission prior to 1948.

Lindsey and his lieutenants found ways to overcome these bureaucratic obstacles. Their quota was quite a large one, but as their work expanded, they hired local citizens who did not need any special residence permits. Missionaries could also enter the country as tourists. They would renew their tourist status after three months and then travel in and out of the country as needed in order to retain their tourist status.[8] The Baptists also used the services of volunteers who came for short periods of time and evangelical students who worked part time for the mission.

Israel's sociological, cultural, and ideological infrastructure had changed dramatically since the 1920s, 1930s, and 1940s. The population had grown rapidly. No longer the small, ideological pioneer society of the British period, Israel was now being shaped by a mass immigration, beginning in the late 1940s and 1950s, that within a decade tripled the country's Jewish population. Most of these immigrants were either

Holocaust survivors from Eastern Europe or immigrants from Middle Eastern or North African countries.[9] The percentage of the latter group grew considerably, comprising almost half of the Jewish population by the early 1960s. Absorbing mass waves of mostly poor immigrants, Israel underwent a period of economic hardship. Food rationing was in effect from the late 1940s until the mid-1950s. In addition, there was a severe shortage of housing: new immigrants often resided for years in shanty towns *(ma'abarot)* that lacked paved roads, electricity, running water, or heating. Among the immigrants were some mixed couples and Jews who had converted to Christianity in Europe or North America.

Missionaries found that Israelis were relatively open to their presence, although there was also resentment and anger.[10] Many missions operated in the poorer neighborhoods of Israeli cities, offering relief services and conducting educational programs for children. Lindsey, however, sought to propagate Christianity among members of the country's social, political, and cultural elite. Hence, in sharp contrast to other missions, the Baptist centers were located in the more fashionable areas of Israeli cities, such as Rehavia in Jerusalem and Dizengoff Street in Tel Aviv.

Looking for ways to reach the young, educated Hebrew-speaking Israelis, Lindsey established Dugit, a Baptist Israeli publishing house, which, among other things, published translations into Hebrew of Roland Brinton's works on Martin Luther and the Reformation. The Baptist mission opened a chain of bookshops in Israeli cities, including one in the heart of Tel Aviv, where evangelistic and scholarly Christian literature was displayed. Another Baptist evangelizing enterprise was the bilingual journal *Bayahad* (Together). Lindsey published extensively in *Bayahad* under the name of Reuven Lud. Other Baptist missionaries who wrote for the journal included Dwight Baker and Chandler Lanier.

In articles and in a number of books, Lindsey expressed his views on Israel's role in history.[11] Although he maintained that he did not necessarily follow the dispensationalist messianic interpretation of Scripture, his understanding of the Jewish people and its role in history was very similar to that of dispensationalist premillennialists. For Lindsey, the Jews were the Chosen People, and he believed that God's promises for the rejuvenation of Israel in its land were still valid. In his vision, the Jews were to convert to Christianity and accept Jesus as their Savior before they could be fully rehabilitated.[12] Like many other missionaries to the Jews, he saw his mission as transcending the mere spreading of

Christianity to unchurched people. To evangelize among the Jews in Israel was to take part in a historical, divinely inspired plan, the rejuvenation of God's chosen nation and land.[13] According to Lindsey,

> The Jews... one day [will] be spoken of as having come into Christ's kingdom (Romans 11:26)... A certainty is that a relationship exists between Jewry and God's plan of world salvation... The Jews are a remnant body in spiritual decline who nevertheless remind themselves and the world of God's beginning of redemptive history....[14]

Lindsey was convinced that the Jewish people could not redeem themselves on their own and were in urgent need of accepting Christianity as the force that would reform, heal, and secure their private and national well-being. Current Israeli society, he complained, was hedonistic, imitating as it did the materialistic, Western styles of living.[15] The Baptist missionary did not care for the secular character and ideology of the Israeli elite. During the 1950s, when Zionism was very much the ideology of the nation, Lindsey spoke about the failure of Zionism, as promoted by the older generation of leaders, to capture the hearts of the younger generation. Christianity, he believed, could fill the existing spiritual and religious vacuum.[16]

During the 1950s and 1960s, the Baptists succeeded in establishing a network of congregations in Israel, both among Hebrew- and Arabic-speaking people. Much of Lindsey's energy during these years went into opening new mission branches, purchasing land and property, building schools and bookshops, and recruiting and maintaining a cadre of workers and volunteers. For example, Lindsey was instrumental in purchasing and building the Baptist Village on the Yarkon River (not far from Tel Aviv), which served as a boarding school for Jews and Arabs, a convention center, and an agricultural farm. Real estate in Israel during the period was relatively inexpensive, which helped the Baptists to expand.[17] The Board for International Missions of the Southern Baptist Convention financed much of the growing enterprise in Israel; Lindsey mustered additional support from others, including the Federation des Eglises Evangeliques Baptistes de France and William Criswell, the influential pastor of the First Baptist Church of Dallas, Texas.

In line with the desire to approach young, educated Israelis, Lindsey concluded that there was a need to use terminology and language that would be more familiar to them. Together with others, Lindsey compiled a *Dictionary of Messianic Terms,* which was intended to help missionaries in writing, preaching, and presenting the Christian evangelical cause in Hebrew.[18] This dictionary offered attractive words for common Christian terms—one of them, which was to create something of a revolution in the Israeli missionary vocabulary, was *meshihi* (messianic), which came to replace the more familiar *nozri* (Christian). Lindsey and other missionaries were well aware of the instant resentment aroused by the term "Christian." *Meshihi* essentially meant Christian, but it had a completely different connotation, referring to the eschatological aspect of the Christian evangelical message that the Baptists were trying to promote. The idea was to shift the meaning of "Christian" from a term denoting an alien, hostile religion to one suitable to a new, hopeful, biblically oriented, and messianic religion. Other terms were also changed, invented, or adapted along the same lines; for example, the Baptists used the term "house" instead of "church" when relating to their own prayer meetings, making use of the biblical phrase, "My house shall be called a house of prayer for all nations." Whereas the new vocabulary did not help to bring about a large movement of converts during the 1950s and 1960s, it was instrumental in the following two decades, when there was a marked increase in the number of Jewish conversions to Christianity in Israel.

Lindsey was also dissatisfied with existing Hebrew translations of the New Testament. For decades, missionaries had mainly relied on Franz Delitzsch's late-nineteenth-century translation from Greek into biblical-like Hebrew. As a scholar of the New Testament, Lindsey found many inaccuracies in Delitzsch's work, and he also considered the translation to be archaic, stiff, and alien to the Israeli culture of the day. Thus it came to pass that Lindsey initiated the translation of the New Testament into modern Israeli Hebrew, a task that occupied him, alongside his other responsibilities, for well over a decade.[19]

In the course of this project, Lindsey came to believe that the Synoptic Gospels were originally written in Hebrew and were translated only later into Greek. The original Gospel, he concluded, was that of Luke—which contained fewer antisemitic remarks than did the Gospels of Matthew and Mark. These later gospels, he claimed, relied on Luke in its original form and on an additional source, "Q." This theory fit nicely with the Baptist missionary agenda in Israel, since it enabled missionaries to present the New Testament as being essentially devoid of antisemitism.[20] It also served as a cornerstone for a new school of New Testament studies that consisted of the very unlikely match of evangelical Christians and Orthodox Jews. The group, known later as the Jerusalem School of New Testament Studies, included Lindsey and some other evangelical scholars residing in Jerusalem, mostly members of the Baptist congregation, and a number of Orthodox Jewish Israeli scholars. Among the latter were several Hebrew University professors, notably David Flusser, a New Testament scholar, and Shmuel Safrai, a historian of Judaism during the Second Temple period. These Jewish scholars were particularly interested in comparing the Gospels and Jewish teachings of the Mishnaic period. Thus Jews and Christians, albeit for different reasons, were interested in emphasizing the Jewish origins of early Christianity.

The association between evangelical missionaries and Orthodox Jewish scholars seemed strange enough. Even more amazing, however, was the encounter between the Southern Baptists and the Canaanites—the latter a small ideological-cultural group that originated in the 1930s and 1940s, whose best-known member was Israeli poet Yonatan Ratosh.[21] Standing outside the Zionist consensus of the day, the Canaanites advocated the building of a Hebrew nation and culture that was entirely divorced from traditional Judaism. Among other things, they demanded the separation of synagogue and state in Israel. Although they had only a very small following and no political power, the Canaanites influenced Hebrew poetry and Israeli art.[22] Rumor also claimed that there were tendencies among some members of the group to practice "neo-pagan" rites.[23] Notwithstanding, Lindsey established close connections with several Canaanite ideologues, including Yonatan Ratosh.[24] He hired Zvi Rin, Ratosh's brother, to translate books published by the Baptist publishing house. He also published articles in the Canaanite magazine, *Alef*, in which he advocated the idea of separation of church and state. "The mutual attraction between the Canaanites and the Baptists derived from the latter's views in religious matters," wrote Rin. "They were the only Christian group whose language of prayer was Hebrew. . . . I was also attracted to the Baptist outlook that religion was a personal faith, and not an inherited one . . . similarly, I was enchanted by their advocacy of complete separation of church and state. . . ."[25]

Lindsey and others were chafing at the limitations that had been imposed on them. They could propagate the Gospel freely, publish their materials and build congregations, and yet the system at large was not working in their favor. Religious affiliation in Israel was not a matter of choice; it was recorded at birth or upon immigration, and was henceforth part of the official identity of all Israeli residents. Rabbinical, church, and Sharia (Muslim) courts had exclusive authority over their constituencies in matters of marriage, divorce, burials, and, at times, legacies and custody issues. Moreover, Jewish Israeli children were receiving religious education as part of the official public school curriculum. The Baptists were not competing in an open market of religion.[26]

In the mid-1950s, a group of secular Israelis (among them Uzi Ornan and Zvi Rin) established the League for the Prevention of Religious Coercion *(Haliga Limeniat Kfia Datit)*. Lindsey joined, but later resigned in the wake of criticism on the part of both Christians and Jews.[27] The Southern Baptist convention passed a resolution: "Believing in the complete separation of church and state . . . we join with all who support the principle of religious freedom anywhere in the World, especially in Spain, Israel and Italy, and throughout Latin America."[28] It is doubtful, however, if Baptist leaders and activists were aware of the fact that their representative in Israel was joining with secular Israelis, including the Canaanites, in seeking the desired separation of church and state.

Another group with which Lindsey established a rather curious relationship was the anti-Zionist American Council for Judaism, which was founded in the late 1940s to oppose the establishment of a Jewish state. Members of this elitist (albeit not very influential) group believed that "nationality and religion are separate and distinct" and rejected "the concept that the State of Israel is the national homeland of the Jewish people."[29] Lindsey exchanged letters and views with Elmer Berger, the executive director of the Council.[30] On most issues, the two men disagreed. Lindsey, of course, was in favor of the establishment of the State of Israel; moreover, he saw Jewish religion and nationality as inseparable. The common ground between Berger and Lindsey was the rejection of the notion that secular Israeli culture could replace religion.[31] For Lindsey, it was desirable that the ideological and religious beliefs guiding Israel should become Christian evangelical ones.

Although formally accountable to the Southern Baptist church, Lindsey pursued an amazingly independent course of action in Israel. For example, he became attracted to the charismatic Christian movement, which advocated personal manifestation of the divine in the believer's life, a more expressive and spontaneous religious service, and, in some instances, healing. Under his leadership, the Baptist House in Jerusalem, as well as other Baptist congregations in the country, turned charismatic, even though the Southern Baptist Convention was in principle a non-charismatic denomination. Indeed, in other countries, Baptist missionaries and ministers had been asked to resign because of charismatic leanings. The anomalies and paradoxes did not end there. Within Baptist congregations in Israel, groups were organized to hold separate English- or Hebrew-speaking services. Participants at the Hebrew services included converted Jews as well as evangelical expatriates. The English-speaking congregations were also atypical; not only were they charismatic, but also many of their members were not Baptist, belonging to other American and European Protestant, sometimes liberal and mainline, churches.

Paradoxically, the Southern Baptists were sponsoring a missionary who, on a number of issues—including biblical exegesis and prayer—deviated from the usual Baptist approach. He certainly did not follow Baptist norms in choosing people and ideological groups with which to associate, or in defining his public image. As a charismatic minister, Lindsey practiced healing and exorcism;[32] his reputation was such that even some Jews with no intention of converting requested his services. Despite such unorthodox practices, he was careful to update the Foreign Mission Board at the Richmond, Virginia, headquarters on developments in the Israeli enterprise.[33] One of the pragmatic changes he inaugurated was moving the weekly worship services to Saturdays rather than Sundays in order to make Baptist houses more accessible to Israelis, whose work week in the 1950s and 1960s left only Saturday (the Jewish Sabbath) free, and for whom Sunday worship was associated with an alien religious tradition.

Lindsey was also capable of personal boldness. In 1961, he slipped across the Jordanian-Israeli border in order to help an Arab youth who wished to return to West Jerusalem. Salem Edward Jumad had been left behind by his parents during the 1948 War of Independence and had been brought up in a Baptist school. When it was learned that his family was in the Jordanian-held sector of the city, the Baptists arranged for him to visit his family. He crossed the border legally for a two-day visit, but his family refused to allow him to return. He wrote to the Baptists expressing a strong desire to continue his education at their school, and Lindsey crossed the border in an attempt to smuggle the boy back to the Israeli side. In the course of this adventure, he stepped on a mine, and consequently lost a leg. After the Jordanians had put him under hospital arrest, the Israeli government intervened to obtain his release and "repatriation." This incident served to enhance Lindsey's image in Israel, where he was looked upon as a *sabra* and *hevreman*—one of their own. The secular press offered enthusiastic praise for what was seen as a brave act of self-sacrifice.[34]

With his missionary intent often overlooked, Lindsey became an accepted participant in Israeli society, and he enjoyed the friendship and trust of that very elite whose beliefs and lifestyle he criticized so vehemently. He was invited to serve on a special government committee intended to promote Christian pilgrimage to Israel, and he served as a judge in the International Bible Contests initiated by Prime Minister David Ben-Gurion. He was interviewed several times by Israeli journalists.[35]

While there was much resentment, particularly among Orthodox Jews, toward missionary activity, and various attempts to harass missionaries, many Israelis (particularly secular ones) were not much bothered by their presence. They did not fully appreciate the scope and nature of the missions, assuming that very few Jews, if any, actually converted to Christianity from genuine conviction.[36] It was believed that those Jews who did convert did so because of Christian promises of economic support.

Baptist missionary gains in Israel were, in fact, very limited in the period from the late 1940s until the 1970s, estimated to be no more than a few hundred converts.[37] This should not be surprising. Whereas missions in America were advocating a message that represented the values, norms, and beliefs of a large segment of society, in Israel Christianity was a minority religion and evangelical Christianity had no particular standing or influence. Moreover, under the charismatic leadership of David Ben-Gurion, and despite the severe economic shortages, the early years of the state were basically marked by a sense of national optimism and pride. Zionism served not merely as a political agenda but as an all-encompassing ideology that provided a hopeful outlook on the course of Jewish history. Non-Zionist outlooks, such as those advocated by Communists or ultra-Orthodox Jews, were regarded as completely marginal to the mainstream. Under such circumstances, there was almost no chance that Israelis of the social elite would accept Christianity.

As noted, much of the missionary efforts in Israel were directed toward the struggling new immigrants. But even here, missionary gains were minimal. Although many children of immigrants sought a new cultural framework and set of values to replace that of their parents, they looked to the mostly secular Israeli culture. The mission's messages seemed to them alien and irrelevant. Older immigrants, especially those from North Africa or the Middle East, were even less open to changing their set of beliefs; the synagogue was the center of their social, communal, and spiritual lives. They had much to lose by converting to Christianity, and very little to gain. Even when new immigrants approached the missionaries to seek aid or economic assistance, they had no desire to commit themselves to accepting Jesus as their Savior. Such evangelical terminology was completely incomprehensible to most of them.

Lindsey was well aware of the difficulties that converted Jews faced in Israeli society.[38] Since there was no separation of synagogue (or church) and state, Jews who accepted Christianity had to choose: they could reveal their decision to embrace Christianity, register as Christians, and be regarded by the authorities as Christians, or they could choose to keep that fact a secret and be registered as Jews. If they chose the latter, they had to live their lives under the jurisdiction of the rabbinate, including marrying as Jews and being buried as Jews. Most chose that option rather than openly declare themselves as Christians. Many of these Christian Jews were not really "in the closet"; they were members of evangelical congregations and lived their lives within the evangelical subculture in Israel. In some cases, however, Jews accepted the Christian evangelical faith but kept it secret, neither joining evangelical congregations nor interacting with fellow Christian believers. Such persons, often members of Orthodox communities afraid of arousing social resentment, lived something of a double life, revealing their belief only to a few people that they could trust completely.[39] One does not know, of course, the exact number of such persons. Baptists pointed, at times, to the existence of such people as an indication that the number of Jews who had accepted the Christian faith in Israel was larger than their recorded numbers.[40] Carl F. H. Henry, editor of *Christianity Today*, visited Israel in the early 1960s and described a group of crypto-Baptists in Haifa whom he met.[41] Ironically, in those cases where Jews who joined the Baptist congregations asked to be registered as Christians in order to be exempt from army service, they were denied such an option because the Baptists were not officially recognized as a *millet*, a religious community holding its own ecclesiastical courts.[42]

The only way missionaries could have turned their mission into a great numerical success was, in the words of the secretary of the International Hebrew Christian Alliance, "by turning into a travel agency."[43]

Many Israelis in the 1950s and 1960s, immigrants from Eastern Europe, the Balkans, North Africa, or Middle Eastern countries, felt that their lot might have been rosier if they emigrated to Western, more affluent countries. Many approached the missions inquiring whether they would help them emigrate and settle in a Western country and expressing interest in converting to Christianity pending future emigration.[44] There was a prevailing assumption in Israeli society that missions were willing to bestow large material benefits on converts. In actuality, missions did not possess the economic resources many Israelis assumed they did. The mission's budgets, although generous by Israeli terms, certainly did not include any bonuses for the newly converted. Contrary to the Jewish stereotype, missionaries such as Lindsey were interested in sincere converts and not in mere opportunists, whose obvious motivation was economic benefit. In addition, since their premillennialist view of history held that the Jews' return to Israel was part of God's plan for the End Times, they could not, in principle, support the idea of assisting Jews to leave the country.

Although the actual number of converts was relatively small in the 1950s and 1960s, Lindsey and his friends did not see their efforts as wasted. Living and evangelizing in Israel during the early years of the State seemed of itself fulfilling and rewarding. They were "sowing the seed" for the future. Moreover, considering the legal and social obstacles, and the ideological and cultural mood of the country, many saw reason to be satisfied with relatively modest numbers of converts. Those Jews who did convert filled missionaries with an enormous sense of satisfaction and joy. They were, for the most part young, independent people in the prime of life, looking forward to building families and careers. Lindsey also found his scholarly and literary work, which were closely tied to his missionary agenda, to be immensely rewarding. He had not made an extensive number of converts, but had built tools, in his translation of the New Testament into Hebrew, his scholarly work on the Synoptic Gospels, the *Dictionary of Hebrew Christian Terms,* and the sponsorship of Hebrew-speaking congregations, that helped bring about a larger movement of converts in the 1970s and 1980s.

Lindsey remained in Israel until the mid-1980s, maintaining his good standing with Israeli society and his close relationship with the Orthodox scholars of the school of New Testament studies he had established. His interest in actual evangelization declined, and he devoted

## The Ambiguous Missionary

more time and energy to his scholarly pursuits. Whereas the 1950s and 1960s were years of growth and expansion for the Baptists in Israel, the 1970s were not. A new vigorous movement of Messianic Jews—converts to Christianity who wished to retain their Jewish and Israeli identities—became the missionary movement par excellence in the country. Although officially unaffiliated with the Baptists, this new movement fulfilled Lindsey's vision of converting young educated Israelis. It made extensive use of the Hebrew Christian terminology he advocated, the new translation of the New Testament, and the interpretation he and his friends in the Jerusalem School of New Testament studies gave to these texts.

The Israeli press wrote favorably about Lindsey and his role in the country once again in 1978 on the occasion of U.S. President Jimmy Carter's visit to Israel, when Lindsey preached on the significance of the creation of the State of Israel and its special role in history. In his newspaper interviews, Lindsey expressed his confidence that Carter, who attended the service, shared his views.

After his retirement in the mid-1980s, Lindsey returned to Oklahoma. His health deteriorated rapidly, and he died in 1995.

A number of factors created the unusual, often paradoxical reality in which Lindsey operated in Israel. A major factor was the non-separation of synagogue and state, which led, at times, to the development of incredible, even bizarre, alliances and friendships. It also made for a strange relationship between Lindsey and the Israeli government, which sought, for political reasons, to build a friendly atmosphere with missionaries like himself, who, the government believed, represented large segments of Christianity.

The unusual character of the Baptist missionary endeavor in Israel was also shaped by the fact that Lindsey and his friends did not treat Israel as just another country. Influenced by a messianic premillennialist outlook, they believed that they were evangelizing in a country where the great drama of the End Times was about to unfold, and among a people who they believed were destined to play a crucial role in that drama. Their interests in the people and the country were much broader than trying to convince individual Jews of the truth of the Christian message. In their eyes, they were witnesses to developments that had global, historical significance. They had their own vested interests in the country, which made them an interested party in the drama. Lindsey's aim was to try to influence the course of events, to educate the Jews as to how to better fulfill their historical role, whether it resulted in immediate conversions or not.

## Notes

1. See, for example, Louis T. Talbot and William W. Orr, *The New Nation of Israel and the Word of God* (Los Angeles, 1948); M. R. DeHaan, *The Jew and Palestine in Prophecy* (Grand Rapids, 1950); William L. Hull, *The Fall and Rise of Israel* (Grand Rapids, 1954); George T. B. Davis, *God's Guiding Hand* (Philadelphia, 1962); John Walvoord, *Israel in Prophecy* (Grand Rapids, 1962).

2. See *The Chosen People* 55, no. 2 (Nov. 1949): 16–17; Harold Sevener, *A Rabbi's Vision*, (Charlotte, N.C., 1994) 162–76.

3. George T. B. Davis, *Sowing God's Word in Israel Today* (Philadelphia, 1953).

4. On Israel's policy in its early years toward the Christian churches, see Saul Colbi, *History of the Christian Presence in the Holy Land* (Lanham, Md., 1988), 163–84; Herbert Weiner, *The Wild Goats of Ein Gedi* (Garden City, N.Y., 1961), especially 12–15, 29–111. Cf. also Gavriel Zeldin, "Catholics and Protestants in Jerusalem and the 'Return of Jews to Zion,' 1948–1988" (Ph.D. dissertation, Hebrew University of Jerusalem, 1992).

5. See Sergio I. Minerbi, *The Vatican and Zionism* (New York, 1990).

6. During the 1948 war, David Ben-Gurion, Israel's first prime minister, sent a telegram to Israeli army officers, ordering them to use severe, indeed draconian measures to ensure the security and well-being of Christian institutions. See Israel State Archive, Case 2397, folder 3, document H/A/15092. See also *Recording of the Provisional Government Meetings*, 28, Israel State Archives, Jerusalem. This is a declaration regarding religious freedom, adopted by the Provisional Government, May 23, 1948, eight days after the establishment of the State of Israel.

7. In one extreme case in the early 1960s, the police were sent to break up anti-missionary demonstrations. See Per Osterlye, *The Church in Israel* (Lund, 1970). Osterlye's account is written from a distinctly Protestant missionary point of view.

8. Cf. Carl F. H. Henry, "The Christian Witness in Israel," Part 1, *Christianity Today* 5, no. 22 (July 31, 1961): 22–23. Henry complains about the quota system. For various means used by missionaries to gain residence in Israel in that period, see, for example, Glora Ulysses, International Missionary Council, to George Sadler, Foreign Mission Board of the Southern Baptist Convention, 12 Nov. 1954. The letter, along with many of Lindsey's papers from the 1950s and 1960s, was given by him to Mr. Kim Jin-Hae, a Ph.D. candidate at the Hebrew University of Jerusalem. Copies are in the collection of Yaakov Ariel.

9. On the transition that took place in Israel's early years, see, for example, Varda Pilousky, ed., *Transition from "Yishuv" to State* (Haifa, 1988).

10. *The Chosen People* 61, no. 9 (May 1956): 11.

11. For example, Reuven Lud [Robert Lindsey], "Kriat am Adonai al-pi Habrit Hahadasha" (The nation of God according to the New Testament), *Hayahad* 25 (April 1965): 4–5; Robert Lindsey, "Salvation and the Jews," *International Review of Missions* (1972): 20–47.

12. Robert Lindsey, "The Jews and the Christian Hope" (unpublished manuscript, n.d., Lindsey's personal papers); see also Zeldin, "Catholics and Protestants," 230–36.

13. See, for example, Lindsey's report to the 13th Annual Conference of the UCCI, 28–30 Oct. 1969, p. 3.

14. Lindsey, "Jews and Christian Hope."

15. For example, see the talk given at the annual conference of the United Christian Council in Israel, 14 Nov. 1958, Jerusalem. Quoted by Zeldin, "Catholics and Protestants," 230.

16. This theme is repeated in Lindsey's correspondence.

17. On the nature of Baptist activity in Israel in this period, see, for example, "Report on the Executive Committee Summary of Meetings for the Years 1958–1959," compiled by Baptist activists in Israel (copy in the collection of Yaakov Ariel), and Dwight L. Baker, *Baptists Golden Jubilee: 50 Years in Palestine-Israel* (unpublished typed manuscript, archives of the Southern Baptist Convention, Richmond, Va.). I am grateful to the Archives for sending me a copy of the manuscript.

18. Robert Lindsey, ed., *Munahim meshichiim notzriim* (Jerusalem, 1976). Editorial work on the publication began in 1963.

19. Robert Lindsey to Dr. Goerner of the Southern Baptist Mission Department, 16 April 1960.

20. For an early summary of Lindsey's theory, see Robert Lindsey, "Summary of Conclusions of Research into the Synoptic Relationship," *Hayahad* 3, no. 17 (November-December 1963): 2, 7; some of Lindsey's books on the topic are idem, *A Hebrew Translation of the Gospel of Mark* (Jerusalem, n.d.); idem, *A New Approach to the Synoptic Gospel* (Jerusalem, 1971).

21. Yaacov Shavit, *The New Hebrew Nation* (London, 1989).

22. Everyman's University, *Hakvutza haknaanit: sifrut veedeologia* (The Canaanite group: literature and ideology) (Tel Aviv, 1987).

23. See Uri Avnery, *Milhemet hayom hashvi'i* (The seventh day war; Tel Aviv, 1968), 145–80.

24. David Klatzker, "Israeli Civil Religion and Jewish-Christian Relations: The Case of the Baptists," *Jewish Civilization: Essays and Studies* 3 (1985): 135–52.

25. Svi Rin to Yaakov Ariel, 30 July 1996.

26. See Robert Lindsey to Lillian E. Williams, 28 September 1959, Lindsey's personal papers; also see "Baptist Cites Israeli Discord," *Norman Oklahoma Transcript,* 24 June 1960, 8, and Dwight L. Baker, *Baptists Golden Jubilee,* 9, 11.

27. Klatzker, "Israeli Civil Religion," 143.

28. A copy is in Lindsey's personal papers.

29. On that organization, see Samuel Halperin, *The Political World of American Zionism* (Detroit, 1961), 86–92, 301–309, 351–52, and Thomas A. Kolsky, *Jews Against Zionism: The American Council for Judaism* (Philadelphia, 1990).

30. See such correspondence in Lindsey's personal papers, for example, Elmer Berger to Lindsey, 22 July 1953 and 20 January 1954, and Robert Lindsey to Elmer Berger, 11 August 1953.

31. Robert Lindsey to Elmer Berger, 30 May 1953.

32. Shachar Ilan, "Megaresh hashedim holech habayta" (The exorcist goes home), *Kol Ha'ir,* 9 January 1987, 25–27. On the charismatic nature and practice of Baptist congregations in Israel, see Chandler Lanier, *The Renewal of the Church in Israel* (unpublished manuscript, collection of Yaakov Ariel), which describes healing as a common practice among Baptists in Israel. Lanier was a missionary in Israel in the 1960s and 1970s.

33. See, for example, the correspondence of Lindsey and the Board in Richmond, Va., Lindsey's personal papers.

34. Cf. Weiner, *Wild Goats of Ein Gedi,* 69–70; see also Editorial, *Haboker,* 4 May 1962; Uri Kesari, *Ha'aretz,* 26 Oct. 1961; G. Ben Ari, "The Baptists Believe in Freedom of Religion," *Maarivcedilla* 21 September 1961; Gabriel Stern, "A Tragedy within a Tragedy," *Al Hamishmar,* 27 September 1961.

35. In the 1970s, the Hebrew daily, *Ha'aretz,* carried a series, "A Week in the Life of One Person," in which noted public figures were asked to describe their week, and Lindsey was asked to contribute.

36. See, for example, L. Ben Or to the Department for Christian Churches, 10 June 1952. Ben Or, then director general of the Ministry of Education, voiced the opinion of many when he wrote, "I have never looked and do not look today either on missionary activity as a dangerous thing," Israel State Archive, file 29/1/100, container G 5817/19.

37. Menahem Ben Hayim, former secretary of the Messianic Jewish Alliance in Israel, estimated that in the early 1960s there were no more than 300 Jewish members of evangelical congregations in the country, which included those who had converted outside of Israel. Menahem Ben Hayim, interview by Yaakov Ariel, July 1994, Jerusalem.

38. Ibid. The association of evangelical churches in Israel appointed a special committee and organized a conference to discuss the issues involved, in which Lindsey expressed his resentment about the situation.

39. Cf. Zola Levitt, *The Underground Church of Jerusalem* (Nashville, 1978), and Carl. F. H. Henry, *Confessions of a Theologian* (Waco, Tex. 1986), 233.

40. Aaron J. Kligerman and Nate Schaiff, "Destination Israel," *American Hebrew Christian* 42 (Fall 1956):9–11; Levitt, *The Underground Church of Jerusalem,* 95.

41. Henry, *Confessions,* 233.

42. See Judith Hibner, Ministry of the Interior regarding the case of Jaachim Boin to Robert Lindsey, 23 November 1964, Israel State Archive, file 29/1/74, container G 5815. Lindsey tried to intervene on behalf of Boin's daughter to obtain exemption from army service.

43. H. L. Ellison, "Christian Missions and Israel," *The Hebrew Christian* 26, no. 1 (Spring 1953): 26.

44. Cf. Weiner, *Wild Goats of Ein Gedi,* 67.

# American Olim and the Transfer of Innovation to Palestine, 1917–1939

Joseph B. Glass
*Hebrew University of Jerusalem*

American Jewish immigrants to Palestine (*olim,* sing. *oleh*) between the two world wars were agents of innovation, transferring technologies, skills, and ideas to the Jewish homeland.[1] As such, they constituted part of the process of the land's upbuilding, its modernization, and the creation of a new society within its boundaries. Their move to Palestine also reflected the olim's relationship with American society and the changes America had undergone up to and during that period, particularly with respect to American industrial-age capitalism and the social ills that attended it. A response to the woes of American society was not a radical, but a gentle and even benign construct, that might be called "Social Zionism." Their role, as they perceived it, was to utilize their resources (both financial and human capital) for the betterment of a Jewish society.

## The Immediate Development of Palestine's Infrastructure

World War I brought about British control over Palestine and a promise for the development of a Jewish homeland there as outlined in the Balfour Declaration. This, at least during the first years of British rule, inspired calls for action by American Zionists to prepare the ancient homeland for its settlement by a mass of Jewish immigrants. Prior to the war, Palestine was undergoing an accelerated process of modernization.

The war arrested this process and even set it back significantly. To prepare for large-scale migration, immediate action was needed. American Zionist leader Justice Louis D. Brandeis outlined this principle in the Zeeland Memorandum, where the objective of Zionism was defined as follows: "to populate Palestine within a comparatively short time with a preponderiong body of many self-supporting Jews who will develop into a homogeneous people with high Jewish ideas; will develop and apply there the Jewish spiritual and intellectual ideals; and will ultimately become a self-governing commonwealth." However, there were immediate hurdles that needed to be overcome before such goals could be realized. Brandeis explained:

> The land is (in the main) now in a condition which would prevent the individual, even if he owned it free, from gaining there a living by individual investment or effort. That is, he could not raise a crop upon it for lack of water or of drainage or because of malarial conditions. He could not build a house upon it, by felling of trees thereon or nearby. He could not utilize it as the site of a factory, for lack of power, there being neither wood, coal nor oil available. Certain indispensables to making a living thereon and therefrom, possible, must be supplied in some way by community action. Water, water power, health (i.e., elimination of malaria), drainage. These, beside roads, and the intellectual and spiritual needs of a Jewish population are indispensable to the development desired.[2]

Thus, investment and expertise in the development of this infrastructure were required as a preliminary step before mass settlement. Such expertise could be readily found in the United States. Accordingly, the Zionist Society of Engineers and Agriculturalists was organized at the American Zionist Convention in Baltimore in June 1917, "to utilize the technical training of Jewish Engineers, Agriculturalists and Scientists in behalf of the agricultural, industrial and economic development of Palestine."[3] The background for their organization was, on the one hand, Brandeis's conviction that such work was essential for the development of Palestine and, on the other, the widely shared view that the necessary personnel was not to be found in Palestine. The society's plan of action called for the recruitment of sanitary, industrial, hydroelectric, construction, mining, and topographical engineers, plus agricultural experts. Membership as of November 1919 totaled 324 [see Figure 1]. Significant strides were made in the improvement of health conditions immediately after World War I. The American Zionist Medical Unit

Cover of Memorandum to the members of the Zionist Society of Engineers and Agriculturists, New York, September 1919 (CZA F25/298)

was organized in 1916 to provide medical assistance and relief to the war-torn Jewish population of Palestine. In June 1918, the forty-four member unit departed from the United States. Included in their ranks under the leadership of Eliyahu Lewin-Epstein, were twenty nurses, a dermatologist, obstetricians and gynecologists, an orthopedist, pediatricians, dentists, a pharmacist, ear-nose-and-throat and eye specialists, a sanitary engineer, social workers, and five administrators. The pharmacopeia and supplies included 2,000 cases of medicines, two ambulances, eight vehicles, gallons of anti-louse fluid, surgical instruments, blankets, linen, and clothing—enough equipment to open a fifty-bed hospital. From their arrival in Palestine in August 1918 until November of that year, they dealt with emergency care for the civilian population. Later, they tended to various local health needs. The unit established the basic foundations for medical services in Palestine, activating hospitals throughout the country. One important innovation was the introduction of an x-ray institute in Jerusalem. Medical activities were expanded to include preventive as well as curative medicine, as well as public health education services.[4]

American olim also played an important role in the eradication of malaria. Israel Kligler and Louis Kantor, two American experts who were recruited after 1918, were instrumental in the battle against this chronic parasitic disease. The Russian-born Kligler (1889–1944), a bacteriologist by training, left the United States for Palestine in 1920 with the Hadassah Medical Unit. His approach to dealing with the problem differed from the accepted view, which called for enormous sums for the drainage of swamps. Since the Zionist Executive did not have the funds necessary for such a large-scale project, the anti-malarial campaign proposed by Kligler emphasized prevention: detection and treatment of carriers of the parasite; an anti-mosquito campaign, including the use of pesticides to kill mosquito larvae; distribution of quinine prophylaxis; and education of the public.

Brandeis, unable to convince Chaim Weizmann and the Zionist Executive to support even this modest plan, obtained $10,000 from Hadassah (founded in 1912). Work was first conducted in the Migdal-Degania area west of the Sea of Galilee, where the incidence of malaria among Jewish workers had reached an alarming 95 percent. The success of Kligler and his anti-malarial unit attracted the attention of the League of Nations, which sent a special commission to Palestine to report on the project.[5] Kantor, a sanitation engineer, was also a member of the American Zionist Medical Unit. Under British High Commissioner Sir Herbert Samuel, Kantor directed squads of inspectors for an anti-malaria campaign.[6]

The anti-malaria campaign and the American Zionist Medical Unit are examples of activities initiated by American olim, whose expertise helped lay the groundwork for large-scale migration to Palestine. American olim, however, played a very limited role in the actual preparation of the land for settlement—its survey, mapping, and parceling. The fault lay not in any lack of desire, but in the political situation in Palestine, where the British military government had halted all land transactions until the reopening of the land registry. Government lands, those inherited by the British administration from the Ottoman regime, were not made available for immediate Jewish settlement. Furthermore, Jewish-rented or owned lands were subdivided and prepared for settlement by their owners—the Jewish National Fund, the Jewish Colonization Association, private owners, and the American Zion Commonwealth. The Zionist Society of Engineers and Agriculturalists was thus left with no territory to plan for settlement, even though they were fully prepared to do so. The society's president, Boris Kazmann, had devised a plan known as the "unit system," which entailed the planning of settlement units of groups of 100,000, by first determining the

> necessary food, shelter, clothing, other commodities including machinery, tools, equipment and materials leading to the creation of indispensable agricultural, industrial and public utility developments in order to make the unit self-sustaining, as far as economically feasible.[7]

To this end, the society distributed to its members an outline of proposed settlement projects.

David Ben-Gurion was also among those who deemed the American contribution of skilled manpower to be consequential to the immediate development of Palestine following the war. Ben-Gurion, Yitzhak Ben-Zvi, and Pinhas Rutenberg had traveled the length and breadth of the North American continent during the war recruiting young Jews for the Jewish Legion, a special unit of the British army.[8] Ben-Gurion regarded the enlistment and service of American Jews in these battalions not simply as a contribution to the liberation of Ottoman Palestine, but as an immigration movement. In his personal history of Israel he elaborated, observing that the largest *aliyah* to come in the wake of the Balfour Declaration was, in fact, that of the Jewish Legion from the

United States, which numbered more than 4,000 men. Not all of these Americans remained in Palestine after the war, partly because of the apathetic attitude of the Zionist Executive, concentrated then in the Zionist Commission which went to (Eretz) Israel in 1918. The commission did not offer any assistance to the American volunteers who wished to remain in the Land of Israel.[9] Ben-Gurion was clearly disappointed that proper provision was not made for the demobilized American Jewish troops, although other factors were also involved, including the negative attitude of the British government.

Following the war, Poale Zion, the Zionist labor group led by Ben-Gurion, sought to promote the recruitment of competent and experienced workers from the United States. America could provide builders, metal-workers, carpenters, mechanics, cobblers, tailors, and sailors. If there were none of the latter, Ben-Gurion suggested, American Jews could enlist in the American navy or merchant marine so that they could acquire experience before their eventual immigration. Such American recruits would not only strengthen the position of Poale Zion in Palestine, but also contribute to the development of the land.[10]

Following the establishment of the British civil administration in Palestine in 1920, there was a need for skilled and unskilled English-speaking workers in various positions. Chaim Weizmann hoped to attract individuals from North America. He sent a telegram to the Zionist Organization of America:

> Confidential: Zionist Commission reports opportunity. Government employment [in] Palestine [for] two hundred skilled, one hundred unskilled, English-speaking, medically fit, unmarried labourers [in] building trade. No promise definite job or privileged treatment. Please cable how many desirous emigrating [under] those conditions.[11]

Since the total number of American Jewish immigrants to Palestine in 1921 was only 150, it does not appear that the plan ever materialized. It is probable that the human reserve, which included mainly former Jewish Legionnaires, was unwilling to be caught up in another round of uncertainty and false promises. Some of the demobilized Legionnaires, as Ben-Gurion later noted, had waited to settle in Palestine, only to find no job opportunities or assistance, and thus had returned to America.

During the immediately preceding period, from January 1919 to the end of May 1920, 1,836 family heads, representing 6,001 persons residing in North America, had applied for immigration to Palestine.

The occupations of the would-be settlers included 30 agricultural experts, 124 teachers, 63 architects and engineers, 159 in the medical professions, 21 social workers, 2 accountants, and 10 administrators. (For a complete list, see Appendix 1, p. 277.)[12] Most of the applicants did not actually immigrate; those who did, however, helped to lay the foundations for further development in Palestine.

## Creation of a New and Better Society

In a letter written in 1919 to his friend and confidant in Zionist affairs, Bernard Flexner, Brandeis outlined his views for the development of a new and better Jewish society in Palestine. American involvement was needed, he wrote, not only for the sake of financial assistance but also for ideas that might shape the new society:

> If America is to do for Palestine what we dream, and Palestine for its Jewish Hinterland in America, there must be created a dynamic nexus between the Palestinian development and the Jewish intellectuals and idealists here. These must be made to feel that they share, not mere Palestinian burdens, but the joy of solving in its social and political laboratory, problems which, being universal, are occupying their thoughts or dreams. In other words, we must secure support for Palestine—from the intellectual Zionists—by enlisting their professional interests; bearing in mind that business, too, should be a profession, and that all Jews are potentially both intellectuals and idealists. Through the Palestinian Health Service, with its socialization of medicine, we ought to secure and hold the active interest of Jewish physicians and social workers; and through land nationalization and the cooperative movement, the interest of those who seek by these means to reduce, in America, the evils of landlordism and of industrial exploitation; and through other of our activities—corresponding groups of American Jews.[13]

American Jewish groups and individuals shared a common goal of creating a progressive Jewish society in Palestine, largely through its partial Americanization. They differed in terms of just which route they favored towards this goal and they were selective in choosing which aspects of American society they wanted to transfer to Palestine. In certain circumstances, Palestine was something of a laboratory setting for social ideas that found no acceptance in America at that time.

American Zionist leader Justice Bernard A. Rosenblatt (1886–1969), for instance, explained his worldview as follows:

> A Social Zionist is one whose idealism is not satisfied merely with the creation of a Jewish state, but who is determined to build a model state in the Holy Land—freed from economic wrongs, the social injustices and the greed of modern-day industrialism. While he may not be prepared to endorse the full program of any particular radical school, yet he purposes to utilize the truths of all schools in building the new Commonwealth in Zion.[14]

Acting on these views, Rosenblatt founded the American Zion Commonwealth, a land purchasing and development company, and participated in other activities in conjunction with this perception of a socially progressive, developed economy.[15]

Poet and educator Jessie Sampter emigrated to Palestine in 1919 and encountered there a society that she believed needed to be transformed. According to her biographer, Bertha Badt-Strauss, Sampter spoke of "Errors in Utopia." The first of these "errors" was the all-or-nothing approach taken in Palestine toward Judaism—either extreme Orthodoxy or the absolute rejection of Judaism. The second error, which bitterly depressed her and which she tried to put right, was "the failure of the Western Jews to accord social justice to their Yemenite brothers." To improve their plight, Sampter organized evening classes for Yemenite working girls.[16]

Deborah Kallen established an elementary school in Jerusalem, the School of the Parents Education Association (better known as the Kallen School). "Our aim," she explained, "was to create a school environment that would produce situations typical of everyday life. The school was conducted as a miniature community with a school bank, a store, a library, kitchen and garden—with its components of community life."[17] Her brother, Horace Kallen, later noted that "the notions of teaching and learning Miss Kallen brought to the Jewish homeland on her arrival in 1920 were still in the experimental, pioneering stage even in her own country. John Dewey's *Democracy and Education* had been published only in 1916, and the preoccupations of World War I had held back its impact on schools in the United States."[18]

Concurrent with Kallen's arrival, American educator Alexander M. Dushkin was involved in various aspects of education in Palestine during the years 1919–1922. He later outlined his activities in his memoirs:

> [David] Yellin invited me to teach English in the Hebrew Teachers Seminary in Zikhron Moshe, which he founded and conducted. I agreed to do

so, but on condition that I also be permitted to teach a course in pedagogy to senior students. In those days, teachers seminars were normal schools, *écoles normales*—secondary schools plus a smattering of methodology in the teaching of Hebrew language and literature. It was my privilege to be the first to introduce American progressive educational ideas to Jerusalem teacher trainees—the progressive philosophy of John Dewey, the project methodology of Kilpatrick, the psychology and measurement techniques of Thorndike, etc. I remember the excitement of the public lecture, in which I brought before the students and the teachers the then popular book *New Schools for Old* by John and Evelyn Dewey.[19]

Dushkin returned to Palestine for the years 1934–1939 and was appointed associate professor at the Hebrew University of Jerusalem, where he established the Department of Teacher Training and the University Secondary School. In 1949, he settled permanently in Israel.

The socialization of medicine mentioned by Brandeis was considered a particularly progressive leap forward, in that it would allow everyone, irrespective of socioeconomic status, to receive basic medical services. Henrietta Szold, who headed Hadassah activities in Palestine from the time of her arrival in 1920, was involved in the process of the amalgamation of the health care funds of Ahdut Ha'avoda and Hapo'el hatza'ir. Her position, which included control over Hadassah funding and services for the two funds, allowed her leverage over these rival groups. According to Marlin Levin, Szold "put her foot down and issued an ultimatum that the two would amalgamate or else."[20] This resulted in the formation of the Kupat Holim of the Histadrut, a precursor of national health insurance. Americans were only beginning to dream of such a program—which is unrealized to this day. Szold's actions clearly illustrate the attempt by Americans to create a system of social welfare, one that could not be established in the United States, but was possible in the new-old Zion.

Social pioneering also found expression in the design of the landscape. In a project funded by Bertha Guggenheimer, Hadassah established a playground in the Old City of Jerusalem so that "the children . . . Jews, Moslems and Christians, . . . should have a satisfactory wholesome place for outdoor recreation and play." Activities included games, handwork (basketry, weaving, modeling, carpentry, and embroidery), light and heavy athletics, and dramatics. Children received a daily health inspection. A sanitary water system and showers were installed at the playground. The equipment—including swings, seesaws, giant slides, basketball courts, and sand boxes—was sent from the United States. In line with Guggenheimer's social and political worldview, it was hoped that if children of different backgrounds learned to get along early in life, they would continue to do so as they grew older. The concept gained popularity and such playgrounds were opened throughout the country.[21]

Menachem Mendel Freidman of Norfolk, Virginia, was an American entrepreneur who took the initiative in improving working conditions at a Jerusalem-based factory. In the wake of a survey of local cigarette manufacturing, Freidman entered into a partnership with a local producer in 1921. The factory, with six employees, had originally consisted of one room. Freidman relocated the business to a five-room site in the Succat Shalom neighborhood, which met the requirements of government health department standards.[22]

For many American olim, in short, the renewal of Palestine was not just the development of a refuge for persecuted Jews of Eastern Europe, and later Central Europe. Nor was it the development of a spiritual center as outlined in the Zionist philosophy of Ahad Ha'am. Instead, it was the construction of a utopia—not necessarily along socialist lines, but along the principles of "social justice." This was a peculiarly American construct that sought to incorporate the best of America while at the same time righting the injustices of capitalist society. Particularly during the first years of British rule, American olim were motivated by the prospect that, by introducing certain innovations, some developed in America, they could be social pioneers.

## Upbuilding and Modernization of Palestine

An enormous technological disparity existed between the United States and underdeveloped Palestine. In many instances, the role of American olim was to attempt to narrow the gap, using skills they had acquired in their previous home.

Some American Zionists even chose a particular vocation with their future aliyah in mind, ascertaining its suitability for the Zionist enterprise and the absence or paucity of trained practitioners.[23]

Intent on migrating to Palestine, Gershon Agronsky (Agron) approached Arthur Ruppin in 1914 and asked him which career—agriculture or engineering—would best benefit the Zionist enterprise. Ruppin, the head of the Palestine Land Development Company, grappled with the question but was unable to give a clear-cut answer. As it turned out, Agronsky's career took another direction entirely: journalism. In 1915, he began contributing articles to the Philadelphia *Jewish World*. Two years later, he became editor of the Zionist organ, *Dos yiddishe folk*. After moving to Jerusalem, Agronsky worked as a correspondent and in various press-related positions until he became editor-in-chief of the *Palestine Post* in 1932.[24]

Zionist youth movements gave their members information and indispensable preparation for life in Palestine. Movement leaders were attuned to the needs of the Yishuv. For example, Yosef Baratz of Kibbutz Degania, an emissary *(shaliah)* to the Zionist labor movement in America, suggested to members of Kvutzat Gordonia from Philadelphia that they specialize in poultry farming. The movement sent nine members to Petaluma, California, a center for poultry farming, in 1937. Each member specialized in one of the stages of poultry breeding and raising. Five members migrated as a group to Palestine in 1929, remaining together for two additional years.[25] Specialization in this field and the importation of the leghorn hen and other superior breeds led to production standards almost comparable to those in the United States. Figures from the mid-1930s show that the average hen in the kvutza laid 150 eggs a year, at a time when the Arab peasant's yield averaged a maximum of 70 to 80 eggs.[26] American olim may not have been solely responsible for this difference, but they presumably had an impact.

Not all American halutzim (pioneers) specialized in a vocation that was deemed especially needed in Palestine. Many, like their American Jewish counterparts today, chose more academic fields. In the mid-1930s, Avraham Revusky, a journalist for New York's Yiddish-language daily, the *Morgen zhurnal,* suggested that American pioneers

> would be much more valuable in the building of Palestine if every one of them before leaving the United States prepared himself thoroughly in some trade which could be usefully practised in Palestine. Palestine has an excess of college-trained engineers and architects; there is also an inexhaustible source of unskilled laborers in the poverty-stricken ghettos of Eastern Europe. Yet there is an actual lack of practical electricians, automobile mechanics, plumbers, experienced bricklayers, carpenters, and sundry qualified factory workers. In all these trades, as well as in special branches of agriculture, American experience is highly valued and appreciated. . . . [N]o country can supply such quantity and quality of

corporals of labour as the United States, which serves as the supreme source of technical knowledge for all backward countries in the process of growth.[27]

In an address delivered before the Second Annual Conference of the Palestine Land Development Council in 1923, Brandeis took a slightly different tack: "The greatest of all Palestinian resources is the human resource; I mean this not only spiritually, but economically," he declared. "What may we not expect from the Jewish mind, Jewish persistence, Jewish ingenuity and Jewish capital, when employed in a country which is congenial, in a climate which is admirable and in surroundings which will call out the best that is in men."[28]

In the field of industrial development, many American olim realized the practical contributions, particularly of facilitating immigrant absorption and fostering the growth of a higher standard of living that could be obtained through industrialization. Typically, their projects can be described as industrialization through the utilization of a skilled labor force operating advanced machinery, rather than through labor-intensive operations.

An early example of American initiative was the Palestine Knitting Works, established in 1921 as the first power-driven plant in the Middle East. Operating with state-of-the-art machinery, the plant produced scarves, shawls, sweaters, blankets, underclothing, dress materials, ties, and other clothing from wool, artificial silk, and a mixture of the two.[29] The factory was founded by Alexander Landsberg, a former Jewish Legionnaire. Following the war, Landsberg returned to America to settle his affairs, selling a long-established business in Brooklyn. He returned to Palestine via Poland, where he purchased a completely equipped knitting factory. Landsberg also arranged for the immigration of a staff of mechanics to install and operate his plant. His old friend and Zionist coworker, Robert Kesselman, assisted in setting up the plant in Jerusalem's Kerem neighborhood, negotiating with the customs office and with national authorities, and generally promoting support for "home industries." One of Landsberg's difficulties was his lack of sufficient working capital. Another was his decision to use artificial silk; he soon discovered that there was greater local demand for woolen goods. Eventually, however, his business expanded to an annual production of £E 10,000, with twenty-five workers. Demand for the factory's products was so great that

## THE SIGN OF QUALITY MADE IN סמל שׁל איכות

**HASOREG** / הסורג

MEDALS AWARDED 1924-5 PALESTINE זכו במדליות תרפ״ד-ה

## ALL KINDS OF KNITTED GARMENTS
IN
# SILK,
# WOOL,
AND
# COTTON
FOR
## MEN, WOMEN
### and CHILDREN

Ladies Underwear
in Artificial Silk

Netting, Underskirts,
Knitted Neckties

## HASOREG KNITTING WORKS, LTD.

Ramath-Gan (Tel-Aviv)   o   o   Telegr. Addr.: Hasoreg Ramathgan Tel-Aviv,   o   o   Code A.B.C. 5th edition

Advertisement for Hasoreg Knitting Works, founded by American Alexander Landsberg (*Palestine and Near East Economic Magazine*, 1931, p. 320)

Advertisement for "New Marbadia," a carpet company developed with American capital (*Palestine and Near East Economic Magazine*, 1931, p. 320)

it could have employed three shifts, but the lack of skilled labor restricted the staff to one fully-staffed and one partially-staffed shift.[30]

Another example of American attempts to utilize technology was the American Fruit Growers of Palestine, Inc. The growers believed that modernized, mechanized packaging of citrus fruits would increase the fruit's value and result in lower labor costs. Working conditions, moreover, would be improved with the arduous manual labor being replaced by more skilled work. The group established a 1,200–square-meter plant on a plot in Petah Tikvah in 1921. A 26–meter-deep well was dug to supply the necessary water. A 40–horsepower motor powered the fruit washing and brushing machines, conveyer belts, and machines that sorted the fruit according to size, a method used in California. The labor was needed for quality control, wrapping the fruit, and placing it in crates.[31]

After less than two years of operation, the company had incurred debts of over £E 2,262. The reason, according to Moshe Novomeysky, was that "after the first year, when a certain portion of the oranges were slightly damaged during the packing . . . the colonists refused to expose their product to risks, unless adequate security was afforded by the factory. The latter, however, could not give any such guarantee because of a lack of funds." In a letter to the Anglo-Palestine Bank in January 1923, one of its creditors, company president L. J. Lippman, explained that the plant was engaged in reorganizing and was attempting to increase its liquid capital. These efforts, however, were unsuccessful, and the property and inventory were put up for sale.[32]

A different direction for industrial development was specialization. One of the most successful American enterprises established in Palestine was the American Porcelain Tooth Manufacturing Company, Ltd., which flourished despite predictions of an insufficient local market. Samuel Simon Bloom, born in Lithuania in 1860, had immigrated in 1882 to the United States and had slowly built up a prosperous artificial tooth factory. He developed strong Zionist sympathies, visiting Palestine and taking an active role in fund-raising. Already at the 1909 Federation of American Zionists convention in New York, he expressed his intention to open a branch factory in Palestine.[33]

Bloom was affiliated with the Brandeis group and supported its approach to building Palestine through both national and private initiative. Relocating his factory to Palestine, he decided, would foster the growth of the Jewish economy and provide employment for local inhabitants and future immigrants. Accordingly, Bloom settled in Pales-

**Table 1.** Palestinian Exports of Artificial Teeth and Industrial Products for Various Years

| Year | Export of Artificial Teeth, £P | Industrial Exports, £P | Artificial Teeth as a Percentage of Industrial Exports |
|---|---|---|---|
| 1930 | 10,325 | 365,350 | 2.82 |
| 1932 | 13,429 | 312,392 | 4.30 |
| 1934 | 28,585 | 294,243 | 9.71 |
| 1936 | 34,431 | 417,078 | 7.72 |
| 1938 | 30,732 | 639,604 | 4.80 |

Source: Government of Palestine, *Statistical Abstract of Palestine, 1937–1938* (London, 1939), 74–75

tine in 1926, locating his factory on Maged Street in the Nahalat Itzhak neighborhood of Tel Aviv, where there was cheap labor available. Eighty percent of the employees were young women, aged fourteen to twenty, who were engaged in physically easy and clean work. The demand for artificial teeth at that time exceeded the supply.[34]

By February 1927, Bloom's plant employed forty-two workers and was operating at 50 percent capacity, producing 15,000 teeth a day. But conditions in Palestine were not conducive to production, since the raw materials—feldspar, gold, and platinum—had to be imported with an import duty of 12 to 15 percent. Bloom, in a "very bitter" act of protest, announced the closing of his factory (in which he had already invested £P10,000), arguing that completed artificial teeth were being admitted customs-free to Palestine, and that it was illogical to tax the raw materials.[35] Notwithstanding the difficulties, Bloom kept his factory going. His product had gained a reputation with the British dental community and was much in demand. By 1934, approximately 180 workers were employed and the product had taken an important place in the country's export economy. (See Table 1 and Figure 3).[36]

Louis D. Brandeis took pride in this particular enterprise. He noted that "the sale of £P 10,000 (in 1930) of artificial teeth to England is an indication of what Jewish ingenuity, courage and determination can achieve for Palestine."[37]

A final example of American attempts at industrialization is the

Interior of the American Porcelain Tooth Manufacturing Company, 1931 (CZA photograph collection 696)

Meshi concern. Meshi's founder was Isaac Sacks of Paterson, New Jersey, who owned a similar artificial silk factory in the United States. Established in Ramat Gan in 1932, Meshi was intended both to provide employment for a large number of workers, decent wages, and proper working conditions in a modern factory. To ensure a sufficient supply of energy for the factory and other new developments nearby, the Palestine Electric Corporation set up a transformer near Ramat Gan; Sacks himself purchased £P 4,000 worth of shares in the utility. Further assisting the new factory, which was expected to employ 100 workers, were tax exemptions and reduced water rates provided by the Ramat Gan Council.[38]

Sacks eventually invested more than £P 150,000 in Palestine, £P 77,320 of that in the factory. Despite the benefits outlined above, the factory operated at a disadvantage. Labor for Japanese producers cost one-fifth of what it cost local producers. High duty on raw material and low tariffs on manufactured goods further hindered the growth of this

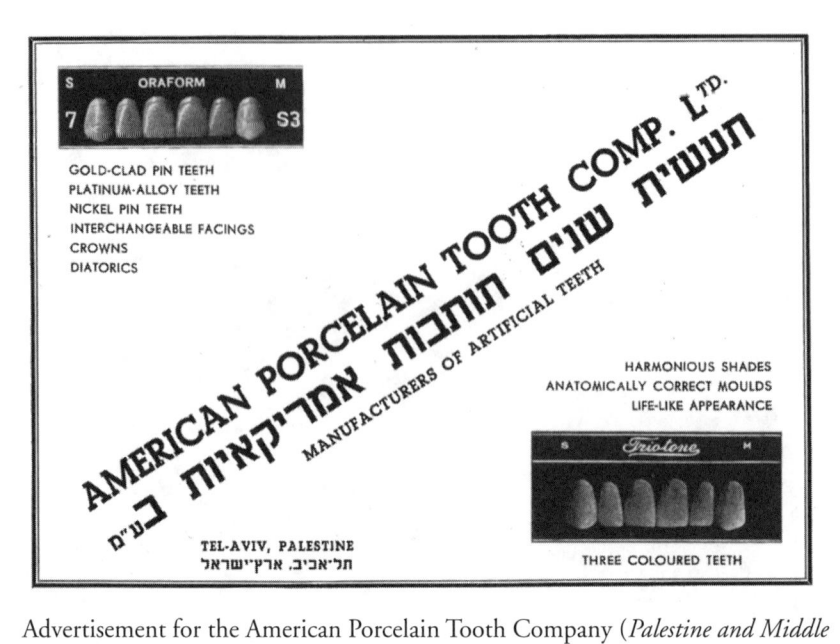

Advertisement for the American Porcelain Tooth Company (*Palestine and Middle East Economic Magazine,* 1938)

industry. By 1933, however, there were sixty-six mechanical looms in the factory, with another twenty en route from the United States.[39]

To allow for more efficient production, Sacks also established a second factory, Argaman, for dying textiles. This allowed for control of a number of phases of production. Nonetheless, both factories had limited success during their first years; their losses were offset by profits from Sacks's citrus orchards. Only during World War II did the two factories become profitable, when the importation of foreign silk was virtually halted because of difficulties in international shipping.[40]

### Instruction, Education, and the Diffusion of Technology

Americans could transfer technology, but this did not necessarily result in its diffusion and the desired improvement of conditions in Palestine. Realizing this, a number of American olim put aside their personal advancement and took on the task of training others. For example, following World War I, Louis Kantor noted the difficulty "in obtaining installation [of house sanitation and plumbing] in proper workmanlike manner, as no plumbers were available. Tinsmiths, locksmiths, and blacksmiths undertook the work with faulty results."[41] To improve the situation, Kantor (who, as previously noted, was one of the heads of the anti-malaria campaign) began to instruct a group of local plumbers. Later, he traveled to various towns and gave classes to architects, plumbers, and engineers.

Notwithstanding the progress that had been made in the field of medical care, it was clear that the local population needed to be trained to provide these services. A continuous flow of olim trained in nursing and other fields could not be expected, and even if they did arrive, their integration and acculturation would take a number of years. In November 1918, forty Jewish women began studying nursing in a program based on the American curriculum. In his history of Hadassah, Marlin Levin outlined certain difficulties between the European and American approaches:

> The European physicians at Rothschild [Hospital] had their own idiosyncracies. They objected strongly to a three-year period of training for nurses, which they thought was overlong. They considered theoretical classroom work a waste of time. On the Continent, nurses learned all they knew in the wards, and were never required to utter more than an obedient "Yes, sir" or "No sir." And here was Hadassah teaching them to give intramuscular injections, to take blood pressure, to do all sorts of preventive work that was the private preserve of the physician.[42]

Henrietta Szold personally took an active role in the development of the Hadassah Nurses Training School. The first class of 22 nurses graduated in 1921. Ten years later, the school had produced 135 registered nurses.

Accounting was another profession strongly influenced by American olim. Robert Kesselman arrived in Palestine in 1919 and was employed by the Department of Public Works until 1926, when he established his own firm. According to his biographers:

> One of the main difficulties with which Kesselman had to contend during the first years of his private accountancy business was the lack of trained assistants. Each man he wished to employ in his office he had to train and teach. . . . [I]n his fifteen years' work as private accountant in Palestine, he trained many dozen, perhaps even hundreds, of boys and men for good jobs. Sometimes, especially in later years, he used to say, "I am tired of just teaching all the time." Nevertheless he went on teaching

Straus Medical Center, Jerusalem, circa 1935 (CZA Keren Hayesod photograph collection)

and training. He imbued his staff not only with much practical knowledge in all branches of accountancy and auditing but also with the ethics of the profession. He often spoke to them about professional ethics of accountancy which, he held, must be as clean and holy as that of a priest.[43]

Instruction in the field of agriculture was particularly important, and American agronomists played an important role in the process of advancing more productive methods. Nathan Fiat, for example, received his M.Sc. at California University. After coming to Palestine, he lectured on poultry husbandry and beekeeping at the Mikveh Israel Agricultural School (1928–1937) and Herzliya College (1933–1937). He then took up the position of principal at the Kadoorie Agricultural School.

Although Hebrew was the lingua franca of the Yishuv, mastery of the English language was necessary in order to communicate with British government officials. Sylva Gelber (a Canadian) recalled that "I took my tenuous steps into the world of urban wage earners by seeking a few young people who might wish to improve their knowledge of the English language. Quite apart from its cultural value, English was essential in a country administered by Britain."[44] A large number of American olim found employment in English-language instruction and other vocations that required proficiency in English. Following a period of employment with the American Zion Commonwealth, Nellie Straus Mochenson (1892–1933) moved to Tel Aviv to teach English at the Herzliya Gymnasium. She later edited the English section of the Hebrew daily, *Davar*.[45] American Itzhak Avinoam (Grossman), an expert in literature and pedagogy at New York University, also taught English at the Herzliya Gymnasium. Language instruction, of course, included not only the transfer of proficiency, but also cultural values.

Poale Zion in America understood that Palestine could not be developed unless the halutzim were properly equipped. During 1920–1921, the organization collected money, machinery, and tools for the Palestine Workers' Fund. Altogether, the campaign yielded equipment valued at $250,000. Accompanying the shipment to Palestine was "Chaver Kesselman" of Cincinnati, an engineer with expertise in farm equipment, who was sent to provide instruction to the halutzim.[46]

An important project developed by the Hadassah organization was *Tipat Halav* (A Drop of Milk), a program for infant and child welfare. Something similar had originally been developed for the underprivileged neighborhoods of New York, with funding provided by the American Jewish philanthropist Nathan Straus. The architect of the program in Palestine was an American-born nurse, Bertha Landsman, who founded the first infant and mother welfare station in Jerusalem in 1921. Landsman drew upon her experience in America at the Straus center in New York, but adapted the project to local conditions and culture. Infant mortality at that time was high: as of 1922, 144 Jewish children out of every 1,000 died before their first birthday. By 1930, the mortality rate had dropped to 69 per 1,000, in part because of the care provided by Tipat Halav. Twenty-two stations were in operation by 1931. Impressed by its success, the British Mandatory government adopted a similar program for the Arab population in Palestine, and also implemented programs in Cairo, Amman, and Baghdad.[47]

Dietician Julia Aronson arrived in Palestine in 1920. She had been drafted by Henrietta Szold to teach nutrition at the nursing school, but also went out into the field. Pioneers at Migdal, for example, were suffering from mouth diseases caused by poor nutrition. Aronson provided them with guidelines for healthier and more economical diets.[48]

Searchlight on Hadassah (*Palestine and Near East Economic Magazine*, 1938)

## SEARCHLIGHT

THE essence of Life is change, and the essence of a programme to preserve Life lies in its dynamic quality, its ability to meet new demands, to enlarge or contract its activity in one field or another as Life dictates. If one reviews the work of Hadassah in 27 years of service in Palestine, one feels in it this vital quality of movement and adaptability.

Hadassah accepted responsibility for the health section of the Foundation pro-

Corner: Child welfare is one of the main objects of Hadassah, for which it has established an extensive system of medical and non-medical services.

Arc (from top downwards): 1. In the school eye clinic, infected children receive daily treatment.
2. The Henrietta Szold School of Nursing supplies the country with a corps of highly trained nurses.
3. Orthopedic class in the Hadassah Nathan and Lina Struas Health Centre in Jerusalem.
4. Supervised play in one of the Guggenheimer Playgrounds administered by Hadassah.
5. A Youth Aliya group arrives at the port of Tel Aviv.

## ON HADASSAH

gramme during the World War because devastated Palestine itself called for medical help, and the World Zionist Organization recognized that malaria, trachoma, typhoid, cholera and dysentery had to be wiped out in order that the pioneer, the road labourer, the farmer, the builder might begin his work of construction.

*Hospitals*

Its first task was to open hospitals in the main cities of Palestine where

Corner: New Hadassah University Medical Centre on Mount Scopus, Jerusalem—for healing, teaching, and research.

Arc (from top downwards): 1. Oriental mother receiving prenatal care in one of Hadassah's infant welfare stations.
2. A complete system of clinics is attached to Hadassah's hospitals.
3. Lessons in first aid are given by the nurses of Hadassah's School Hygiene Department.
4. Feeding and teaching are combined in the School Luncheons activity.
5. Children in Meir Shefeye receive agricultural training.

These two examples illuminate the comprehensive approach to health and welfare that was characteristic of American Zionists. A third example was the Straus Health Centre, whose cornerstone was laid by the second High Commissioner for Palestine, Field Marshal Lord Plumer, on March 2, 1927. In an address given at the ceremony, Straus explained that

> the laying of the cornerstone of a Health and Welfare Centre in Jerusalem is the realization of my fondest dreams, the crowning satisfaction of all that God has given me the means and the will to do for the alleviation of suffering and of aiding my fellow men. Through this Health and Welfare Center we shall endeavor to introduce some of the latest American methods of sanitation and hygiene in the Holy Land, which are bound to prove of the greatest benefit to all its inhabitants, regardless of race or creed.[49]

Plans for the Health Centre were prepared by a local architect, Benjamin Chaikin, with the assistance of a mostly American professional committee. Before final approval, the blueprints were reviewed by a New York hospital expert. The three-story structure, simple in outline and built around an inner garden court, is built of roughly cut rose-tinted Jerusalem limestone. At its opening, the ground floor housed a model of a pasteurization plant, the Straus Soup Kitchen, a department of nutrition, and a prenatal and infant welfare station. In addition, the first floor had a lobby used for health exhibits. To the left of the lobby were the school hygiene department, the dental clinic, the public health reading room, and the council room. To the right were the administrative offices, the department of health education, the adult health examination clinic, and the lecture hall. The upper floor was given over to the day nursery, the corrective gymnasium, two club rooms, and showers. Large terraces leading off of the nursery and gymnasium were used for outdoor play and gymnastic drill. (See Figure 4.)[50]

## Conclusion

This paper has outlined different aspects of the influence of American olim on the development of Palestine between the two world wars. It is necessary to place this influence in perspective. First, it was limited in scope, mainly because of the small number of olim. Between 1919

**Table 2.** American Immigration to Palestine, 1919–1939

| Period | American Citizens | Total Jewish Immigration | Percent of Total Jewish Immigration |
|---|---|---|---|
| 1919–1923 | 601 | 35,101 | 1.71 |
| 1924–1931 | 1,158 | 73,435 | 1.58 |
| 1932–1939 | 4,261 | 186,097 | 2.29 |
| 1919–1939 | 6,380 | 294,633 | 2.17 |

Source: A Gertz, ed., *Statistical Handbook of Jewish Palestine, 1947* (Jerusalem 1947), 100

and 1939, American citizens accounted for approximately 2.2 percent of the total Jewish immigration to Palestine (see Table 2).[51] Of these immigrants, between a quarter and a third were affiliated with the ultra-Orthodox community. Residing in segregated communities, their influence was quite limited. In addition, approximately half of the American olim had been born outside the United States and thus may have been less influenced by American society than were American-born olim.

American olim, moreover, were not the only source of American innovation. American know-how was conveyed to Palestine indirectly through scientific literature, and directly through scientific interchange and by human agents.[52] Apart from olim, there were also residents of Palestine who studied in America, and American experts who visited Palestine.[53]

It should also be noted that American olim appear to have played a more important and dominant role during the earlier interwar period. This is best observed with regard to the medical professions, where the early role of American physicians was eclipsed by German Jewish doctors in the mid-1930s. In 1932, there were 476 licensed physicians in Palestine. This number jumped to 1,849 in 1935, mainly as a result of the migration of German-speaking Jewish doctors (68 percent of the doctors had been educated in Germany, Switzerland, and Austria). As a result of this impelled migration, the medical profession became dominated by Jews from Central Europe. As Doron Niederland has ably argued, these immigrants did not need to assimilate. By sheer numbers, along with expertise and experience, they were able to effect change, becoming responsible for developments in surgery, radiology, psychiatry, pharmacology, and medical research.[54]

As products of a free immigration, American olim had a greater stake in the transfer of technologies, ideas, and values. In their minds, they were in Palestine in order to shape a society they wanted to live in. In this regard, it is noteworthy that the majority of their endeavors were not limited to the Jewish population. Rather, the olim used their resources for the betterment and benefit of the entire population of Palestine.

As John A. Jackson has explained: "Although migration is expressed through the actual movement of individuals from A to B, that movement contrasts and compares two whole societies which continue to exist in encapsulated form in the migrant individual whose experience straddles and to an extent reconciles each to the other."[55] American olim in the interwar period illustrate this observation. Indeed, a powerful motivation for their aliyah was the hope that "America" could not only be brought over, but also improved upon, in a new Jewish society.

## Notes

1. For a detailed discussion of American Jewish immigration and settlement between the two world wars, see Joseph B. Glass, *From New Zion to Old Zion: American Jewish Immigration and Settlement in Palestine, 1917–1939* (Detroit, 2002).

2. Louis D. Brandeis, "The Zeeland Memorandum," *Statement to the Delegates of the Twelfth Zionist Congress on Behalf of the Former Administration of the Zionist Organization of America* (New York, 1921), 51–57.

3. *Bulletin of the Zionist Society of Engineers and Agriculturalists* 1, no. 1 (Nov. 1919), Central Zionist Archives, Jerusalem [henceforth CZA], F25/298.

4. Marlin Levin, *Balm in Gilead: The Story of Hadassah* (New York, 1973), 35–64. For a list of the American Zionist Medical Unit personnel, see Henrietta Szold, New York, to Albert Lucas, New York, 13 November 1919, Central Archives for the History of the Jewish People, Jerusalem [henceforth CAHJP], P3/1037.

5. Israel J. Kligler, "The Fight Against Malaria," *Menorah Journal* 11, no. 5 (October 1925), 497–501; Zvi Saliternik, "Notes," *Cathedra* 32 (July 1984): 182–89 (in Hebrew); see also Louis D. Brandeis, Washington, D.C., to Jack Mosseri, n.p., 24 Sept. 1919, in *Letters of Louis D. Brandeis*, vol. 4, ed. by Melvin I. Urofsky and David W. Levy (Albany, 1971–1978), 427; Louis D. Brandeis, Washington, D.C., to Julian William Mack and Bernard Flexner, n.p., 6 October 1921, in ibid., vol. 5, 19; Levin, *Balm in Gilead*, 78, explained that "with methods proven in Panama during the construction of the canal, new cases were reduced by 90 percent." Other sources, including Kligler, do not draw a comparison to the American experience in Panama.

6. Levin, *Balm in Gilead,* 77–78; Solomon J. Weinstein, Jerusalem, to Marcus Esterman, Haifa, 5 October 1920, CZA L65/478.

7. *Bulletin of the Zionist Society of Engineers and Agriculturalists* 1, no. 1 (November 1919), CZA F25/298. The bulletin included the following list of completed and fairly advanced projects: *Public Utilities*—national shipping, dock, and harbor development; receiving and distributing stations; hospitals, markets, slaughter houses and refrigerating plants; water power development, sewage disposal plants, water supply, highways and railroads. *Agriculture and Agricultural Plants*—fertilizers, creameries, poultry raising, fruit packing, canning, preserving and evaporating, vegetable packing and preserving, agricultural byproducts, sorghum plant, peanut industry, sugar factory. *Industrial*—textiles, clothing, shoes, tanning factory, salt plant and utilization of byproducts of Dead Sea, olive oil plant, cement mill, brick kilns, trim mill, furniture.

8. Elias Gilner, *War and Hope: A History of the Jewish Legion* (New York, 1969); Samuel Rodman, "Ha-Gedud Ha-Ibri," *Kadimah* (New York, 1918; rpt. 1977), 15–22.

9. David Ben-Gurion, *Israel: A Personal History* (New York and Tel Aviv, 1971), 42, 843.

10. David Ben-Gurion, Jaffa to the Center Committee of Poale Zion in America, n.p., 10 October 1919 (in Hebrew), in *Ben-Gurion's Letters,* vol. 2, edited by Yehuda Erez (Tel Aviv 1971–1974), 8–11.

11. Telegram, Chaim Weizmann and [?] Cohen, London, to Zionist Organization of America, New York, 18 November 1920, in *The Letters and Papers of Chaim Weizmann,* vol. 10, edited by Leonard Stein (Oxford, 1968), 88.

12. Palestine Service and Information Bureau, Zionist Organization of America, "Statistical Report on Applicants and Registrants for Immigration to Palestine from America," New York, 31 May 1920, CZA F25/33. The report does not differentiate among country of residence in its listing of occupations. Included in the report were 733 applicants from Canada, one from Australia, 10 from South America, and 14 not reported.

13. Louis D. Brandeis, Washington, D.C., to Bernard Flexner, n.p., 12 February 1919, *Letters of Louis D. Brandeis,* vol. 4, 380–81.

14. Bernard A. Rosenblatt, *Social Zionism (Selected Essays)* (New York, 1919), 13.

15. Bernard A. Rosenblatt, *Two Generations of Zionism: Historical Recollections of An American Zionist* (New York, 1967).

16. For further discussion of American women in Mandatory Palestine see Joseph B. Glass, "Immigration of American Jewish Women to Eretz Israel, 1918–1939," *Women in the Yishuv and Zionism: A Gender Perspective,* ed. Margalit Shilo, Ruth Kark, and Galit Hasan-Rokem [Hebrew] (Jerusalem, 2001); Joseph B. Glass, "On American Jewish Women's Place in the Promised Land: Their Spatial Distribution and Locational Decisions in Palestine, 1917–1939," *Untold Stories: American Jewish Women in the Yishuv and Early State of Israel,* ed. Shulamit Reinharz and Mark A. Raider (Hanover, Mass., in press); Bertha Badt-Strauss, *White Fire: The Life and Works of Jessie Sampter* (New York, 1956), 68–70.

17. Bertha Schoolman, "3 American Pioneers in Israel," *Hadassah Newsletter* 36, no. 5 (January 1956): 15.

18. Horace M. Kallen, *Utopians at Bay* (New York, 1958), 264; Schoolman, "3 American Pioneers in Israel," 4, 15; Elisha Efrat, *Deborah Kallen: Her Life and Work* (in Hebrew; Jerusalem, 1959), 13–21. Among those employed at the school was Fanny Soyer, an American graduate of the Teachers' Institute at the Jewish Theological Seminary. See Ezra Mendelsohn, "An American Educator in Eretz Israel: Three Letters from Fanny Soyer to Rebecca Letz" (in Hebrew), *Cathedra* 72 (June 1994): 97–98. The school never had a permanent location, moving from Abyssinia Street to the Rehavia neighborhood and then to the Hadassah hospital compound on the Street of the Prophets in 1939. At that time, it was renamed the Julian W. Mack School and Workshops. It remained in operation until 1948.

19. Alexander M. Dushkin, *Living Bridges: Memoirs of an Educator* (Jerusalem, 1975), 38.

20. Levin, *Balm in Gilead,* 80. Michal Hagitti, in "A Rest-Home for Agricultural Laborers in Jerusalem," 1919–1923" (in Hebrew), *Cathedra* 30 (December 1983): 98, downplayed the role of Hadassah.

21. Irma L. Lindheim, *Parallel Quest: A Search of a Person and a People* (New York, 1962), 21–22; *Hadassah Newsletter* 8, no. 21 (29 June 1928): 3–5.

22. Menachem Mendel Freidman, "Memoirs" (in Hebrew), Tel Aviv University Archives, Tel Aviv, T-11/263, 128–29; Moshe Novomeysky, "The Industries of Palestine, Its Conditions and Prospects," *Bulletin of the Palestine Economic Society* 4–5 (May 1942): 16.

23. German Jews also prepared themselves prior to emigration to Palestine. See Nachum Gross, "The Absorption of University-Educated Immigrants in the 1920s and Hydrological Research" (in Hebrew), *Zionism: Studies in the History of the Zionist Movement and of the Jewish Community of Palestine* 12 (1987): 132–39.

24. Agronsky (1893–1959) was born in the Ukraine and immigrated with his family to the United States in 1906. He joined the Jewish Legion in 1918 and was demobilized in Palestine. Gershon Agronsky, Philadelphia, to Arthur Ruppin, Jaffa, 17 May 1914; Arthur Ruppin to Agronsky, 4 June 1914, CZA A209/12; Arthur Ruppin, *Three Decades of Palestine: Speeches and Papers on the Upbuilding of the Jewish National Home* (Jerusalem: 1936), 88–149.

25. Yaacov Levin, "Kvutzat Gordonia in Philadelphia," *Pioneers from America: 75 Years of Hechalutz, 1905–1980* (Tel Aviv, 1981); Kenneth L. Kann, *Comrades and Chicken Ranchers: The Story of a California Jewish Community* (Ithaca and London, 1993), 22–27.

26. Avraham Revusky, *Jews in Palestine* (London, 1935), 39, 136.

27. Ibid., 273.

28. Louis D. Brandeis, *Brandeis on Zionism* (New York, 1942), 134–35.

29. Anon., "Trade and Commerce in Our Land," *The Judean* 3, no. 8 (January 1923): 177; anon., *Rough Notes of the Secretary for Trade and Industry of the Palestine Zionist Executive* 8 (9 December 1923): 2–3.

30. *Rough Notes,* 2–3; Naomi Patai and Raphael Patai, "A Builder of Zion:

The Life and Letters of Robert D.(Reuven David) Kesselman," CZA A168/13, 255; Palestine Knitting Works, "Statement of Income, Profit & Loss, for the period of four months, from September 1 to December 31, 1922," CZA S8/2093.

31. Copy of Certificate of Registration of the American Fruit Growers of Palestine, Inc., 23 March 1923, CZA A417/33; A Levontein, "Report on the American Fruit Growers of Palestine, Inc. Packing House," 3 Av 5683 (16 July 1923), CZA S1/680.

32. Novomeysky, "Industries of Palestine," 16; L. J. Lippman, New York, to Anglo-Palestine Bank, Jerusalem, 8 January 1923, CZA L51/188; George C. Cobb, American Vice Consul in Charge, Jerusalem, to Emanuel Mohl, Jerusalem, 3 March 1923, CZA S1/680; M. Freidenberg, Jerusalem to the President, District Court as Chief Execution Officer, Jaffa, 14 August 1924; Philip Vadas and Jacob Behor, n.p., to the President, District Court, Jerusalem, n.d., CZA A417/33.

33. Julius Haber, *The Odyssey of an American Zionist: Fifty Years of Zionist History* (New York, 1956), 167.

34. S. S. Bloom, Tel Aviv, to S. Patterson, Director of Customs, Excise and Trade, Jerusalem, 20 February 1927, CZA S25/525 (reference to this file graciously provided by Michael Brown); "Artificial Teeth," *Palestine and Near East Economic Magazine* 1, no. 2 (15 July 1926): 84; David Tidhar, *Encyclopedia of the Pioneers of the Yishuv and Its Builders* (in Hebrew), vol. 1 (Tel Aviv, 1947), 204.

35. Frederick H. Kisch, n.p., to S. Patterson, Director of Customs, Excise and Trade, Jerusalem, 27 February 1927, CZA S25/525; "Artificial Teeth Factory," *Palestine and Near East Economic Magazine* 2, no. 4 (26 February 1927): 91; cf. S. S. Bloom, Tel Aviv, to the Executive Council of the Zionist Organization, London, 3 April 1927, CZA S25/525

36. *Palestine and Middle East Economic Magazine* 8, no. 1 (January 1933): 42; David Gurevich, *Statistical Abstract of Palestine, 1929*, (Jerusalem, 1930), 159–65.

37. Louis D. Brandeis, Chatham, Massachusetts, to Maurice Beck Hexter, n.p., 7 Sept. 1930, *Letters of Louis D. Brandeis*, vol. 5, 453.

38. *Palestine and Middle East Economic Magazine* 7, nos. 12–13 (August 1932): 330; ibid., 7, nos. 14–15 (September 1932): 374–75.

39. N. J. Thischby, Jerusalem, to the Chairman, Standing Committee for Commerce and Industry, Government of Palestine, Jerusalem, 22 November 1933, CZA S8/2093a. Sacks paid an average of 250 mils for an eight-hour day. Labor costs per 100 yards of silk fabric were £P 4 in Palestine compared to £P 0.8 in Japan.

40. Tidhar, *Encyclopedia of the Pioneers*, vol. 1, 420.

41. Louis Kantor, "Ten Years of Public Health Engineering in Palestine," *Palestine and Middle East Economic Magazine* 7–8 (1933): 314; Levin, *Balm in Gilead*, 77–78.

42. Levin, *Balm in Gilead*, 67–68; Henrietta Szold, Jerusalem to the Hadassah Chapters of the United States and Canada, 9 December 1920, CAHJP, P3/851.

43. Patai and Patai, "A Builder of Zion," 256.

44. Sylva M. Gelber, *No Balm in Gilead: A Personal Retrospective of Mandate Days in Palestine* (Ottawa, 1989), 41.

45. Alice L. Seligsberg, "Nellie Straus Mochenson," *Hadassah Newsletter* 18, no. 6 (March 1938): 109, 118.

46. Jacob Katzman, *Commitment, The Labor Zionist Life-Style in America: A Personal Memoir* (New York, 1975), 151–56.

47. Levin, *Balm in Gilead*, 81–86; "Familiar Letter from Palestine": Henrietta Szold, Jerusalem, to the Chapters of Hadassah in the United States and Canada, 3 August 1922, CZA 125/10.

48. Dushkin, *Living Bridges*, 47–53; Levin, *Balm in Gilead*, 75–76.

49. *Hadassah Medical Organization, The Nathan and Lina Straus Health Centre, Jerusalem, First Annual Report (October 1930–September 1931)* (Jerusalem, 1932).

50. Ibid.

51. The number of American olim was apparently higher than the figures provided in this table. See Glass, *From New Zion to Old Zion,* introduction, for a detailed discussion of American immigration statistics. Jews, it should be noted, were not the only immigrants to Palestine during this period. Altogether, 31,352 non-Jews immigrated to Palestine between 1920–1944, of whom 583 were non-Jewish American citizens. See David Gurevich and Aaron Gertz, ed., *Statistical Handbook of Jewish Palestine, 1947* (Jerusalem, 1947), 115.

52. For an example of a study that investigates various avenues for the diffusion of American influences, see Baruch Rosen and Ionel Rosenthal, "American Influences on the Development of the Pasteurized Milk Industry in Eretz Israel" (in Hebrew), *Cathedra* 71 (March 1994): 35–60.

53. Palestinian residents sent for training in the United States, particularly in agriculture, were at first mainly the sons of the farmers from the First Aliya (1882–1900), although their ranks also included members of the Sephardi elite and halutzim from the Second Aliya (1900–1914). American Jews were their sponsors. The training took place in California, which closely resembled Palestine in climate, geologic formation, and agricultural problems. A group known as the "Californians" began to study in the United States before World War I and remained there until the cessation of hostilities. At that time, nine of them received the assistance of Baron Edmond de Rothschild and the Jewish Colonization Association to settle in the "model colony" of Binyamina. There, the "Californians," including an expert in irrigation and a veterinarian and animal husbandry expert, instructed local farmers in agricultural methods imported from the United States. See Ever HaDani [A Feldman], *Binyamina* (in Hebrew) (Binyamina, 1953), 40–67. Eldwood Mead and Robert Nathan were two visiting American experts who attempted to influence the development of Palestine. According to S. Ilan Troen, the activities of these experts "reflected an attempt to export a quintessential American ethos of capitalism, efficiency and individualism." In his view, "American experts were not merely exporting socially-neutral technologies but the social and economic experience of America's development of its own frontiers." See S. Ilan Troen, "American Experts in the Design of Zionist Society: The Reports of Eldwood Mead and Robert

Nathan," *Envisioning Israel: The Changing Ideals and Images of North American Jews,* ed. Allon Gal (Detroit and Jerusalem, 1996), 193–96.

54. Doron Niederland, "Influence of German-Jewish Immigrant Doctors on Medicine in Eretz Israel, 1933–1948" (in Hebrew), *Cathedra* 30 (December 1983): 111–60.

55. John A. Jackson, *Aspects of Modern Sociology: Migration* (London, 1986), 2.

# Armchair Travelers to the Holy Land

## The Travel Accounts of Rev. J. Lynch, OSF

Margaret M. McGuinness
*Cabrini College*

"Poor," "immigrant," "needy," and "uneducated" are terms often used by chroniclers of American Catholic history during the late nineteenth and early twentieth centuries. The Catholic population of the United States increased by about 10 million between 1880 and 1910, an increase due primarily to immigration from southern and eastern Europe. The newcomers tended to be poor, unskilled peasants. They did not speak English and were usually illiterate. Bishops and priests found a way to help such needy Catholics by building a system of charity and social services designed to prevent them from becoming destitute.[1]

The clerical leaders of American Catholicism had to raise a great deal of money in order to provide for the material *and* spiritual wellbeing of needy Catholics. One hierarchical concern that transcended class boundaries was providing a religious education for all American Catholics. In 1884, when the Third Plenary Council convened in Baltimore, it was obvious that the issue of parochial schools was a priority of the bishops.[2] One-fourth of the decisions generated by the council involved the building and maintenance of parochial schools. Local pastors were to establish parish schools where none existed, the laity were to support these schools, and parents were to enroll their children in them. The final vote on this issue approved a resolution that such schools were to be built within two years; any pastor who did not comply with this request was subject to removal from his parish.[3] All of this would, of course, cost money.

In addition to an educational system (that would become the largest alternative to the American public school), other services were instituted to aid the immigrants. Leaders of American Catholicism created and administered a system of hospitals, social settlements, orphan asylums, and homes for the aged.[4] The results were impressive: an observer of Catholic life in Chicago commented that it was "patent that the Roman Catholic church is unexcelled in charities."[5]

If this system of social services was to operate efficiently, money had to be found for its establishment and maintenance. Not all American Catholics were poor. Jay P. Dolan has observed that the American Catholic community "had a large middle class made up of American-born sons and daughters of Irish and German immigrants," and cited one study of early twentieth-century American Catholics that estimated that 20 percent of this population was engaged in middle-class, mainly low white-collar, occupations.

> Beneath this group were blue-collar working-class Catholics, people employed in skilled occupations, many of whom owned their own homes. These two groups, the white-collar middle class and the skilled blue-collar working class, made up a large part of the Catholic community at the turn of the century. These were the people who were sending their sons and daughters to college in increasing numbers in the late nineteenth and early twentieth centuries; these were the ethnic and religious leaders in the community.[6]

Similarly, David J. O'Brien notes: "The story of American Catholicism... was never simply one of an immigrant church over against non-Catholic America, for the church the immigrant found when he arrived was already deeply rooted in the American soil."[7] There was a part of the Catholic population in the United States that had a little "extra" money. Not rich, by any means, they were the donors for the various charitable projects undertaken by their local ordinaries, priests, and religious communities.[8] By the closing decade of the nineteenth century, some had even been asked to contribute to projects and institutions located in other parts of the world, including the Holy Land.

In February 1891, Pope Leo XIII issued a pontifical letter on the shrines of the Holy Land. The pontiff was worried that the amount of money being raised for the upkeep of the holy places was insufficient, since the Franciscans had recently assumed a number of building projects, including the Chapel of the Flagellation on the Via Dolorosa (1838) and two chapels on the Mount of Olives (that at Bethfage in 1883 and the Dominus Flevit in 1891). As travel became easier, more and more faithful Catholics desired to make a pilgrimage to the Holy Land. The pope noted that money to maintain and preserve the sacred shrines was traditionally derived from three sources: offerings made by pilgrims at the various sanctuaries, collections taken by friars on fundraising missions, and specific collections for the Holy Land. Leo XIII ended the letter by announcing he was placing all funds raised for this purpose under the guardianship of the papacy. Implied in the pope's letter is the view that as more Catholics went on pilgrimage to the Holy Land, more money would be needed to maintain the shrines.[9]

In light of this development, middle-class American Catholics came to be viewed as potential donors. The Franciscans had to convince these Catholics, many of whom knew virtually nothing about the most sacred places of their tradition, that their donations were for a very worthy and special cause. Although their sons and daughters may have been given a grand tour of Europe, such travel probably did not include the Holy Land. More important, those Catholics themselves had never visited any of the Holy Places, and were unaware of their significance for Catholicism.

One avenue used to educate devout Catholics about the Holy Land was what amounted to a travelogue serialized in the *Franciscan Tertiary* in the 1890s.[10] The author and pilgrim, Father J. L. Lynch, OSF, described and commented on the region's sights and sounds for the magazine's readers.[11] Lynch's account appeared in the monthly magazine over the course of a dozen-and-a-half issues.[12] During this time, Lynch regaled the magazine's readership with an eyewitness account of the holy places, as well as providing his own interpretation of the current conditions a nineteenth-century pilgrim would find in this holiest of lands. He reminded English-speaking Catholics that the work of the friars was crucial to preserving Christian historic tradition. For instance, prior to his arrival in Jerusalem, Lynch wrote, "In Nazareth, the care of the entire Catholic population is in our hands; and all the holy spots there recorded are in our charge."[13]

Karen Armstrong contends that during the latter half of the nineteenth century, "Western travelers arrived in Palestine in search of facts. Unlike the pilgrims of old, they were not there to explore the sacred geography of the spirit but to find historical evidence that their faith was true."[14] As a Franciscan writing for an English-speaking Catholic readership, Lynch painted a portrait that placed the shrines of the Holy Land within the context of the life and work of Jesus of Nazareth. He took his readers from Bethlehem, where Jesus was born, to Calvary, where he died. "Calvary is all sorrow, Bethlehem all joy, Nazareth all peace, Mount Sion, where He held his 'Last Supper,' all love."[15]

American Catholics of the late nineteenth century were familiar with a Eucharistic spirituality. Catholic theology teaches that Jesus suffered and died for the world, but is present in the Eucharist under the signs of bread and wine. Through the sacrifice of the Mass and reception of the Eucharist, American Catholics were reminded (at least weekly) that Jesus was indeed the suffering Savior. An additional way for Catholics to remember the suffering of Jesus was by participating in the devotional rite known as the Stations of the Cross. This practice, popular among American Catholics from most immigrant groups, reminded the devout how Jesus physically suffered while he was on earth.[16]

When Lynch wrote about following the Stations of the Cross on the Via Dolorosa, he knew that his readers—albeit thousands of miles away—could relate to what he was saying and feeling. Perhaps they would even appreciate the implied connection he made between the ancient world and their communities in the United States at the dawn of the twentieth century:

> We have for once in our lives, wended our way along the same road that Jesus carried His Cross; we have followed Him along it from Pilate's Hall to Calvary. . . . What wonder is it then, that the children of St. Francis who, Friday after Friday, for over seven centuries, have performed this same devotion, should have spread it throughout the length and breadth of Christendom.[17]

During the Stations of the Cross devotions at their local parish, American Catholics unable to visit the Holy Land could remind themselves that devout pilgrims in another part of the world were actually following the paths where Jesus walked on his way to die.

Lynch and his party found accommodations in lodgings and hospices administered by Catholic religious orders in and around Jerusalem. His advice to prospective pilgrims was to avoid "hotels" managed by "schismatics" and "infidels." Stopping in Jaffa prior to his arrival in

Jerusalem, Lynch wrote: "There are two or three hotels in Jaffa where the traveller may put up, if he prefers to do so rather than stay in the Convent; but there is this difference, especially for the Catholic: he feels himself a perfect stranger, a prey to the schemes of wily Asiatics."[18] Inherent in this statement was the idea (common among American Catholics at this time) that one is always better off dealing with one's "own kind" if at all possible.

The serialized reports aimed at enlightening the educated layperson about some of the region's complicated history. While ruminating about the history of Jaffa, Lynch provided a rudimentary (albeit romantic) timeline for the "armchair traveler" to the city: "Here once came the fleets of Hiram of Tyre, with their loads of cedar for Solomon's temple; here came the Crusaders with Louis of France, a Franciscan Tertiary, to rest his army; here too, Napoleon rested. . . ."[19] Several months later, upon climbing to the summit of Nebi Samuel in order to attain a good view of Jerusalem, Lynch wrote: "Here it was the soldiers of Godfrey of Bouillon caught sight of Sion. Here their banners waved in the breeze. Here their cries of joy made Moslem hearts tremble away in Jerusalem."[20]

In August 1892, just prior to the publication of his Holy Land travelogue, Lynch informed his readers what they would be finding in subsequent pieces:

> Tertiaries will be glad to follow me in spirit through the spots so hallowed by a God-Man's presence, and so loved by their Holy Founder, who came there himself, and in his poverty left his children that inheritance, the guarding of these sacred spots—an inheritance which they have never abandoned, and which even today, as well as for the past seven centuries, they, and they alone, have guarded and preserved, both from the greed of the Moslem as well as from the fanaticism of the schismatical Greek, so that the children of the "west" might and may pray at the cradle of Bethlehem as well as near the tomb of the Crucified.[21]

Lynch's background material on the Christian shrines of the Holy Land reflected Christian legends still prevalent at the end of the nineteenth century. Helena Augusta, mother of the Roman emperor Constantine, was responsible for many of the Christian discoveries of the fourth century. Writing about the Church of the Holy Sepulchre, Lynch repeated the common view that the Basilica was planned by Helena, the mother of Constantine, and was partially destroyed when Jerusalem was sacked.[22] (The church was destroyed several times before falling into Moslem hands again in 1187.)

Lynch's description of the church was a clear appeal to his readers' emotions, as well as to their sense of history and tradition:

> There it is; its large heavy door, near which we perceive a Moslem soldier, recalls a time other than the present. The ornaments are all Gothic. The work of the Crusaders is seen in the sculpted bosses, in the tracery in the massive tower to our left. It is sad to see, as if an incarnation of victory over the Christian soldier, the Moslem guard just a step within.[23]

The readers of the *Franciscan Tertiary* may have had a somewhat limited knowledge of the history of the Holy Land and its region, but if they were the recipients of a Catholic school education, they had at least a dim memory of the Crusades. The series of Catholic attempts to capture the Holy Land from the Moslem "infidels" was familiar territory, and readers following Lynch's journey were reminded of this era in medieval history.

The history of the Crusades covers many years, and is quite complex (in many ways, we are still living with their legacy today). Suffice it to say that by 1187 the Muslims had regained control of Jerusalem. Lynch informed his devout readers that since then, Catholics had been restricted in worshipping at their sacred places. In fact, some Christian shrines and churches had been transformed into Islamic sites. Upon arriving in Ramleh (on the way to Jerusalem), Lynch told his readers that the city came into view "with its lofty tower, which once belonged to a Christian church. Now it is a minaret of a miserable mosque."[24] While there, Lynch wrote, he had been "accosted by what seemed to me a fanatic Turk" who offered him coffee. Even the Moslem infidels, he wrote reassuringly, respected and loved the Franciscans. "It was strange to be so kindly greeted by a Moslem; but there the Fathers are loved by all, as they show kindness to all."[25]

In contrast to the friar's obvious hostility to the Islamic presence in the Holy Land, one finds surprisingly little anti-Jewish sentiment in Lynch's pilgrimage account. Lynch does, however, describe his sadness over how the Holy City of Jerusalem had suffered as the result of being administered by non-Christians. While visiting the Valley of Josaphat, he wrote: "They are so bare and bleak these Moslem and Jewish cemeteries." In the same installment, when looking back towards Jerusalem after leaving, he lamented, "How lonely the 'Holy City' looks! What a picture of ruin!"[26]

It was the Eastern Orthodox Christians, however, who bore the brunt of Lynch's hostility. Their presence in the shrines of the Holy Land was a source of anger and bitterness, marring an otherwise ethereal pilgrimage. Even if lay readers did not appreciate the reporter's invective, priests and bishops reading Lynch's "travel diaries" could empathize with his views. Roman Catholic bishops in the United States had not welcomed Eastern rite colleagues with open arms when they began emigrating to America in the late nineteenth century. The Eastern rite clergy brought with them a different liturgical rite (as opposed to the Latin rite practiced by Roman Catholics in the United States) and permitted a married clergy.[27]

Clearly Lynch considered the Greek Orthodox and Armenian Churches to be quite different from Roman Catholicism. In his view, the only solution was for those "schismatics" to accept the authority of Rome. Until such time as this took place, the Church of the Holy Sepulchre would have to be shared among different rites within Christianity. Lynch assumed a prayerful tone as he wrote: "Heaven grant that better days may dawn, and that Greek and Armenian may enter the fold they have left, and then, as brothers, shall we pray willingly by their side."[28]

In a later installment, when describing the "House of Caiphas," he wrote: "The place is now occupied by an Armenian Church. This Sanctuary, for such, indeed, it is, once belonged to the Franciscans, but Schismatic intrigues and Turkish greed have combined to take this place from Catholicity."[29] Lynch was saddened that Mass could not be offered at this site, but consoled readers with: "We can still celebrate Holy Mass on Calvary, on Christ's Tomb, in Gethsemani, in Bethlehem, in Nazareth, and with the few, I can say, unimportant Sanctuaries held, or rather robbed from us, in Jerusalem, every hallowed spot in the Holy Land is still in the possession of the Catholic Church."[30]

The Franciscan's travelogue expressed his contempt for Protestantism as he neared the end of his travels. "Ignorant of the country, of its language, of its traditions, a stranger in the East, Protestantism, in trying to make believe that the traditions of many of the Holy Places are monkish superstitions, merely shows forth its own gross stupidity."[31] His enmity was sure to resonate with American Catholics, who were having their own unpleasant experiences with Protestants.

Lynch's series on the Holy Land ended in 1893, the same year that another Franciscan, Charles Vissani, established *The Crusader's Almanac.* This magazine was devoted exclusively to the Christian shrines of the Holy Land. Between 1897 and 1899, the heirs of Francis would invent a more visual and experiential way to bring the Holy Land to American Catholics—they would complete the Monastery of Mount St. Sepulchre, which included a full-scale reproduction of the Church of the Holy Sepulchre in Jerusalem. The friars of this Washington, D.C. monastery even organized group pilgrimages to the "Holy Land" in America. Catholics without the financial means to travel to the Middle East needed only to travel to the nation's capital to enjoy a vicarious experience of the Holy Land. Perhaps some of these American pilgrims gained their first views of the "real" Holy Land by reading Lynch's accounts in the *Franciscan Tertiary.*

## NOTES

1. See Aaron I. Abell, *American Catholicism and Social Action: A Search for Social Justice, 1865–1950* (Garden City, N.Y., 1960); Richard Linkh, *American Catholicism and European Immigrants (1900–1924)* (Staten Island, N.Y., 1975).

2. A plenary council is a meeting of all of the archbishops and bishops of a country.

3. See, for example, Jay P. Dolan, *The American Catholic Experience: A History from Colonial Times to the Present* (New York, 1985), 262 ff.; James J. Hennesey, SJ, *American Catholics: A History of the Roman Catholic Community in the United States* (New York, 1981). From the theological perspective, the parochial school system allowed parents to "hand on the faith," while the "practical" reason was that American public schools were looked upon as Protestant. See Dolan, *American Catholic Experience,* 276.

4. Dolan, *American Catholic Experience,* 321ff.

5. Quoted in ibid., 328.

6. Ibid., 147–48; the *U.S. Catholic Historian* 13 (Summer 1995) centers on social activism, with articles on Catholics and labor unions, social settlements, and children's social services.

7. David J. O'Brien, "The Ambiguity of Success," in *The Renewal of American Catholicism,* ed. David J. O'Brien (New York, 1972), 89.

8. Recent research has begun to focus on the Catholic middle class during the latter half of the nineteenth century. The winner of the 1995 Notre Dame Studies in American Catholicism award is a manuscript entitled "Beyond Ethnicity: Victorian Catholics and the Crisis of Americanization," by Paul G. Robichaud, CSP.

9. Pope Leo XIII, quoted in "The Sanctuaries of Jerusalem and the Franciscan Missions of Palestine," *Franciscan Tertiary* 1 (July 1891): 507–10.

10. *The Franciscan Tertiary* was published under several names (all similar) over a period of years in the late nineteenth and early twentieth centuries (hence we find several volumes number "one.") Teresa Schafer, reference librarian at St. Bonaventure University, Buffalo, New York, has informed me that the magazine originated in Dublin, Ireland, but was intended for all English-speaking Catholics. Issues of *The Franciscan Tertiary* consulted for this article were found at the Archives of the Archdiocese of Philadelphia and the American Catholic Historical Society, St. Charles Borromeo Seminary, Philadelphia.

11. Franciscan priests and brothers use the initials OFM or a variant (OSM for sisters) following their names. Tertiaries are secular members of the order who follow a modified rule; they may be married.

12. Previous to its series on the Holy Land, the magazine had published accounts of Lynch's travels to other parts of the Middle East where the Franciscans operated.

13. Rev. J. L. Lynch, OSF, "Franciscan Missions in Syria, Palestine and Egypt," *Franciscan Tertiary* 1 (February 1892): 697.

14. Karen Armstrong, *Jerusalem: One City, Three Faiths,* (New York, 1996), 361.

15. Lynch, "In and Around the Holy City," *Franciscan Tertiary* 2 (April 1893): 375.

16. Joseph P. Chinnici, OFM, contends that both the celebration of the Eucharist and devotions such as the Stations of the Cross did more than remind Catholics of Jesus; they "helped make the church a community that could unite the rich and the poor, the person and the institution, the male and the female, the Irish, the American, and the German, time and eternity." Joseph P. Chinnici, OFM, *Living Stones: The History and Structure of Catholic Spiritual Life in the United States* (New York, 1989), 78.

17. Lynch, "In and Around the Holy City," *Franciscan Tertiary* 2 (March 1893): 346–47. In all the issues, Lynch's article took the same title, as each article formed a segment of a single report.

18. Lynch, *Franciscan Tertiary* 2 (September 1892): 151.

19. Lynch, *Franciscan Tertiary* 2 (October 1892): 186.

20. Lynch, *Franciscan Tertiary* 2 (December 1892): 250.

21. Lynch, "Franciscan Missions in the Moslem Empire," *Franciscan Tertiary* 2 (August 1892): 124.

22. "By the middle of the fourth century," Armstrong notes, "Christians tended to believe that she rather than Constantine and Makarios had supervised the excavations at Golgotha. It was also said that she had discovered the relic of the cross on which Jesus had died." Armstrong, *Jerusalem,* 387.

23. Lynch, *Franciscan Tertiary* 2 (January 1893): 272.

24. Lynch, *Franciscan Tertiary* 2 (October 1892): 187.

25. Ibid., 188.

26. Lynch, *Franciscan Tertiary* 3 (May 1893): 12–13.

27. During the late nineteenth century, American bishops were divided over many issues. They were united, however, in excluding any sort of married clergy.

At the same time, the bishops wanted to maintain jurisdiction over Oriental Rite Catholics. They were successful in both areas. "On April 12, 1894, Propaganda [Fide] issued a circular letter to all bishops of the Latin Rite. Oriental prelates, it said, were ordered not to send a priest to the United States or other Latin Rite territories, unless he was celibate or widowed, had obtained the permission of the bishop of the place to which he was going, the written authorization of the Propaganda, and the proper faculties of his own bishop," Gerald P. Fogarty, SJ, *The Vatican and the American Hierarchy from 1870 to 1965* (Collegeville, Minn., 1985), 62–63.

28. Lynch, *Franciscan Tertiary* 2 (February 1893): 310.
29. Lynch, *Franciscan Tertiary* 2 (April 1893): 377.
30. Ibid.
31. Ibid., 378.

# The Franciscan Monastery in Washington, D.C.

"The Holy Land of America"

David Klatzker
*Temple Ner Tamid, Peabody, Massachusetts*

---

By recovering and scrutinizing a wide variety of physical objects—from architecture and paintings to embroidered samplers, calendars, and greeting cards, among other things—scholars are today revealing how, time and again, Americans have pressed the material world into the service of their religious beliefs. As students of American popular culture see it, the Durkheimian dualism of the sacred and the profane has obscured the more typical mingling of spirituality and materialism. Along these lines, they reject the distortion that Protestant piety is focused only on the Word, while Catholic devotion is made incarnate in things, although no one doubts that there are differences in nuance between the two Christianities.[1]

Research into the America–Holy Land relationship has much to contribute to this new wave of material culture studies. For the Protestant founders of America, an interest in the Holy Land was a natural extension of their religious and national self-understanding. To think of America as a new "promised land" did not quench, and may even have deepened, their thirst for physical contact with the places familiar to them from the scriptures. A small number of Americans managed to travel to the Holy Land in the nineteenth and early twentieth centuries, although the journey was expensive and time-consuming. Once they arrived in the land of their imaginings, they were usually appalled by the conditions there: the flies, the trachoma and other rampant disease, the frightful poverty. The experience awakened most travelers to the discrepancy between their idealizations and the reality of things as they really were.[2] It was much easier, and far more pleasant, to bring the Holy Land to America by purchasing vicarious substitutes such as water from the Jordan River, marble chips from Jerusalem, and paintings, stereographs, and photographs of the biblical landscape. Artists, photographers, and entrepreneurs were pleased to oblige their customers' desire for the romantic and picturesque.[3]

But there was yet another option for material concretization of the Holy Land. Palestine could be transported to America by constructing safe, sanitized, and easily assimilated replicas of the sacred places.[4] The two best-known examples of this phenomenon are the 1874 "Palestine Park" at Chautauqua, New York (a 350–foot topographic model of biblical hills, cities, and bodies of water), and the much larger "Jerusalem" of the 1904 St. Louis World's Fair (an 11–acre compound, contoured to resemble the hills and valleys of the Holy City, filled with full-scale models of such structures as the Church of the Holy Sepulchre and the Western Wall, and peopled by one thousand actual Palestinian natives).[5] There can be no doubt that exoticism and the fun of playacting brought many visitors to these elaborate "stage sets"—thus, adult visitors to Chautauqua often wore oriental dress, and World's Fair patrons pretended that they were shopping in the *souk*. But the creators of these places always underscored the fact that this make-believe was intended with the utmost seriousness. Their aim, they insisted, was to teach "useful" information about biblical geography, history, and customs. If they had been questioned more deeply, perhaps they would have admitted that they hoped to revivify the Bible, so distant in time and cultural space from modern America, and to resolve doubts about its authenticity.

In the same period, American Catholics constructed their own "Holy Land of America," as the Franciscan Monastery in Washington, D.C., is called. Unfortunately, access to the Franciscan archives has been restricted and only a few sketchy histories of the monastery are available; but the fact that even Catholic scholars are unfamiliar with the Washington "Holy Land" is due mainly to the sea change in Catholic belief and practice after Vatican II, a transformation so massive that it makes the symbols and values of the Franciscan monastery seem strange, and even a bit embarrassing.

"The Holy Land of America"

In 1880, the Italian-born Charles A. Vissani, OFM, established the Franciscan Commissariat of the Holy Land for the United States, located at first in New York City.[6] Like the commissariats in other countries, its chief duty was to raise funds for the shrines, parishes, schools, orphanages, and hostels in the Holy Land that were staffed by the Franciscans—the fabled "Custodia Terrae Sanctae" founded by St. Francis of Assisi in 1217, when he visited the territories conquered by the Crusaders.[7]

Father Vissani started a magazine, *The Crusader's Almanac* (1893).[8] The first issue announced a "new spiritual Crusade for the rescue and preservation of the Holy Shrines of Palestine." Catholics wishing to be enrolled in this "Army of the Holy Cross" were asked to contribute at least twenty-five cents a year to the work of the Commissariat. Children and the deceased could also be enlisted. The major benefits of membership were special masses said on the donors' behalf by Franciscan fathers in the Holy Land, and plenary indulgences (total remission of temporal punishment due to sin) "on Christmas and Easter and in the hour of death, and a partial one every Friday." This was a spiritual reward equal to what actual pilgrims to the Holy Land would receive. Also, small souvenirs of Palestine were given in gratitude to anyone who would sell almanacs, certificates, and medallions. Such items were not to be regarded lightly: it was suggested that miraculous cures could be obtained by applying the blessed Crusader's Medal.[9]

A less traditional argument for supporting the work of the Franciscans turned on the contemporary American interest in historical preservation:

> Let us take George Washington's birthplace. What is not being done to preserve the house where he first saw the light? To keep in good order the ground where he played in childhood? His last home? Societies have been established, and ladies of every state have claimed their right to display their zeal in memory of the liberator of America. No blame is to be laid on them; nay, they deserve praise from every sensible man. But what should we think of Catholics who acknowledge Jesus as the Redeemer, who pretend to love Him, to be His faithful children, and still are so indifferent to preserve His sacred monuments?[10]

These various appeals for donations, in addition to the traditional Good Friday collections from churches all over the United States, became a major source of support for Franciscan activities in the Holy

Land.[11] Over the next century, funds collected by the American Franciscans would be used to build a 100–room addition to the Casa Nova hostel in Jerusalem, a new pilgrim house ("Our Lady of America") in Nazareth, and the Basilica of the Transfiguration on Mt. Tabor.[12] However, the most remarkable construction project of the American commissariat was undertaken right at home, in Washington, D.C., from 1897 to 1899—the impressive Monastery of Mount St. Sepulchre.

Located on a large plot in suburban Brookland, near the recently opened Catholic University of America, the monastery was largely the achievement of Vissani's successor, Godfrey Schilling, OFM. Its construction, involving many skilled Catholic laborers, was mainly financed through the purchase of model "building stones" that were sold at 10 cents each ($1.00 per row), a cost within reach not only of the Catholic middle class but also the working poor.[13] The monastery church was designed in a modified Byzantine style, with a floor plan in the shape of a five-fold cross—an emblem found throughout the building—representing the five wounds of Christ, and also establishing a connection to the Holy Land by recalling the coat of arms of the Crusader Latin Kingdom of Jerusalem. Over the front entrance are inscribed the arms of Godfrey de Bouillon, rescuer of the Holy Sepulchre from Muslim hands.[14]

The church building contains a full-scale reproduction of the Holy Sepulchre in Jerusalem, incorporating an antechamber and tomb. Other chapels within the same edifice recreate the grotto of the Annunciation in Nazareth, and the grotto of the Nativity in Bethlehem. In the "Gethsemane Valley" to the south of the monastery are faithful copies of the grotto in Gethsemane, a typical Jewish tomb, and the tomb of the Blessed Virgin. The chapel of the Ascension in the valley closely resembles the medieval Crusader church (now a Muslim mosque) on the Mount of Olives.[15]

On September 17, 1899, more than 10,000 people attended the dedication of the monastery. The solemn ceremonies were conducted by Cardinal Gibbons and Msgr. Martinelli, the papal delegate to the United States. In a lengthy description of the event, the *Washington Post* emphasized the medieval pageantry and display, which conveyed the "coming of age" of the American church and its desire to create an identity based on architecture. The *Post* noted the careful attention to detail shown by the builders:

The foremost ecclesiastical architect of Rome, Senor Aristides Leonori, has given his best efforts. For the purpose of making them exact facsimiles, he visited Bethlehem, Nazareth and other sacred spots, taking measurements and keeping in mind the character of stone and structure.... One of the grottoes representing the inner and outer portions of the Sepulchre has a piece of the actual stone of the Sepulchre, brought from Palestine by special dispensation.... The reproduction of the Stable at Bethlehem is perfect in every detail, with a small stone manger in which the child was laid, and the defacement which modern vandalism has wrought.... The inner tomb [of the recreation of the Holy Sepulchre] shows the great marble slab placed there to keep the relic hunters from chipping away the stone. The slab also bears the crack, which was placed in the original to keep the Turks from carrying it away.[16]

The fact that the Washington replicas are based on places mentioned in the New Testament, rather than sites associated with the Hebrew Bible, probably tells us something about Catholic Bible-reading habits. Most Catholics would likely say that Jesus' presence in Palestine made the land "holy." However, not all of the Franciscan reproductions are based on places in the Holy Land; for example, there is an exact duplicate of the shrine near Assisi in Italy where St. Francis established his order. The Franciscans probably found the Holy Land too limited a spatial focus for their devotional aims—wherever in the world they find themselves, the life of St. Francis is set up as a model of inspiration.

Within the church building, as is typical in Catholic shrines, realistic paintings are used to commemorate biblical events. For example, two flights of stairs above the Holy Sepulchre, by the Altar of Tabor, is a huge bas-relief with portable figures of Jesus, Moses, and Elijah, modeled after a picture by Gustave Doré; the figures can be moved to convert the Transfiguration into the Resurrection.[17] However, it seems especially noteworthy that the Franciscans made an effort to balance indoors and outdoors types of spirituality. Outside of the church, they erected stone Stations of the Cross and planted rose gardens. The quiet, pastoral atmosphere encouraged an imaginative identification with Christ's passion. The experience of interiorization, not the image of the literal place, was the apparent object of the way of the cross. Perhaps the beauty of the monastery grounds was also intended to show that nature holds transcendental value—a characteristically American religious notion.

With almost militaristic organization, the Franciscans initiated large group pilgrimages to this new complex of American shrines. These pilgrimages were not strictly regulated by the liturgical calendar, but took place throughout the year. According to the Franciscans, about 60,000 pilgrims visited the monastery in a representative year, 1916.[18] Although pilgrimage served an essentially old-fashioned, conservative function, it was undoubtedly encouraged by America's transformation into a modern, leisure-oriented society in which tourism played a major role. In 1931, a large structure, Pilgrimage Hall, was erected as a rest station for visitors to the Washington site.

The appeal of the Franciscan monastery extended beyond Catholic circles. As the century progressed and fears of Catholicism receded, a larger proportion of Protestants began to visit. After World War II, Protestants comprised about 60 percent of the total number of pilgrims and tourists. In response to this new situation, the brothers and lay "Knights of Mount St. Sepulchre" who guided visitors had to be prepared to answer general questions about the Catholic faith.[19] However, unlike the Protestant creators of Chautauqua and the St. Louis World's Fair, the Franciscan tour guides do not appear to have ever placed much emphasis on teaching the history or geography of the Holy Land—there is an almost total lack of such information in the published descriptions of Mount St. Sepulchre. Inspiration, not education, was the point of a visit to the monastery. Ideally, visitors were to abstract themselves from the real world in which they lived in order to partake in a series of events that took place nearly 2,000 years ago; to bridge across the centuries and become one with Christ.

Similarly, the monastery's "Holy Land Museum" did not stress pedagogy. Over the years, the Franciscans acquired Palestinian arts and crafts that were put on display. These included chalices and icons as well as non-religious curiosities, such as a decorated game table and a mother-of-pearl Great Seal of the United States. These diverse objects formed a meaningful whole only in terms of a sentimental attachment to the Holy Land. At the nearby gift shop, the souvenirs for sale also appear to have focused on religious experience. Olive-wood crucifixes and picture postcards of the duplicate shrines made attractive tokens of heightened moments at the American "Holy Land."[20]

Did the Franciscan installation in Washington tend to displace the original holy places in the minds of the visitors who came there? On the contrary, the American shrines may have enhanced the supposed authenticity of the traditional loci in the Holy Land, just as copies of

"The Holy Land of America"

the Statue of Liberty or the Liberty Bell institutionalize the originals on which they are based. For their part, the Franciscans never abandoned their efforts to encourage religious pilgrimage to the real Jerusalem. A typical appeal read:

> Many say that they cannot go on a pilgrimage to Jerusalem. It is too far; the cost is too great; business cares or other worries keep them at home. That is often true, indeed; but everyone can do his share. The good work of the [Franciscan] Crusade cares for the pilgrims who have reached Palestine, shelters them, and in fact makes many pilgrimages possible.[21]

From the very beginning of the monastery, the Franciscans also intended to train English-speaking personnel for work in the Holy Land (appropriately, at a time when the American church was focusing much of its attention on the education of clergy).[22] Students at the "College of the Holy Land" were able to supplement their study of oriental languages, scripture, and biblical archaeology at the Catholic University. In 1901, ten students (out of about twenty) were taken on a pilgrimage-tour of the Holy Land. As of 1967, some sixty-five American friars had been sent to work in the Holy Land. These Americans, representing a variety of ethnic groups, were an important counterweight to the heavy Italian and Spanish coloration of the Franciscan establishment.[23]

The Washington monastery-church was also used to mark contemporary events in the Holy Land. During mass at Christmas 1917, for example, General Allenby's recent capture of Jerusalem was celebrated by the Franciscans. A letter from Cardinal Gibbons was read in which he rejoiced in the triumphant return of the holy places to Christian control.[24]

The "Holy Land of America" does not attract large numbers of visitors today. Christians of all denominations are more likely to visit the largest Catholic cathedral in America, the National Shrine of the Immaculate Conception (begun in 1920 and not completed until 1959), which is only about a mile away from the monastery.[25] But even without competition from another shrine, it is likely that the Franciscan monastery would have lost much of its cachet. The anti-modern impulse that characterized immigrant Catholic spiritual life provides a context for understanding the popularity of the Washington monastery in its heyday, from the turn of the century to about the 1940s—a period when Catholic immigrants and their children frequented ethnic-religious shrines and pilgrimage centers all across the United States. As the immigrants became more firmly rooted as Americans, they eventually abandoned many European-style devotions and expressions of *communitas*.[26]

There are many parallels from the same period that show American Catholics reproducing the holy places of the land of Jesus, thereby revealing an impulse to reach beyond the local and ephemeral to the transnational and transtemporal. The 1870s complex of duplicate shrines at the University of Notre Dame in Indiana includes a Holy Sepulchre and a Tomb of the Blessed Virgin.[27] The 1883 St. Anthony's Chapel in Troy Hill, Pittsburgh, Pennsylvania, contains a reliquary holding "a splinter of the True Cross and a piece of stone from the Holy Sepulchre": the altar "is said to contain a fragment of the table of the Last Supper."[28] The Benedictine abbey of Saint Bernard at Cullman, near Birmingham, Alabama, contains an extraordinarily detailed rock and marble miniature panorama of Jerusalem, carved by a lay brother from Bavaria, Joseph Zoettl (circa 1930).[29]

Interestingly, there is a more recent example of the same phenomenon, "Holy Land, U.S.A.," in Waterbury, Connecticut. The lifetime work of John Baptist Greco, a local Catholic lawyer, it consists of a 170–acre theme park with a chapel, stations of the cross, replicas of catacombs and Israelite villages, which are all fabricated from cinder blocks, bathtubs, and junkyard discards. The exhibit opened in 1957 and was closed to the public in 1984. A struggle over the future of the deteriorating park pitted those who saw it as ugly kitsch against an odd coalition of folk-art preservationists and conservative religionists. While it seems unlikely that "Holy Land, U.S.A." will ever be reconstructed, an illuminated cross on a hillside is still visible today to thousands of motorists on interstate highway I-84.[30]

As the Chautauqua and St. Louis World's Fair replicas of the Holy Land indicate, American Catholics were not alone in believing that, to be absorbed, sacred history must be recreated and reincarnated. The Franciscan monastery differs from the other "Holy Lands" mainly in its medieval architectural aesthetic and in its lack of interest in geographical and historical education. Umberto Eco suggests that Americans appear to crave a past "preserved and celebrated in full-scale authentic copy," although he offers only secular examples such as the colonial reconstructions in Williamsburg, Virginia, and Sturbridge Village, Massachusetts. "The American imagination," writes Eco, "demands the real thing and, to attain it, must fabricate the absolute fake"; he calls this "a philosophy of immortality as duplication."[31] With less cynicism and more respect for the mentality of average people, we can affirm Eco's insight and apply it to American material religion. By trying to uncover the motivations behind the various efforts to recreate the Holy Land in America, we learn not only how Americans have revered the Land, but also how they have situated themselves along the flow of history by affirming the value of the past.

## Notes

1. Material studies are a growth industry. Works of interest include John Dillenberger, *The Visual Arts and Christianity in America* (New York, 1989); Jenna Weissman Joselet, *The Wonders of America: Reinventing American Jewish Culture, 1880–1950* (New York, 1995); the online "Material History of American Religion Project" (http://www.materialreligion.org); Colleen McDannell, *Material Christianity: Religion and Popular Culture in America* (New Haven, 1995); David Morgan, ed., *Icons of American Protestantism: The Art of Warner Sallman* (New Haven, 1996); Leigh Erica Schmidt, *Consumer Rites: The Buying and Selling of American Holidays* (Princeton, 1995); Thomas J. Schlereth, *Cultural History and Material Culture: Everyday Life, Landscapes, Museums* (Charlottesville, 1992).

2. See David Klatzker, "American Christian Travelers to the Holy Land" (Ph.D. dissertation, Temple University, 1987).

3. See John Davis, *The Landscape of Belief: Encountering the Holy Land in Nineteenth-Century American Art and Culture* (Princeton, 1996); Yehoshua Nir, *The Bible and the Image: The History of Photography in the Holy Land, 1839–1899* (Philadelphia, 1985).

4. Moshe Davis was eager to see research on this aspect of the America–Holy Land relationship. His classic essay "The Holy Land in American Spiritual History" shows how broadly he conceived of the religiocultural dimension of America–Holy Land studies; see Moshe Davis, *With Eyes Toward Zion*, vol. 4: *America and the Holy Land* (Westport, Conn.), 11–42.

5. See Lester I. Vogel, *To See A Promised Land: Americans and the Holy Land in the Nineteenth Century* (University Park, Pa., 1993), 213–15; John Davis, "Holy Land, Holy People? Photography, Semitic Wannabes, and Chautauqua's Palestine Park," *Prospects* 17 (1992): 241–71; idem, *Landscape of Belief*, 88–97.

6. A brief biography of Vissani appears in *Franciscan Monastery Washington, D.C. Diamond Jubilee, 1899–1974* (Washington, D.C., 1974), 9.

7. *The Custody of the Holy Land* (Jerusalem, 1981), 8–15.

8. The magazine was earlier called *The Pilgrim of Palestine* (1885) and later retitled *The Messenger* (1888), then *The Advocate* (1889). Copies of the earlier newspapers do not seem to have survived. However, the full series of the *Crusader's Almanac* is available at the Commissariat of the Holy Land in Washington. According to the Franciscans, by the turn of the century, it was being published in

Polish and German as well as in English, with a combined circulation of 50,000 to 100,000.

9. *Crusader's Almanac* 2, no. 1 (1894): inside front cover.

10. *Crusader's Almanac* 7, no. 3 (April 1899): 7.

11. Pope Leo XIII issued a brief encouraging the Good Friday collections, *Salvatoris ac Domini Nostri,* in 1887. See Godfrey Hunt, OFM, "The Holy Land and the Good Friday Collection," *Ecclesiastical Review* 8 (March 1918): 241–48.

12. *Crusader Almanac* 4, no. 3 (1896): 12; ibid., 6, no. 1 (1898): 8; ibid., 32, no. 4 (1924): 5–9.

13. *Franciscan Monastery Washington D.C. Diamond Jubilee,* 18.

14. See the copious architectural descriptions in *The Franciscan Monastery: The Holy Land of America* (Washington, D.C., 1985) and Fremont Rider, *Rider's Washington* (New York, 1924), 423–35.

15. *The Franciscan Monastery,* 20.

16. *Washington Post,* 18 Sept. 1899.

17. Rider, *Rider's Washington,* 425.

18. *Crusader's Almanac* 24, no. 4 (July 1916): 8010.

19. *Franciscan Monastery Washington D.C. Diamond Jubilee,* 87.

20. Ibid., 49, 92–99.

21. *Crusader's Almanac* 10, no. 1 (1901): 2. For more details, see David Klatzker, "American Catholic Travelers to the Holy Land, 1861–1929," *Catholic Historical Review* 74, no. 1 (January 1988): 55–74.

22. This may have been viewed by the Catholic hierarchy as the major justification for the creation of the monastery. See Robert D. Cross, "The Meaning of the Holy Land to American Catholics in the 19th Century," in *With Eyes Toward Zion,* vol. 2: *Themes and Sources in the Archives of the United States, Great Britain, Turkey, and Israel,* ed. by Moshe Davis (New York, 1986), 339, n. 6.

23. Adalbert Callahan, OFM, *Medieval Francis in Modern America: The Story of Eighty Years, 1855–1935* (New York, 1936), 343–44; *New Catholic Encyclopedia* (New York, 1976), 4:11.

24. *Crusaders's Almanac* 26, no. 3 (April 1918): 15.

25. *Crusader's Almanac* 24, no. 4 (1916): 8–10; *Catholic Shrines and Places of Pilgrimage in the United States* (Washington, D.C., 1992), 121. It may be significant that this book is a publication of the Office for the Pastoral Care of Migrants and Refugees of the United States Catholic Conference. Do native-born American Catholics today feel the same interest as the foreign-born in visiting places of pilgrimage?

26. See Joseph P. Chinnici, OFM, *Living Stones: The History and Structure of Catholic Spiritual Life in the United States* (New York, 1989); Robert A. Orsi, *The Madonna of 115th Street: Faith and Community in Italian Harlem, 1880–1950* (New Haven, 1985); Ann Taves, *Household of Faith: Roman Catholic Devotions in Mid-Nineteenth-Century America* (Notre Dame, Ind., 1986).

27. McDannell, *Material Christianity,* 158.

28. J. Anthony Moran, *Pilgrim's Guide to America* (Huntington, Ind., 1992), 65.

29. Francis Beauchesne Thornton, *Catholic Shrines in the United States and Canada* (New York, 1954), 220–21.

30. Nick Ravo, "Kitsch Crusade: Artists Rally for Holy Land," *New York Times,* 3 August 1988, B1.

31. Umberto Eco, *Travels in Hyperreality: Essays* (San Diego, Calif., 1986), 6, 8.

# Jerusalem, Vilna, Chicago

## Gedaliah Bublick's Wartime Dilemma

Gershon Greenberg
*American University*

In the wake of the Holocaust, leading voices of the Mizrahi religious-nationalist movement turned even more intensely toward the land of Israel as the sole remaining hope for the future of the Jewish people. In Palestine, for example, Shlomo Zalman Shraggai (1899–1994) wrote that the appropriate response to the disaster was to channel all Jewish concern into restoring the Jews to Israel. The root of the Jews' historical and contemporary catastrophe, he wrote, was the metahistorical alienation between Jacob-Israel and Esau. Beginning from Israel's condition of landlessness and its inclination to misdirected quests for redemption, the Jewish condition had catalyzed Esau's hatred into an explosion. Jews bore indirect responsibility for the Holocaust, in Shraggai's view, insofar as they had not embraced Zionism fully, and with it, a chance for their own land-based redemption. Thus, the end of the Holocaust—objective historical facts notwithstanding—coincided in Shraggai's mind with the end to landlessness as a viable Jewish option.[1]

In America, Aharon Petshenik (1904–1965?) enunciated an apocalyptic response: the Holocaust was a by-product of redemption, functioning as the cleansing away of a generation that was incapable of restoring and moving to the land. As a result of the catastrophe, another generation would arise, which would have the courage to respond to the onset of redemption by taking over the land.[2]

Gedaliah Bublick, perhaps the leading Mizrahi ideologue in wartime America, responded differently. In the wake of the Holocaust he turned to the land of Israel and to America simultaneously.

Bublick was born in Grodno, Russia. He moved as a child to Bialystok and attended yeshivot in Lomza and Mir. In 1901, under an arrangement with the Jewish Colonization Association in Paris, he led a group of Bialystok Jews to join the pioneer Moisesville Colony in Argentina. He remained for three years, teaching at the local school. In 1904, he left for Chicago, and from there went on to New York. He visited the land of Israel briefly in 1920, and again from 1925 to 1928. On his return trip, he stopped to attend the world Mizrahi congress in Danzig. Years later, in 1945, Petshenik recalled Bublick's enthusiastic address dwelling on Mizrahi's accomplishments in the land of Israel and urging new efforts in developing the religious life there. In his address, Bublick had criticized the placement of a picture of Ahad Ha'am in a Mizrahi youth center. Ahad Ha'am, he declared, was irrelevant to Mizrahi's struggle against secular nationalism.

Back in New York, Bublick was appointed president of the American Mizrahi organization, which he had helped to establish in 1911. He served for four years and continued as honorary president until his death. His duties included representing the organization at the 21st Zionist Congress in Geneva in 1939. Bublick also helped to found the American Jewish Congress, and in 1918 served as its vice-president. Finally, he was a prolific journalist. His outlets included *Der id* and *Dos idishe togblat,* both of Warsaw, and *Idishe vokhentsaytung* in London. He edited and wrote for *Dos idishe togblat* (New York) beginning in 1915, and continued as contributing editor after it merged with *Der morgen zhurnal.*[3]

## Israel as Religion and Polity

Bublick's earliest work was an essay on "Hebrew Nationalism," published in *Ha'shiloah* in Berlin in 1898–1899. In this essay, Bublick described the Hebrew nation in terms of a dialectical relationship between the whole and its individual components. Nationality was a collective "I" composed of individual "I's." As the individual body was composed of many parts, each with its own special life, yet dependent upon the whole for existence, so every nation was composed of individuals who essentially derived their existence from their collective and mutual solidarity. Each person, in other words, was a "limb" of the body, drawing both moral and physical existence from the community. In the specific case of Israel, the nation's inner identity was defined in terms of the revelation of the Torah, assuming two primary forms of expression: religion and land-based polity. Although both were indispensable for Israel's ongoing existence, they could—and did—serve alternately in the course of history. Ultimately, the two forms would be integrated, and there would be a nation of Israel that lived through Torah and that assumed political form.

Bublick outlined four stages in the path of alternation between religion and polity. During Israel's first era, its spiritual-religious culture was suspended while the landed, political aspect dominated the national identity. Indeed, when the ten tribes were exiled from the land in 722 BCE, they were left without the spiritual wherewithal to resist assimilation, and thus disappeared. Religion emerged as the political reality of the land became destabilized. The turn to religion, represented by the prophet Jeremiah, became increasingly intense. By the time Nebuchadnezzar attacked, religion was strong enough for Israel to endure, even despite the loss of the land in 586 BCE. Religion's vitality was demonstrated again after Israel returned from exile in 538 BCE (when religious considerations motivated the Hasmonean revolt against the Greeks), persisting under Roman oppression, and for centuries thereafter.

The role of religion changed in the modern period. In the nineteenth century in Western Europe, religion declined in tandem with the rise in assimilation. Whereas Israel had once assumed the form of religion to survive, it now took on the form of Zionist politics. As Bublick pointed out, religion did remain vital among Jews of Eastern Europe, and their tie to the nation did not require any change in form. Notwithstanding, he argued, a global shift had occurred, and even those who were rooted in religion (himself included) were obliged both to recognize and to support the political reawakening.[4]

Thus, in Bublick's view, Israel's two basic aspects, political and religious, which had alternated in the past, would ultimately synthesize in the establishment of a religious nation in the land of Israel. Indeed, they had never been mutually exclusive; even when religion had dominated during the long period of exile, the people had drawn spiritual sustenance and hope from the idea of the land. The two forms were inherent to the essence of the nation, not only potentially but in the sense that without one or the other, the nation would die. Although religion's hold had been loosened during the nineteenth century, Bublick, in the era of political Zionism, sought a political reality that would capstone the entire history of Israel: a landed reality that was steeped in religion. As he put it in 1923:

> A land of Israel without Jewishness, a land of Israel which is little more than a slavish imitation of what the *maskilim* saw in the countries they were in before they came to the Jewish land—this is not the land of Israel that the Jewish people can accept. The Jewish people have always recognized and will always recognize only a land of Israel that is at one with the Torah of Israel.[5]

Noticeably absent in Bublick's scheme was any messianic overlay to his view of history's path, and any exploration of the role of the diaspora once the final coalescence took place. Bublick's depiction resembled an earlier uncited work by Heinrich Graetz, *Die Konstruktion der juedischen Geschichte* (1846), in which Graetz had identified preexilic history up to 586 BCE in terms of national, political, and social life. The struggle to actualize God, Graetz argued, unfolded within the political context. Afterwards, when the sociopolitical structure dissolved after 70 CE, religion emerged to dominate. Graetz described the post-70 CE era as one of reflection. Whereas Israel labored previously to consolidate according to world-historical values, namely polity, it now sought to distinguish itself among the rest of the world. Leaving behind its geographical isolation in the Near East, surrounded by mountain, desert, and sea, Israel went out into the world to be stimulated into self-definition. What did the near future hold? Graetz looked forward to the coalescence and synthesis of the political and religious-reflective stages into a religious state in Eretz Israel. For Graetz, the idea of land, polity, and religion was potentially present in Israel from the beginning, a Hegelian-like idea awaiting unfolding in empirical reality. Jewish history was now on the verge of culmination, where the three would be realized in a final synthesis.[6]

Bublick brought his views forward indirectly in an admiring portrayal, published in 1921, of Avraham Yitzhak Hakohen Kook (1865–1935), the chief rabbi of Palestine. For Kook, while exilic Judaism in the past drew its nourishment from images of the land that reflected its holiness, these images now had to be transformed into reality. Presumably because of changing conditions in the world, imagination could now subordinate itself to action. For Kook, nationalism and religion were inseparable: the spirit of God was present in the land, the language, Jewish history, and custom. Accordingly, the polity he sought was immersed in Torah-holiness. The fact that religionists and nationalists sought to exclude one another from the endeavor did not endanger the relationship. On the contrary, such denials implied prior and mutual recognition. Pious Jews, Kook believed, had to reach out to secularists and make efforts to link political nationalism with religion. For his own part, Kook preferred free-spirited nationalists over Jews who were disinterested in building the land; in his view, even violators of the halakhah who loved Israel and the land, and who wanted to build the nation, were to be preferred to pious Jews who sat on the side. Yet the goal was synthesis—and for Kook, such synthesis assumed messianic dimensions. The soul of the pious would be mended, he said, by making holy the violator's soul, while the soul of the violator would be mended by receiving the influence of the pious. The light of the messiah awaited the rapprochement: once bound together in the light, Israel would be ready for redemption. Although Bublick did not share Kook's messianic temperament, the melding of piety and Zionist nationalism in Kook's philosophy was at the center of his own program.[7] Moreover, Bublick concurred with Kook's positive approach to nonreligious Zionists. Herzl and Nordau were acceptable to the Orthodox, he wrote in 1923, because they were committed to building a Jewish state and made no presumptions about any new attitude toward religion. Ahad Ha'am, by contrast, was unacceptable:

> The Orthodox were liberal and did not demand that Herzl and Nordau and other free Zionists become Orthodox. But the Darwinist Ahad Ha'am in fact wanted Herzl and Nordau to believe in his "culture" and did not want to concede that one could be a Zionist solely by virtue of desiring to build up the land of Israel. The most dangerous fanatic is the radical fanatic, who wants to void Judaism from the Jewish nation, a nation that is holy and has a generations-long history. He cannot tolerate it when someone voids his new creation, "nationalism without Judaism."[8]

Salient aspects of the religious-nationalist synthesis are evident in Bublick's January 1941 synopsis of Ben-Zion Dinur's *Sefer hatsiyonut* (1938), in which he cited classical proto-Zionist texts that reflected his own views. The onset of the religious polity in the land, Bublick wrote, did not depend upon divine intervention in history but rather upon human initiative. Yehuda Halevi and Nachmanides believed that the prerequisite for redemption was that Israel *wanted* to be redeemed, and that this was evidenced by acts of restoring the land. In *Sefer shimush,* Ya'akov Emden (1697–1776) advocated action to restore the land— "Shake thyself from the dust, arise and sit down, O Jerusalem" (Is. 52:22), according to Emden, referred to the real labors and sufferings of the population of Jerusalem as they sought to rebuild the city. Redemption would follow the rebuilding.[9] In his biblical commentary, *Aderet Eliyahu,* the Gaon of Vilna (1720–1798) wrote that the verse, "But unto the place which the Lord your God shall choose out of all your tribes to put His name there, even unto His habitation shall ye seek, and thither thou shalt come" (Deut. 12:5) should be interpreted to mean that Jews first had to take the land of Israel by force, and then God would agree to their possessing it.[10] Bublick even cited the radical views of Yehonatan Eybeschuetz (1696–1794), as expounded in his *Ya'arot devash.* For Eybeschuetz, Jewish life without the restored House of David was pointless. Expulsion from the land, which was precipitated by Israel's sins, meant descent from life to death. Return to the land meant renewed life. Thus, so long as Jews remained unworthy to return, martyrdom was a suitable response to exile.[11] If Jews really grasped the tragedy of exile, they would be able neither to eat nor to drink, capable only of rolling in the dust of misery.[12] Suicide might have been preferable:

> If our predecessors knew that the exile would last so long, they would have killed themselves in anticipation of the great sorrow and trouble ahead; they would have ended their lives. For "Love is as strong as death" [Song of Songs 8:6]. As it is, we end our lives [little by little] whenever we remember how much good has been removed from us, and how much we have lost, day by day, year by year.[13]

Eybeschuetz explained that suicidal despair was the reason for attempting to predict an imminent end to exile. All of Israel would have been lost if the people realized how long the exile, a result of their own sins, would last.

Bublick's commitment to the uniqueness of Jerusalem was expressed in another work by Emden, *Siddur 'amudei shamayim,* in which he argued that just as no other land could replace the land of Israel, so too no other city could replace Jerusalem. When Jews did try to replace it they met with disaster—for example in Spain. Moreover, their expulsion from countries in which they had tried to establish a new

Jerusalem was an expression of divine righteousness. For Emden, the intent to become oblivious to exile and to mix culturally and racially with other nations was contemptible. Both the nation and the land of Israel belonged to God; the abandoning of one meant the abandoning of the other, and God did not allow this.[14] How, Emden asked, could Jews be so punctilious about mitzvot, even adding to the original commandments, and at the same time neglect the mitzvah of settling the land—"For you will cross over the Jordan and go in to possess the land which the Lord your God is giving you, and you will possess it and dwell in it." (Deut. 11:31)—a mitzvah upon which all of Torah depended?[15]

Bublick added a series of texts which spoke of the uniqueness of the land, and its appropriateness to Israel alone. Ya'akov Krants, the Maggid of Dubno (1740–1804), wrote in *Kol bokhim* that Eretz Israel coincided with Israel's character. It had traits that fit Israel like a tailored garment.[16] Levi Yitzhak of Berditshev (1740–1810) wrote that when Israel was in the land it thrived; when not, it turned desolate—proving that the land was proper to Israel alone.[17]

Bublick, in short, viewed his position as authentic to tradition, from Yehudah Halevi through the eighteenth-century authorities and up until Rav Kook. Nationalism and religion were inherently bound up with one another; Jerusalem was irreplaceable; Israel's identity was tied with the land. At the same time, Bublick's partition of history into religious and political stages meant that the initiative to "take the land" was a function of the dissolution of religion in Western Europe. Likewise, the life-death choice enunciated by Eybeschuetz did not apply, Bublick argued, until the time of Herzl.[18]

## Modernity: From Religion to Political Reality

According to Bublick's Graetz-like structuring of Jewish history, the destruction of the Temple forced Israel into a situation where politics receded and religion ascended—although the attachment to the land remained. In modern times, Israel's voluntary surrender of religion brought about a reversal, in which the nation's survival required it to assume a political identity. In his survey of the premodern period, Bublick did not explore the extent to which the change in form was inherent to the nature of Israel's history, as it was for Graetz. He did not speak of divine leadership, but instead stressed the inevitability of historical forces in the modern period and the need for Israel to initiate actions on its own.

He focused on the dissolution of religion. When Israel originally came to Europe, he argued, they did not assimilate. It was the nature of the lower culture to assimilate into the higher, but not the other way around; and many non-Jews in Europe had yet to reach the higher level of civilization. The Jews were the "elite" to the masses, the "rabbi" to the "bath-house attendant." But in modern times the relationship was reversed. Jews in Germany, England, or America could no longer claim superiority in terms of wisdom, leadership, behavior, literature, or ideals. Whereas earlier the Jews had no incentive to assimilate, and thereby threaten their national existence, now they did. This situation, in Bublick's view, made for the first complete crisis in Israel's history, one that could mean total collapse *(Untergang)*. The solution was to turn to Israel's alternate form, as a polity. Those whose religion was still strong did not need to make this turn, but to the extent that the political restoration had become the central factor in Israel's overall survival, all Jews depended upon it.[19] Those who lost their religion, Bublick implied, should either go to the land or at best be receptive to the religio-national life it had generated.

Throughout the period of exile, the land was a vital source for Israel's religious life. But now, as Rav Kook had said, it was not enough to draw from images of Eretz Israel; the Jews had to unite with the land directly and in political terms. Political restoration also had implications for the diaspora—Bublick anticipated that four out of five Jews would remain outside the land. As noted, the restored polity would have to be based on Torah; indeed, any alienation from the Torah could lead to total collapse. The religious revival would act as a centripetal force, benefitting Jews everywhere. Although Ahad Ha'am was wrong (Bublick thought) in prescribing the establishment of a national "spiritual center" in Palestine prior to the creation of a Jewish state, Bublick was in basic sympathy with the notion of the Land of Israel as a spiritual center for Jews throughout the world. Moreover, Bublick did not think—as did Herzl—that political restoration would put an end to antisemitism. He knew, for example, that when Russian Jews came to America, antisemitism in Russia did not cease. This issue, however, was secondary to establishing a collective entity in the land, which would be steeped in Torah and which would reinforce Jewish religion universally.[20]

Bublick held Herzl in high esteem. Whereas a leading Mizrahi ideologue in the land of Israel, Moshe Avigdor Amiel, had condemned Herzl for helping to generate the intrusion into non-Jewish culture that ultimately provoked the Nazi assault, Bublick's view (published in 1923) was that:

> Political Zionism did not propound any spiritual question. It did not want to break any Jewish tradition and did not want to lead the people [astray] from their historical path. Herzl and Nordau wanted to create the Jewish state and did not want to provide any new Torah to an old nation. To the contrary, both greats of the Zionist movement had great respect for Judaism. And Orthodox Jews repaid them with respect and trust.[21]

During the war years, Bublick praised Herzl's *Der Judenstaat* for touching deeply on the Jewish longing for the land and for lifting the people into the political arena for the first time since the second-century Bar Kokhba rebellion. Herzl had demanded the return to Israel of the land that had been robbed from it and, like Pinsker (1821–1891) in his *Autoemancipation,* was aware that persecution was endemic to the exilic condition. Tragically, Bublick wrote, few Jews had been ready to respond to Herzl's call. Bublick asserted that, had more than just a few Jews considered realistically the future of European Jewry, the result could have been two million Jews living in Eretz Israel at the outbreak of the war, rather than half a million. The wealth belonging to European Jewry could have been used to build the land; instead, Jewish communities in Europe were being destroyed. Herzl, he recalled, had warned of a time when the Jews would have to shake off Europe's dust from their feet.[22]

Again echoing Rav Kook's preference for Zionists who built the state over pious Jews who were indifferent, Bublick was critical of the non-Zionist Orthodox. In his January 1941 review of *Sefer hatsiyonut,* he cited the view of the Gaon of Vilna, who, in his interpretation of Deut. 12:5, had argued that Israel first had to "seek" before God would "choose" to agree to what was done. A similar idea was to be found in Ps. 132:5, "until I find out a place for the land, an habitation for the mighty God of Jacob," which the Gaon of Vilna interpreted as meaning that first Israel had to secure the land before God would agree to dwell in it.[23]

In September 1947, Bublick criticized those among the Orthodox community who seemed to consider their exilic life ideal—one unnamed Orthodox leader had recently given priority to restoring Jewish life in Germany as well as in other bloodied lands—while leaving Eretz Israel to eternity. Did not Moses, Joshua, Ezra, Nehemiah, and the Maccabees, Bublick asked, struggle for the land? Contemporary non-Zionist Orthodox Jews in America were defying the spirit of Tzvi Hirsch Kalischer (1795–1874), Shmuel Mohilever (1824–1898), Eliahu Guttmacher (1795–1874), and Rav Kook. Were these leaders any less pious? Was their messianism any less intense? In citing allegedly religious reasons for refusing to "accelerate the *eschaton*" and in rejecting any cooperation with non-religious Jews, these Jews were taking a positive position on exile and demonstrating an indifference toward the land of Israel. Bublick acknowledged that living in the diaspora was a viable option for Orthodox Jews. He demanded, however, that they share in the overall shift in Judaism's point of gravity to the land of Israel by supporting the Zionist effort.[24]

## The Failure of American Judaism

Judaism in America fit Bublick's depiction of the dissolution of religion in Western Europe. Writing in December 1942, he noted some signs of religious life and expressed the hope that assimilation and materialism were subsiding, yet considered the overall situation to be bleak. Back in the 1920s, he had singled out for criticism the Reform and Conservative movements.[25] During the war, he described the decline on various levels of internal and external religiosity: Jews in America exhibited little longing for *teshuvah* or a thirst for Jewishness in the tradition of "My soul thirsteth for God, for the living God" (Ps. 42:2). Attendance at synagogue services was dwindling down to small *minyanim* for those saying *kaddish,* consisting mainly of older Jews sighing about the youth that didn't come.[26] In April 1942, Bublick wrote that the quantitative increase of Jews in America was proportional to a decrease in the Jewish content of their lives, their sense of *klal yisrael* (world Jewish solidarity), and their attachment to Zion. There was even anti-Zionism among American Jewry (a reference to the American Jewish Committee)—a particularly vicious phenomenon out to destroy what had been built in Eretz Israel.[27] In May 1943, Bublick observed that the frenetic organizational, social, and political activity of American Jewry disguised the absence of any deeper spiritual conviction. This applied not only to assimilated German Jews and Americanized Zionists, but to the Orthodox themselves. Outside of the yeshiva world, the new Orthodox generation lacked the depth of the older.[28] A possible explanation for this, he wrote, was the absence of a cohesive structure, or of modern leaders on the level of an ancient prototype such as Yohanan ben-Zakkai.[29] In former times, he wrote in a succeeding article, the Jews had inner dignity: they prayed, learned, and celebrated in terms of their own values, and did not run after Gentiles by surrendering their culture. But in America, Jews were ready to surrender both their being chosen by God, as expressed in the *kiddush,* and the memory of God's assaults upon their enemy as expressed in the Passover *hagadah,* in exchange for some Gentile goodwill.[30]

In September 1943, Bublick wrote that American Jewry had failed to carry on the tradition of Torah, learning, and holidays. For the first time in history, Jews were so obsessed with material comfort that they were ready to postpone the Sabbath until Sunday, question the words of the prophets, and turn their back on the history of personal sacrifice.[31] The failure of American Jewry in the sphere of religion was so blatant that it was even recognized by the Gentiles. They saw how American Jews failed to bring the faith and national fervor, which accounted for Israel's survival in exile, from Eastern Europe to America. They emulated the Jews of western Europe, with their reform, assimilation, and gravitation toward apostasy. Once the Eastern European source was totally dried up, the Gentiles realized, Jewish assimilation and religious self-destruction would become complete.[32] By June 1946, Bublick had little remaining hope that the Torah-steeped culture of East European Jewry could be recreated on American shores: "Not the Sabbath, not the holidays, not the education, not the religious consciousness, not the city nor the *shtetl,* not the Jewish street of Poland or Lithuania." Whereas Jews in Europe were being killed, the Jews in America were themselves letting Judaism die.[33]

What needed to be done? As the response to Western European assimilation was Zionism, the response to American dissolution had to be political and religious nationalism. Eretz Israel was the only place left where religious Judaism could be grounded and revitalized; elsewhere, Judaism was suspended in mid-air. Yet once Israel had been revived politically, the center in Eretz Israel would help to revive Jewish life in America and in other diaspora communities.[34]

Apart from his critique of American Jewry, Bublick also criticized America more generally for its failure to combat antisemitism. Perhaps out of a sense of impotence, Bublick chose to publish articles in 1943 and 1944 on this theme not in New York, but rather in the Tel Aviv Orthodox weekly, *Ha'yesod*. Bublick wrote that the Nazi assault had split the world into two camps, with the culture of Scriptural civilization (Israel, America, and Great Britain) on one side and anti-Scriptural barbarism on the other. During the crisis, America and Israel inhabited common ground. Yet America had at the same time excluded the defeat of antisemitism from its avowed goal of protecting democracy. Nazism was condemned, but not the antisemitism that was integral to it. All that America offered was "banal and superficial expression of sorrow, devoid of tormented soul and heart." No American leader had come forth to say that upon victory, the war would continue against antisemitism until it was totally eradicated. In Bublick's words:

> Hitler's *Mein Kampf* is based upon hatred of Israel. Why, then, isn't "Our [Allied] War" directed toward the love of Israel, and toward mending the historical antipathy toward the nation of the *Tanakh?* The hatred of Jacob has played a decisive role in the destruction of Europe. Why is the matter of love of Israel so diminished when it comes to rebuilding Europe?[35]

By failing to harness its power to Scripture in its war against Nazism, America was in effect invalidating the very raison d'être for the war. By ignoring the onslaught of antisemitism, it was betraying the Scriptural underpinnings of its own civilization. Bublick conjectured that, had America properly recognized that hatred of Israel was inextricably bound up with hatred for American values of progress, freedom, and democracy, it would have intervened sooner, and much of the disaster could have been averted. Writing after the war's conclusion, in November 1947, Bublick expressed his views much more sharply:

> America has slapped us in the face with her indifference and strange silence [toward the assault upon the Jews]. When the demons twisted the necks of the Jews and choked them, there were no objections. After all, only Jews, no one else, was involved.[36]

In sum, the religious self-destruction of Israel in America, coupled with America's failure to live up to its Scripture-based principles of civilization, reinforced each other in undermining Jewish life in the United States. Religiously and politically, American Jewry had to be redirected toward Eretz Israel. Although Bublick had never negated exile in the manner of an Eybeschuetz—viewing it instead as potentially vital in the religious sense—he saw that its potential was not being actualized in America. Once the polity of Israel was restored, however, it would act as a centripetal force to renew faith even in America.

Up until this point, Bublick's view of American Judaism fit in with his longstanding thinking, from the *Hashiloah* essay on. The nation of Israel had passed from political to religious eras; the modern decline in religion pointed back to the political and, in the end, Jewish history would be capstoned by a political-religious nation in the Land of Israel. The experience of American Judaism folded into this process.

Yet Bublick's perception of America was more complex than suggested by his Graetz-like structuring of Jewish history. In general, Bublick treated other cultures as irrelevant to Israel's identity, arguing instead for the centrality of Eretz Israel. Notwithstanding his criticism of American Jewry, Bublick saw America as a second center for Jewry, in which the community would play an independent role in Jewish history. In various forums, Bublick wrote and spoke enthusiastically about how America (along with England) was founded according to Scripture's principles of civilization: freedom, equality, justice, and democracy, which reinforced and enhanced Israel's own identity.[37] He regarded the "blessed" ground of America as fertile soil for the development of Judaism and for the reinforcement of its Scriptural basis.[38]

In July 1941, for example, he wrote that the conditions for Israel in America were unlike any others in exilic history. They made it possible for Israel to "leap forward." The American government bore the spirit of the Bible, the society offered equality, and the geographic breadth of the country and its varied population created space for Jewish life. Altogether, these conditions allowed for the building of a Jewish population of "great significance," which would form "the main body of the Jewish people outside the Land of Israel in the future."[39]

Earlier that year he had told the 24th American Mizrahi convention in Atlantic City that the country which would rescue the world from slavery would also rescue world Jewry.[40] It was also a refuge, the "only place left for Jews."[41] Beyond rescue and refuge, America's character (as with that of England) was melded to Israel's. The Bible belonged to the social and political fabric of America, finding expression in the Constitution as it had earlier found expression in the Magna Carta. Thus, in a world divided by war, America's struggle against Nazi barbarism and idolatry was essentially a fight for Israel.[42] By defending civilization, America defended Israel.[43]

Bublick expected America to lead the effort to restore the land—if for no other reason, he said in June 1941, than the fact that Israel had given the world, America especially, both its notion of God and the Bible.[44] Committed to justice, America should reverse the injustice of the land's having been stolen from Israel and see to it that "the mountain of the Lord's house shall be established in the top of the mountains" (Is. 3:4).[45] In a subsequent article, Bublick recalled the precedent of William E. Blackstone's petition to President Harrison, four years before Herzl's *Der Judenstaat*. Blackstone had contended that the land should be returned because it was Israel's home, which the nation had cultivated beautifully and from which it had been driven by force. God divided the world according to nations. If now even the Bulgarians and Serbians had their lands returned, why not the Jews? The petition, he noted, had received the support of leading American Gentiles, including John D. Rockefeller, Chief Justice Melville Weston Fuller, James Cardinal Gibbons, and future president William McKinley.[46]

## Vilna in America

It will be recalled that Bublick never excluded the likelihood that the diaspora would remain—and even should remain—after the state had been established. Indeed, he believed that most Jews would not go to Eretz Israel and acknowledged that the Jews' identity was first and foremost a *religious,* rather than a national, political one. During the Second World War, Bublick argued, Israel in America had assumed an identity of its own. His concern was that this modern community carry on the authentic tradition of Judaism—located until the Holocaust in Eastern Europe—through the next millennium.

Speaking of America's five million Jews—four and a half million in North America, and half a million more in South America—Bublick used a phrase that Ya'akov Emden would have recoiled at: he referred to Moisesville as the "Jerusalem of Argentina."[47] This population, he wrote in June 1940, was to be the bridge to the future:

> In a world of storm and destructions, in a time of turmoil and collapse, the nearly five million Jews in America have been called to great deeds, to much effort, to sacrifice in the spiritual sense. They have been called upon to protect Jewish history, so that it will not, God forbid, be torn apart. They have been called upon to be the transmitters who bring to

the future what was holy and precious in the past. The *Keneset Yisrael* of America must become the bridge over which the great portion of Judaism will be carried to our children's children, to Jewish eternity!⁴⁸

At the Mizrahi convention in May 1941, Bublick spoke of Israel's history as one that moved from crisis to crisis, from one *hurban* (destruction) to another—itself an extraordinary act of endurance. With the fall of East European Jewry, America became Israel's new center of gravity. America—Bublick did not say the Land of Israel—was the successor to the heart of Judaism, that of Eastern Europe. New York, Chicago, and Boston needed to become the new Warsaw, Vilna, and Cracow. American Judaism was to bring forth the identical reality—the Torah-based nation—that had prevailed in Eastern Europe, and do so in a way that preserved its character.⁴⁹ In July 1941, he reiterated the point:

> In America there should be a renewal of the Jewish people, who have passed through misfortune and *hurban*. There should be a renewal based on old principles. Here, the people can once again rebuild what was lost. They can create the possibilities for a new future. New York, Cleveland, Chicago, and Boston will be for the future what Cracow, Warsaw, and Vilna were for the past. Here the ancient plan of Jacob will be realized: "If Esau come to the one company and smite it, then the other company which is left shall escape" [Gen. 23:8]. The ancient people which believes in its eternity can begin to rebuild from here, for here is now the best place to build.

Further:

> The population of five million Jews here can and should carry Jewish history forward after the contemporary *hurban*. It can draw new powers from the new ground and become the Jewish exilic home, akin to that of Babylon, Spain, and Poland. America can and should become the central point for Jewish thoughts, feelings, and Jewish life in all aspects of conduct. America can and should carry forward the best traditions of the lands from which Jews have come.

To accomplish this, a strong Jewish consciousness would have to be created, a religious-national life in which (recalling the *Hashiloah* essay) each individual was vital—just as each individual reflected the entire historical experience of Israel and drew life from the whole.⁵⁰

In August 1941, Bublick made it clear that ultimately America was only an "inn," a "refuge for the night," a temporary home. But for now,

America was the "mother of Israel" to which all of the dispersed children would gather. America was now the center, after Asia and Europe. As Israel had once left old Asia for new Europe, now it went from old Europe to America. Coincidentally, as Israel left them, Asia and Europe turned old. And American Israel bridged catastrophe with redemption:

> I cannot help but blurt out this thought: What would happen if America became old; if she settled into a rut, if her people became old? What would happen if the new world became an old world? . . . May such depressing thoughts disappear! Do not tempt Satan. Surely there must indeed be a place on the globe for the Jewish people until their redemption. America, the great, the glorious, is the one place remaining. Here we shall be, between Atlantic and Pacific, until the messiah comes.[51]

In April 1943, Bublick wrote that whereas the land of Israel was to be the principal Jewish community, outside of it, American Jewry embodied the essential part of world Jewry and, therefore, was central. As such, America would be Israel's point of gravity for the next millennium. Israel's first thousand years was spent in its land, the next thousand in Babylon, the next in Europe. The fourth millennium would be in America. Israel's essence as the Torah grounded nation remained unchanging, Bublick argued, which accounted for her unity despite all difficulties; hence, Eretz Israel, Babylon, and the Polish shtetl belonged to the same continuum. Had the Judaism of Eastern Europe torn itself away from that of Babylon, or that of Babylon from that of Eretz Israel, the nation would have been shattered. Now American Jewry had to continue the collective life of Torah-based Israel, since, with the Holocaust, Bublick said, the cornerstone of Israel was to be set in America. Judaism in America was to be the basis for Israel's future identity. It was up to American Jewry not to squander the legacy, but to transmit it intact into the future.[52]

After the war, Bublick continued to reiterate this theme. In November 1945, he wrote that Israel's centers were, in turn, Eretz Israel, Babylon, Europe (Spain and southern France in past centuries, and Poland and Lithuania into the modern period), and America. To be sure, the "center of centers," the ultimate "source of everything Jewish," was the land of Israel. The two centers were not comparable: Eretz Israel was the nation's historical base, the locale of redemption, the symbol and paradigm of Israel's ultimate religious and political character. But America constituted another center where the enduring legacy of the nation would be carried forward. As the next exilic center, America must carry forward the achievement of Vilna, Cracow, Brisk (Brzescz, Brest-Litovsk), Lublin, and Volozhin. As earlier crises moved Israel to new locations, now the Holocaust moved it to America. America "must take upon herself the great responsibility that history, or more correctly, providence, has thrown upon it. The Jews of America have been selected as the new flagbearers of exilic Judaism."[53]

In March 1946, Bublick cited Leo Baeck's comment upon his arrival in America from Berlin, that Eastern Europe had turned into a *gehinnom* (hell) for Jews, and that there was also no future for Jews in Germany. Bublick observed that once Judaism was finished in a country—whether Egypt, Babylon, or Spain—there was no revival. Jewish history always moved forward in different locations. At the same time, the "center of centers" was not America: the Yishuv was small in number but great in significance; the community in America was large in number but not of comparable significance. American Jewry, accordingly, had to continue to turn its eyes to the Yishuv:

> Not that American Jewry should be compared with the Jewish home in the land of Israel. Rather that the Jews of America should build up the land of Israel. [Meanwhile] they should see that Judaism will not, God forbid, collapse (*untergehen*) in the new world, following upon the *hurban* of Europe.[54]

## Conclusion

For Bublick, American Judaism confirmed the modern pattern in which religion dissipated and Israel turned to its land to establish a new religio-political reality. On the one hand, America was to be the location of Israel's heritage for the next millennium; Vilna would be in America, not in the land of Israel. Unlike contemporaries in Palestine such as Amiel and Shraggai, Bublick did not consider the Holocaust to be the categorical end to exilic life. At the same time, he also saw Jewish history, according to his Graetz-like scheme, as moving toward Zion.

Why was Bublick pulled in two separate directions? To begin with, he was neither a metahistorical nor a messianic thinker, looking instead to history for explanations of Israel's fate. Given this mindset, Bublick was perhaps unwilling to place all of the nation's hopes on Eretz Israel, which at the time was not yet secure for Jews. Bublick was also unwilling to see Israel surrender its role in diaspora history: since history was Israel's stage, he wanted the nation to develop positively within it.

Empirical history, however, was inconclusive, which left Bublick's thought two-sided. He did not try to synthesize his thinking about Israel's internal developments with external forces. When Bublick spoke of American Jewry's continuing in the path of Western European dissolution, he had Jewish religious internal dynamics in mind, not associating the decline with the Holocaust (as did, for example, Amiel)—other than to correlate it with America's seeming indifference to world antisemitism. When he spoke of America as the new Babylon, the new Eastern Europe, he was responding to the external threat of the Holocaust. At the very time that he lost hope in the diaspora as a stage for religion, he renewed it in America. He left his ideology divided.

Given his leading position in American Mizrahi, it can only be concluded that Bublick's ambiguity reflected the ambivalence of his listeners. His ideological wartime dilemma was reflected in that of the American Mizrahi movement, which operated, accordingly, both in America and in the land of Israel.

## Notes

1. See Shlomo Zalman Shraggai, *Tehumim* (Jerusalem, 1951–1952); idem, *Zemanim: shabatot umo'adim* (Jerusalem, 1969); idem, *Tahalikhei ha'temura vehageula: perakim bevaayot ha'medina behit'havuta* (Jerusalem, 1958–1959).

2. Aharon Petshenik, "Der mizrahi oyf sheydveg," *Der mizrahi veg* (henceforth *DMV*) 8, no. 3 (November 1943): 7, 13; idem, "Golus un geula," *DMV* 8, no. 6 (March 1944): 5, 13; idem, "Oyfn erets yisroel front," *DMV* 5, no. 4 (March 1944): 3.

3. See Aharon Petshenik, "Der zibetsig-yerigen yubileyam fun Gedaliah Bublick," *DMV* (October–November 1945): 3; A. Leo Gellman and Aharon Petshenik, "Mitoldotav," in *Gedaliah Bublick z"l: ketavim nivharim,* vol. 1 (Jerusalem 1961–1962), 7–9; Editor, "R. Gedaliah Bublick z"l," *Yidishe shtimme* 2, no. 28, whole no. 63 (May 1948): 4; Gedaliah Bublick, "Di kolonye mozesvil: Di yerushalyim fun argentina," *Der morgen zhurnal* 41, no. 12,144 (12 October 1941): 6; Z. M. Kerstein, "Gedaliah Bublick, boyer un kemfer fun ortodoksishen identum," *Der Morgen Zhurnal* (October–November 1945): 2.

4. Gedaliah Bublick, "Hale'umiut ha'ivrit," *Hashiloah,* 5, nos. 28–30 (December 1898–July 1899): 401–07.

5. Gedaliah Bublick, "Di natsionale heym," in his *Min hametsar* (New York, 1923), 401–407.

6. Heinrich Graetz (Berlin, 1936); original publication: idem, "Die Construction der jüdischen Geschichte," *Zeitschrift für die religiösen Interessen des Judenthums* 3 (1846), 81–97, 121–32, 361–68, 413–21.

7. Gedaliah Bublick, "Harav Kook—rov, dikhter un filozof," in *Mayn rayze in erets yisroel* (New York, 1921), 331–38.

8. Idem, "Herzl, Nordau, Ahad Ha'am," in *Min hametsar*, 277–82.

9. Ya'akov Emden, *Sefer shimush* (1758), 58b-59a.

10. Eliyahu ben Shlomo, Gaon of Vilna, *Aderet eliyahu* (Tel Aviv, 1963): Deut. 11:31 [p. 395]; Deut. 12:5 [p. 397].

11. Yehonatan Eybeschuetz, *Ya'arot devash,* vol. 1 (Jerusalem, 1983), 22.

12. Ibid., 253.

13. Ibid., 85.

14. Ya'akov Emden, *Siddur 'amudei shamayim* (Altona, 1743), 1b, as cited in *Sefer hatsionut verishume hatenuah umifaleha begiluiyehem uvehishtalshelutam hahistorit,* edited by Bentsion Dinur (Tel Aviv, 1938).

15. Emden, *Siddur amudei shamayim,* 34b-35a.

16. Ya'akov Krants, *Kol bokhim* 70a, as cited by Dinur, infra.

17. Levi Yitzhak of Berditshev, *Kedushat levi: megilat eykha,* as cited by Dinur, infra.

18. Gedaliah Bublick, "Di shafer un farshpreyter fun tsiyonistishen gedank," *Der morgen zhurnal* 40, no 11,920 (12 January 1941): 6. Bublick drew from *Sefer hatsionut verishume hatenua umifaleha begiluiyehem uvehishtalshelutam hahistorit,* vol. 1: *mevasrei tsiyon,* ed. Bentsiyon Dinur (Tel Aviv, 1938), 3–67. Bublick also cited Elia ben Shlomo Hakohen of Izmir (1650–1729), David ben Aryeh Leb Lida of Lvov (eighteenth century), David Pardo (1719–1792), Yehuda Leb Edel (Slonim), Menahem Mendel of Shklov (c. 1827), Israel ben Samuel of Shklov (d. 1839), Nahman of Bratslav (1772–1811), and Shneour Zalman of Liadi (1740–1803).

19. Gedaliah Bublick, "Farvos der id iz nit geshtorben," in *Min hametsar,* 17–23.

20. Idem, "Virkung fun erets yisroel oyfn golus," in *Min hametsar,* 408–14; idem, "Der lebens-kamf fun der idisher uma," in *Min hametsar,* 422–28.

21. Moshe Avigdor Amiel, *Linevukhei hatekufa: perek histaklut bemahut hayahadut* (Jerusalem, 1943), 3–4, 220–24, 281–85, 306–08; Gedaliah Bublick, "Herzl, Nordau, Ahad Ha'am."

22. Gedaliah Bublick, "Vi di iden darfen shtelen foderungen," *Der morgen zhurnal* 43, no. 12,499 (13 December 1942): 6; idem, "Di vornung amol fun idishen khurbn itst," *Der morgen zhurnal* 43, no. 12,595 (4 April 1943):6; idem, "Amerika hot dem shlisel tsu ale fier problemen. Tamtsis fun referat gehalten bay der konvenshon," [24th American Mizrahi Convention, Atlantic City, May 1941], *DMV* 5, no. 6 (June 1941): 1.

23. Eliyahu ben Shlomo, Gaon of Vilna, *Aderet Eliyahu,* on Deut. 12:5, supra.

24. Gedaliah Bublick, "Ortodoksn vos hobn lib dem goles," *DMV* 12, no. 1 (September 1947): 5.

25. See Gedaliah Bublick, "Kenen iden leben on mitzves hamaasiyos"; idem, "Das amerikaner yudentum"; idem, "Di shteyner in veg fun amerikaner yudentum"; idem, "Di reform in amerika" in idem, *Min hametsar,* 81–86, 369–86; idem, "Kampf fun reform an idishkayt"; idem, "Reform un unzere kinder"; idem, "Konservatives yudentum"; idem, "A shmues mit a konservativen ortodoks," in idem, *Der sakh-hakol in amerikanem yudentum* (New York, 1927), 15–19, 20–24, 40–44, 45–49.

26. Idem, "Di krig hot gevirkt oyf iden in land," *Der morgen zhurnal* 43, no. [12,512] (27 December 1942): 1. Because it is impossible to determine what the correct issue number is, this figure is given in brackets.

27. Idem, "Die enderung fun di amerikaner iden," *Der morgen zhurnal* 43, no 12,611 (25 April 1943): 6.

28. Idem, "Oyberflekhlikayt bay amerikaner iden," *Der morgen zhurnal* 43, no. 12,627 (6 May 1943): 6.

29. Idem, "Mayles un khasroynes in der ortodokse," *Der morgen zhurnal* 43, no. 12,633 (23 May 1943): 6.

30. Idem, "Innerlikhe shvakhkayt fun amerikaner identum," *Der morgen zhurnal* 43, no. 12,621 (9 May 1943):6.

31. Idem, "Selihos shtimen bay iden un nit-iden," *Der morgen zhurnal* 43, no. [12,720] (26 September 1943): 6. Because it is impossible to determine what the correct issue number is, this figure is given in brackets.

32. Idem, "The New Season for Jews," *DMV* 10, no. 5 (February 1946): 5.

33. Idem, "Der mizrahi oyf kumendigen kongres," *DMV* 10, no. 8 (June 1946):5.

34. Ibid.

35. Idem, "Haba'aya hayehudit—even bohan ledemokratia," *Hayesod* 15, no. 436 (13 October 1944): 2; idem, "Al haantishemiut lo hukhraza milhama," *Hayesod* 13, no. 403 (29 October 1943): 2.

36. Idem, "Haomnam rak tehia le'umit?" *Hayesod* 16, no 554 (7 November 1947): 3.

37. Idem, "Amerika hot dem shlisl."

38. Idem, "Selihos shtimen."

39. Idem, "Der goyrl fun idishn folk iz itst oyfn vagshal," *Idishe vokhntsaytung* 4, no. 275 (4 July 1941): 2.

40. Idem, "Amerika hot dem shlisl."

41. Idem, "Naye idishe yishuvim," *Der morgen zhurnal* 41, no. 12,089 (3 August 1941): 6.

42. Idem, "Tsvey bibel lender vas kemfen far der mentshhayt," *Idishe vokhntsaytung* 6, no. 256 (24 January 1940): 2–3.

43. Idem, "Soyne fun iden iz soyne fun mentshhayt," *Idishe vokhntsaytung* 5, no. 232 (5 July 1940): 2–3.

44. Idem, "Amerika hot dem shlisl."

45. Idem, "Amerika oyfn shvel fun unzer heymland," *Der morgen zhurnal* 43, no. 12,487 (29 November 1942): 6.

46. Moshe Davis, to whose memory this volume is dedicated, noted that

Herzl's famous phrase, "a land without a people for a people without a land" was originally Blackstone's. Moshe Davis, "American Christian Devotees in the Holy Land," *Christian-Jewish Relations* 20, no. 4 (1987): 3–20. Gedaliah Bublick, "Vi di iden darfen shtelen forderungen," *Der morgen zhurnal* 43, no. 12,499 (13 December 1942): 6. On Blackstone's *Petition,* see Gershon Greenberg, *The Holy Land in American Religious Thought, 1620–1948* (Lanham and Jerusalem, 1994), 210–16.

47. Gedaliah Bublick, "Di kolonye mozesvil: di yerushalayim fun argentina." Cf. Noah Katsavitch, *Mozesviler breyshis: zikhroynes,* vol. 2 (Buenos Aires, 1935), 208–16.

48. Idem, "Di greste gefahr far iden yetst iz: fartsveyflung," *Idishe vokhntsaytung* 5, no. 231 (28 June 1940): 2.

49. Idem, "Amerika hot dem shlisl."

50. Idem, "Der goyrl fun idisher folk iz itst oyfn vagshal," *Idishe vokhntsaytung* 4, no. 275 (4 July 1941): 2.

51. Idem, "Naye idishe yishuvim in di sud-amerikanishe lender," *Der morgen zhurnal* 41, no. 12,089 (3 August 1941): 6.

52. Idem, "Di akhrayus fun a folk in a goyrldiker tsayt," *Der morgen zhurnal* 43, no. 12,607 (April 1943): 6.

53. Idem, "Di naye role fun amerika in idishen leben," *DMV* 10, no.2 (November 1945): 5.

54. Idem, "Hasal seder eyrope," *DMV* 10, no. 6 (March 1946): 3. I have been unable to identify the Leo Baeck address.

# Appendix: Primary Occupations of North American Applicants for Immigration to Palestine, January 1, 1919–May 30, 1920

### Agricultural

Agricultural Experts  30
Farmers  330
Farm-laborers  17
Foresters  1
Veterinarians  4

### Commercial

Buyers  1
Commercial Experts  3
Manufacturers  42
Merchants  165
Peddlers  40
Real Estate  4
Salesmen  49
Shopkeepers  64

### Educational

Hebrew Teachers  85
Kindergarten Teachers  1
Subject Teachers  38

### Engineers

Engineers, Architectural  5
Engineers, Civil  31
Engineers, Other kinds  27

### Medical

Bacteriologists  1
Dentists  23
Dietitians  3
Hospital Orderlies  1
Nurses  30
Pharmacists  29
Physicians  71
Sanitarians  1

### Social Workers

Cooperatives  1
Employment Experts  2
Investigators  10
Organizers  8

### General

Accountants  2
Administrators  10
Artists  3
Bakers  13
Bankers  1

# APPENDIX

Barbers 2
Blacksmiths 3
Bookbinders 5
Bookkeepers 17
Bricklayer 3
Brickmaker 1
Broker 1
Brushmakers 2
Builders 13
Butchers 10
Button Makers 1
Cap Makers 11
Carpenters 56
Cattle Dealer 1
Chauffeurs 7
Chemists 9
Cigar Makers 3
Clerical Workers 43
Dental Mechanics 1
Domestic Servants 5
Dressmakers 2
Druggists (Wholesale) 1
Electricians 16
Embroiderers 2
Engravers 1
Expressmen 1
Foremen 4
Furriers 4
Harness Makers 5
Hatters 3
Insurance Agents 17
Jewelers 4
Journalists 5
Laborers 67
Laundry Workers 6
Lawyers 5
Librarians 2
Locksmiths 6

Machinists 48
Masons 3
Mattress Makers 1
Milliners 7
Musicians 2
Opticians 3
Painters 28
Paperhangers 2
Photographers 1
Plasterers 1
Plumbers 12
Pocketbook Makers 1
Printers 9
Rabbis 15
Railroad Workers 6
Restauranteurs 4
Secretaries 14
*Shochetim* 14
Statisticians 1
Stenographers 24
Students 33
Tailors 131
Teamsters 5
Telegraphers 2
Tanners 3
Tinsmiths 3
Tool Makers 2
Trunk Makers 1
Upholsterers 2
Umbrella Makers 2
Watch Makers 2
Weavers 6

**Miscellaneous**

Professionals 14
Skilled Laborers 28
No Occupation 8

# Notes on Contributors

YAAKOV ARIEL is an associate professor of religious studies at the University of North Carolina at Chapel Hill. He is the author of articles and books on American religious groups and their relation to the Jewish people and Israel, including the recently published *Evangelizing the Chosen People: Missions to the Jews in America, 1880–2000*.

MICHAEL BROWN is professor of Humanities and Hebrew at York University and the former director of the Centre for Jewish Studies there. He is the author and editor of books and articles on modern Jewish history and literature, including *The Israeli-American Connection: Its Roots in the Yishuv, 1914–1945*.

JOHN DAVIS is the Alice Pratt Brown Professor of Art at Smith College, where he chairs the Art Department and also teaches in the American Studies Program. He is the author or co-author of three books and numerous articles and catalogue essays examining the art and architecture of the United States during the nineteenth century. His current research concerns African-American imagery after the Civil War and New York art institutions around 1900.

STEVEN EPPERSON is the Minister at the South Valley Unitarian Universalist Society in Salt Lake City, Utah. He has also been history curator at the Museum of Church History and Art, program director of the Utah Humanities Council, and has taught at Brigham Young University.

## NOTES ON CONTRIBUTORS

JOSEPH B. GLASS is the academic coordinator of the Halbert Centre for Canadian Studies at the Hebrew University and he lectures at the Hebrew University in the Department of Geography and the Rothberg International School. He is the author, with Ruth Kark, of *Sephardi Entrepreneurs in Eretz Israel. The Amzalak Family, 1816–1918* and the author of *From New Zion to Old Zion. American Jewish Immigration and Settlement in Palestine, 1917–1939.*

GERSHON GREENBERG is a professor of philosophy and religion at The American University, and is the author of *The Holy Land in American Religious Thought, 1620–1948.* He has been a contributing author to the series, *With Eyes Toward Zion,* which, like his own monograph, was published under the auspices of the America–Holy Land Project.

ROBERT T. HANDY, a longtime friend and colleague of Moshe Davis, is Professor Emeritus of Church History at Union Theological Seminary. He has been centrally involved in the America–Holy Land Project and in that capacity edited the volume *The Holy Land in American Protestant Life, 1800–1948,* in addition to essays he contributed to *With Eyes toward Zion: Scholars Colloquium on America–Holy Land Studies* and *With Eyes toward Zion II: Themes and Sources in the Archives of the United States, Great Britain, Turkey, and Israel.*

RUTH KARK, a professor at the Hebrew University of Jerusalem, has written and edited seventeen books and over 100 articles on the history and historical geography of Palestine and Israel. Her research interests include the study of concepts of land, land use, and patterns of land ownership in the Middle East and Palestine/Israel in the nineteenth and twentieth centuries, urban and rural settlement processes, and Western interests in the Holy Land and interactions with its local populations.

DAVID KLATZKER, PH.D., is Rabbi of Temple Ner Tamid of Peabody, Massachusetts. He Studied with Moshe Davis and served as academic liaison in the United States for the America–Holy Land Project of the Hebrew University of Jerusalem.

ELI LEDERHENDLER is the Stephen S. Wise Professor of American Jewish History and Institutions at the Avraham Harman Institute of Contemporary Jewry of the Hebrew University of Jerusalem. Among his recently published books is *New York Jews and the Decline of Urban Ethnicity, 1950–1970*. He also edited volume 17 of *Studies in Contemporary Jewry* (2001), which is titled, *Who Owns Judaism? Public Religion and Private Faith in America and Israel*.

MARGARET M. MCGUINNESS is Professor of Religious Studies at Cabrini College in Radnor, Pennsylvania. She currently serves as co-editor of *American Catholic Studies,* formerly the *Records of the American Catholic Historical Society of Philadelphia*. Her current research focuses on American Catholic attitudes toward the Eucharist and Eucharistic devotions, 1926–1976.

MARIANNE SANUA is an assistant professor of History and Judaic Studies at Florida Atlantic University in Boca Raton, Florida.

JONATHAN D. SARNA is the Joseph H. and Belle R. Braun Professor of American Jewish History at Brandeis University. He also chairs the Academic Advisory and Editorial Board of the Jacob R. Marcus Center of the American Jewish Archives, where he serves as consulting scholar. He is the author, editor, or co-author of seventeen books, including *Women and American Judaism: Historical Perspectives,* with Pamela Nadell (2001); *Minority Faiths and the American Protestant Mainstream* (1997); *Religion and State in the American Jewish Experience,* with David Dalin (1997), and others. He is now completing a new history of American Judaism, to be published by Yale University Press.

MATTHEW SILVER teaches modern Jewish history and world history at Emek Yezreel College, in northern Israel. He completed his doctorate at the Avraham Harman Institute of Contemporary Jewry of the Hebrew University of Jerusalem. His dissertation dealt with American Zionism in Palestine during the Mandate Period.

# Index

*Achavah* Club, 23–24, 30
Adler, Selig, 36, 41
Agron (Agronsky), Gershon, 210–11
Ahad Ha'am (pseud., Asher Ginsberg), 120, 210, 256, 262
*'aliyah* (immigration to Palestine/Israel), 120, 201–31
American Academy for Jewish Music, 126
American Board of Missions to the Jews, 186
American colony (Jerusalem), 12, 75–87
American Council for Judaism, 192
American Fruit Growers of Palestine, 215
American Jewish Committee, 125, 135, 264
American Jewish Congress, 121, 125, 256
American Palestine Exploration Society, 67, 68
American Porcelain Tooth Manufacturing Company, 215
American Zion Commonwealth, 208, 221
American Zionist Emergency Council (AZEC), 138, 140
American Zionist Medical Unit, 202–5

Amiel, Moshe Avigdor, 263, 271
Antonius, George, 175
Armenian Church, 17
Aronson, Julia, 221
Art and visual culture, depictions of the Holy Land in, 50–71, 244, 246–8, 250

Baeck, Leo, 271
Baer, Yitzhak, 25
Balfour Declaration, 124, 164, 167, 201, 205
Baltimore (MD), 233
Baptists, 185–9, 191–5, 197
Baron, Salo Wittmayer, 25, 27, 135
Benderly, Samson, 23, 119
Ben-Gurion, David, 163, 194, 205–6
Ben-Zvi, Yitzhak, 205
Berkson, Isaac B., 118–9, 123, 129, 137–8
Bernstein, Leonard, 143, 148
Bialik, Chaim Nachman, 42
Bialystok (Belostok), Poland, 256
Birmingham (AL), 250
Blackstone, William E., 268
Bloom, Samuel Simon, 215–6
Bloomgarden, Solomon (Yehoash), 23
Brandeis, Louis D., 24, 175; and plans for developing Palestine, 202, 204, 207, 209, 212, 216; and Zionist

# INDEX

Brandeis, Louis D. (*continued*)
  political leadership, 165, 169, 171, 172, 175, 179
Brandeis University, 10, 30, 144
Brooklyn (NY), 9, 119
Bublick, Gedaliah, 255–72.

Carter, James (Jimmy), U.S. president, 197
Catherwood, Frederick, 52, 54–58
Catholics: *see* Roman Catholicism
Catholic University of America, 246
Chaikin, Benjamin, 224
Chautauqua (NY), 53, 244, 248, 250, illus., 54
Chicago (IL), 76, 78, 79, 81, 82, 84, 85, 87, 234, 256
Chipkin, Israel S., 118–9, 123
Church, Frederic, 52, 65–70
City College of New York (CCNY), 119, 135, 137, 151–2
Cohen, Ethel S., 12, 117–55
Cohen, Frank, 12, 117–55
Cohen, Jack J., 118, 152
Cohen, Naomi Wiener, 43
College of the Holy Land, 249
Columbia University, 27, 35, 119, 123, 137
Conservative Judaism, 26. See also: Jewish Theological Seminary of America
Cooper Union, 60
Copland, Aaron, 143, 148
*Crusader's Almanac, The*, 245

Davidson, Israel, 23
Davis, Lottie, 7, 40
Davis, Moshe, 7–10, 16–18, 24–27; and America–Holy Land Studies Project, 10–12, 19, 28–30, 33–34, 36–37, 39–45, 91; on *Achavah* club, 23–24, 30
Degania (kibbutz), 211
*Der id*, 256
de Sola Pool, David, 146, 178

Dewey, John, 208, 209
Dinur, Ben-Zion, 18, 25, 259
*Dos idishe togblat* (New York), 256
*Dos idishe togblat* (Warsaw), 256
Dubnow, Simon, 27
Dugit, 188
Dushkin, Alexander M., 208–9

Eco, Umberto, 250–1
Eliyahu, the Gaon of Vilna, 260, 263
Emden, Ya'akov, 260–1, 268
'En Gev (kibbutz), 117, 144–51, 153
ESCO Foundation: *see* Cohen, Ethel S. and Cohen, Frank
Eybeschuetz, Yehonatan, 260–1

Fairman, James, 52, 59–65
Feisal, emir, 167–8
Fiat, Nathan, 220
Finkelstein, Louis, 27, 41
First World War, 87, 139, 165, 173, 201–2, 208, 218
Flusser, David, 191
Franciscan Commissariat of the Holy Land for the United States, 245
*Franciscan Tertiary*, 235–40
Frankfurter, Felix, 165, 167–8, 170, 172–3, 175–6
Friedenwald, Harry, 12, 15, 165–79
Friedlaender, Israel, 23, 27, 126

Gelber, Sylvia, 220
Gibbons, James (cardinal), 246, 249, 268
Ginzberg, Louis (Levi), 23–24
Goren, Arthur (Aryeh), 31n. 14, 43
Graetz, Heinrich, 258, 261, 267
Grant, Heber J., 113
Great Seal of the United States, 248
Greco, John Baptist, 250
Grinstein, Hyman, 25

Hadassah Women's Zionist Organization, 123, 126, 130, 132, 179; Medical Unit, 204, 209, 219; *See also*: Henrietta Szold

# Index

Harrison, William H., (U.S. president), 268
*Ha'Shiloah*, 256, 267
*Ha'Yesod*, 266
Hebrew University of Jerusalem, 119, 134, 140, 144, 185; Moshe Davis and, 9–10, 25, 29–30, 34
Hebrew Youth Federation (*Histadrut Hano'ar Ha'ivri*), 40
Herzl, Theodor, 259, 262–3, 268, 272
Holocaust, 144, 255, 266, 271, 272
Holy Land, U.S.A., 250
Honor, Leo, 123
Hunter College (CUNY), 43, 127
Hyde, Orson, 93–104, 107–9

Jacobs, Rose E., 118, 123, 129–30, 132
Janowsky, Oscar, 135, 139
Jewish Colonization Association, 256
*Jewish Frontier*, 140
Jewish Legion, 205, 212. See also: First World War
Jewish National Fund, 130

Kaganoff, Nathan M., 36, 41
Kallen, Deborah, 208
Kallen, Horace, 208
Kantor, Louis, 204–5, 218–9
Kaplan, Mordecai M., 11, 23–24, 118–9, 123, 129, 147, 152. See also: Reconstructionist Judaism
Kazmann, Boris, 205
Kellogg, Miner, 58
Kesselman, Robert, 219–20
King-Crane Commission, 174–7
Klausner, Joseph, 25
Klepper, Leah, 123, 126, 129, 134
Kligler, Israel, 204
Kook, Avraham Yitzhak Hakohen, 258–9, 261, 262, 264
Krants, Ya'akov, 261

Labor Zionism, 163, 206
Landsberg, Alexander, 212
Leeser, Isaac, 26

Leo XIII (pope), 234
Lewin-Epstein, Eliyahu, 204
Lindsey, Robert, 185–200
Lipsky, Louis, 23
Lynch, J. L., 235–40
Lynch, William F., 14

Mack, Julian, 165
McDonald, James, 134, 140
McKinley, William, U.S. president, 268
Magnes, Judah L., 23, 43, 119, 130
Marcus, Jacob Raider, 25
Marx, Alexander, 23
*Menorah Journal*, 126
Merrill, Selah, 84, 87
Mizrahi, religious Zionist organization, 255, 256, 262–3, 267, 269
Mochenson, Nellie Straus, 221
Mohilever, Shmuel, 264
Moisesville colony (Argentina), 256
*Morgen zhurnal*, 211, 256
Mormons (Church of Jesus Christ of Latter-day Saints), 13, 91–113
Music and musicology, ESCO Foundation and, 142–50, 152. See also: 'En Gev (kibbutz)

Nathan Straus Health Centre, 224
Nevins, Allan, 27, 28, 29
New York *Kehillah* (Jewish community council), 119
New York University, 142, 221
Nordau, Max, 259

*'olim* (immigrants in Palestine/Israel): see *'aliyah*
Optical industry, in Palestine, 131
Orthodox Church, 17
Orthodox Judaism, 12, 15, 17, 19n. 7, 26, 118–19, 152, 194, 263–5. See also: Bublick, Gedaliah; Mizrahi

Palestine Knitting Works, 212
Palestine riots, 43, 168–70

# INDEX

Pardes Hanna, 132–4, 141
Petaluma (CA), 211
Petshenik, Aharon, 255, 256
Pinski, David, 23
Pittsburgh (PA), 250
Poale Zion, 206, 221. *See also*: Labor Zionism

Radin, Max, 23
Reconstructionist Judaism, 126, 152
*Reconstructionist, The*, 126
Rockefeller, John D., 268
Roman Catholicism, 13, 16, 35, 58–59; and depictions of Holy Land, 236–40; in America, 233–6
Rosen, Ben, 119
Rubinow, I. M., 177
Rudy, William H., 13, 75–87
Ruppin, Arthur, 120, 210–11
Rutenberg, Pinhas, 205

Sacks, Isaac, 217–18
St. Louis World's Fair (1904), 244, 248, 250
Sampter, Jesse, 179, 208
Samuel, Sir Herbert, 205
Sargent, John Singer, 70–71
Second World War, 12, 121–6, 128, 135–6, 150, 186, 248, 268. *See also*: Holocaust
Shraggai, Shlomo Zalman, 255, 271
Silver, Abba Hillel, 138. *See also*: American Zionist Emergency Council (AZEC).
Six-Day War (June 5–10, 1967), 145, 149–50
Smith, George A., 106–8
Smith, Joseph, 103, 107–8, 110–11
Spafford, Anna, 80–82
Spafford, Horatio, 80–81
Spector, Johanna, 144
Straus, Nathan, 221

Szold, Henrietta, 118, 129–30, 166, 209, 221
Szold, Robert, 169, 171, 173, 179

Talmage, James, 109, 111–12
Tel Aviv, 120
*Tipat Halav* (mother and baby clinic), 221
Twain, Mark, 106

Union Theological Seminary, 29, 33–36, 39
United States National Archives, 37, 75
University of Notre Dame, 250
Ussishkin, Menahem, 120

Vatican II, 244
Vissani, Charles A., 245
"Vitamins for Britain," 124–5

Wallace, Edwin, 84–85
Warren, Charles, 67
Warsaw, Poland, 256
Washington, DC, 76, 240, 243–8
Waterbury (CT), 250
Wechsler, Israel, 118
Weizmann, Chaim, 125–6, 136, 164, 167, 204, 206
Widstoe, John A., 109, 111–2
Wilson, Woodrow, U.S. president, 170, 174, 176
Wise, Stephen S., 121, 125
World War I: *see* First World War
World War II: *see* Second World War

Yellin, David, 208
Young, Brigham, 102, 105, 107
"Youth Aliyah," 130, 132–4

Zhitlowsky, Chaim, 23
Zionist Organization of America (ZOA), 165
Zionist Society of Engineers and Agriculturalists, 202, 205